1968 type 912 Coupé
4 cylinders, 1582 cc, 90 hp
2194 pounds, 118 mph

1969 type 911 S Targa
6 cylinders, 2195 cc, 180 hp
2249 pounds, 137 mph

1970 type 914
4 cylinders, 1679 cc, 80 hp
1984 pounds, ca. 112 mph

1972 type 916
6 cylinders, 2341 cc, 190 hp
2006 pounds, 143 mph

1972 type 911 E Targa
6 cylinders, 2341 cc, 165 hp
2370 pounds, 137 mph

1974 type 911 Carrera RS
6 cylinders, 2687 cc, 210 hp
1984 pounds, 149 mph

1974 type 911 Coupé
6 cylinders, 2687 cc, 175 hp
2370 pounds, 140 mph

1976 type 911 TURBO
6 cylinders, 2994 cc, 260 hp
2513 pounds, 155 mph

1976 type 924
4 cylinders, 1984 cc, 125 hp
2381 pounds, 124 mph

1977 type 928
8 cylinders, 4474 cc, 240 hp
3210 pounds, ca. 143 mph

1978 type 911 TURBO 3,3
6 cylinders, 3299 cc, 300 hp
2866 pounds, 162 mph

1979 type 924 TURBO
4 cylinders, 1984 cc, 170 hp
2601 pounds, 140 mph

1980 type 924 Carrera GT
4 cylinders, 1984 cc, 210 hp
2601 pounds, 149 mph

1982 type 944
4 cylinders, 2479 cc, 163 hp
2601 pounds, 137 mph

1985 type 928 S
8 cylinders, 4664 cc, 310 hp
3373 pounds, ca. 158 mph

1985 type 911 Carrera Cabrio
6 cylinders, 3164 cc, 231 hp
2778 pounds, 152 mph

1985 type 944 Turbo
4 cylinders, 2479 cc, 220 hp
2822 pounds, 152 mph

1985 type 959
6 cylinders, 2850 cc, ca. 450 hp
186 mph

 equivalent to the German DIN-PS-values. Kilograms are given in pounds and kilometres per hour are given in mph.

PORSCHE
PORTRAIT OF A LEGEND

Conceived and realized
with a team of authors
and photographers by Ingo Seiff
with
Hoffmann und Campe

TABLE
OF CONTENTS

The term "horsepower" is indicated with hp. The hp-values given are equivalent to the German DIN-PS-values.

Metric weight and speed data have been converted to pounds and mph.

INGO SEIFF

"BELLA MACCHINA"!

No, my heart didn't beat any faster the first time I squeezed in behind the wheel of a 911 Carrera. Nor did my palms begin to sweat. What I was really worrying about was how a novice like myself could get acquainted with this meteor without causing harm. Should I play the tough guy on the autobahn right away or should I start off by putting the Porsche through a baptism of fire on the legendary Nuerburgring?

I wanted to find out if my outlook on life was compatible with the Carrera's character, so I decided on a "tour d'éducation" through classical northern Italy. You see, I'd been told that a Porsche required a certain environment in order to give maximum pleasure. First of all, however, I quite mundanely had to take the car out of the factory yard at Zuffenhausen and drive toward the autobahn by way of Porschestrasse, accelerating up to the second traffic light, where greenhorns traditionally stall the rear engine for the first time. "Let the clutch out very slowly," I'd been prudently advised. That's easier said than done when you're used to the ultrasmooth separation of engine and transmission in a docile, easy-going 6-cylinder car from Cologne. I merged easily into the traffic on local highway B 10 and didn't have any trouble getting onto the southbound autobahn. The six air-cooled cylinders in back of me were roaring to go. European road builders having done a grand job in recent years, the drive down to St. Gotthard in Switzerland was a pure pleasure, the engine humming along at low revs and sounding bored. Speed limits and traffic jams tend to dampen some of the Carrera's verve.

The new Swiss autobahns bypass a lot of tourist highlights, and countless exciting stretches of road that fascinated thousands of sports car drivers for decades have been gobbled up by the bulldozers. Tellplatte, the place where legendary Swiss national hero William Tell is supposed to have shot an apple from his son's head with a crossbow, is now underpassed by the Seelisberg tunnel. I decided to bypass the convenient St. Gotthard tunnel and took the road to the right over the pass that climbs up to an altitude of 6916 feet. Here, I intended to let the Carrera breathe some fresh air and feel at home, but they'd taken the sting out of that route as well. On the south side, the road over the pass had been widened so generously it looked like the runway of a mid-sized airport. You can't impress a Carrera with small-time serpentines of that sort. All you have to do is stay in third, only occasionally shifting down to second. The air-cooled, 6-cylinder boxer engine behind me was rattling and laboring and pretending it was working harder than it was, making it difficult for me to hear the stereo. But who cares about stereo in a Carrera? Isn't the rear engine music enough? All this I had to learn as I went along...

Next morning at seven I filled it up at Porlezza, Lake Lugano. The gas station attendant asked me to put my foot on the pedal in neutral. "Mamma mia!" he enthused as he heard that 231 hp howl. A few minutes later I was in sight of Lake Como, which the French poet Stendhal called "the most beautiful place on earth" over 120 years ago. When traveling was still a luxury enjoyed by only a few, Lake Como was already known throughout the cultured world. Ever since the period of the Roman settlement in the early second century B. C., it has been the resort of emperors, kings, fieldmarshals, cardinals, artists, writers and bonvivants.

Delicately introducing the Carrera into this ancient cultural domain is a matter of tact and discernment.

"BELLA MACCHINA"!

Descending to Menaggio I stayed in second. The sound of the Carrera's engine echoed around the vine-covered hills like a clattering allegro con brio. Coming out of the romantic town I was able to speed up, but the fun didn't last for long; just after you come out of a tunnel you're again forced to slow down. That way you're at leisure to admire all the venerable old villas that were put up here over the centuries by notables like the composers Bellini and Donizetti and the physicist Volta. Just after Menaggio, the Villa Margherita came into view, where Guiseppe Verdi completed his opera "La Traviata." The Villa La Collina rises high above the town of Cadenabbia; here West Germany's first chancellor, Konrad Adenauer, used to relax and here is where he wrote his memoirs. To the south, on the tip of a peninsula, the Villa Arconati, built two hundred years ago by the pomp-loving cardinal Angelo Durini, appeared in the early morning mist. Today, the villa belongs to an American family.

There is no end to villas down here, partly covered with the patina of centuries and sometimes so luxuriantly decorated that Hugh Hefner's Playboy Mansions in Chicago and Los Angeles look like simple cabins in comparison. The ferry took us over to Bellagio, an elegant little town rich in history. Its main landmark is the ancient Villa Serbelloni, today owned by the Rockefeller Foundation, to which it was presented by the German princess Ella von Thurn und Taxis. In Bellagio, the Carrera rolled across cobblestones that had been walked by Leonardo da Vinci, Napoleon, Mark Twain, Henry Wadsworth Longfellow, Franz Liszt, Arturo Toscanini and others.

I parked the Porsche next to the thousand-year-old Basilica of Saint James. I was interrupted several times while having my cappuccino by people asking me to open the hood, start the car, put my foot on the pedal, everybody praising my "bella macchina." It was Saturday night and after a while the first playboys from Milan began arriving. Jealously, their Ferraris, Maseratis and Lamborghinis wheezed past the Carrera's tail end, and the American guests at the Villa Serbelloni who had appeared on the piazza for their aperitifs commended the Porsche with compliments like, "What a nice car!" and, "Typical German craftsmanship!" They said the car didn't look a bit out of place in the romantic environment of this singularly beautiful little square next to Lake Como and that they really couldn't imagine a Lincoln Continental or a Cadillac in these surroundings. Let's face it, they said, a Porsche is a product of the Old World. Thinking of Leonardo da Vinci's stay in Bellagio, we wondered if that brilliant inventor would have appreciated the Porsche's rear engine. That's not the point, my American friends said; with a Porsche you have to talk in terms of a Gesamtkunstwerk, a masterpiece in which all art forms are combined. Small wonder, they said, that a Porsche was among the most admired exhibits in the Museum of Modern Art...

Thus, the popular European conversation about fuel consumption went off on a surprising tangent. How much could it do, how many hp did it have, what the acceleration was like – all that didn't matter any more. What really interested us was what kind of music one could associate with a high-tech product like the Porsche. Richard Wagner's "Ride of the Valkyries" seemed best suited for German autobahns; cruising along L. A. boulevards, James Brown's "Sex Machine" might be in order, and how about Ravel's "Bolero" as a grand finale with your female co-pilot? After all, eroticism does play a part in Porsches.

"Please don't lean against the car unless you're nude!" a 906 owner joked on a poster at a Porsche meeting in Missouri. Sigmund Freud would have had a field day with Porsches, regarding them as phallic symbols, as libido substitutes, as fountains of youth in mid-life crises. These are clichés that the folks at Porsche in Zuffenhausen, Ludwigsburg and Weissach have regarded as obsolete for a long time. All the same, from what I've seen, even a fifty-year-old has no trouble finding pretty female co-pilots as long as he drops enough subtle hints that he's driving a Porsche. Still, Elton John and Bruce Springsteen sound a lot better in my spacious, feeble 1978 6-cylinder car. Obviously, the joyous shout of "macchina potente" referred to my Porsche's 6-cylinder rear engine, not to myself. But what more could a car want than a string of praises running the gamut from "work of art" to "sex machine?" The Porsche entered the realm of the irrational long ago.

For a fair comparison, I repeated my Italian journey with a 944. Unimpeded by the noise of the engine, Samuel Barber's "Adagio for Strings" sounded excellent. There were no Italians asking me to open the hood, no Ferraris or Maseratis acting envious. When friends asked me about my impressions after testing a "new" Porsche, I was able to reply quite candidly: "The 944 is something you can become addicted to, while the 911 was already a legend in its own time." As far as their technical concepts are concerned, the two are light-years apart. All the same, they are both unmistakably Porsche. I wanted to find out why. I suppose that is the reason why I wrote this book.

FROM 40 TO 1100 HP

Question: Professor, what is the secret behind the fame of the Porsche make?

Prof. Porsche: One would have to delve back into the past. As a young boy, I was surprised that my father was known worldwide, more so than any other automobile designer. He always made the news when he transferred from Austro-Daimler to Daimler and later to Steyr. Nobody took any notice when another chief design engineer moved to a different firm. I think the reason for my father's being the focal point of interest was his nature and his modesty.

It was also typical that, whoever he was working for – Austro-Daimler, Daimler or Steyr – people were always simply talking about Porsche designs. The fact that my father himself never built a Porsche car is also of historical interest. He only worked for other firms. My father was not interested in secretive political machinations concerning the development and production of the Volkswagen. He was only interested in the challenge the task presented. We produced our first cars after the war and it was logical that the name Porsche lived on in these automobiles. Logical that a reporter asked me when my father actually died ... When I answered that it was in 1951, a year after we had begun work in Stuttgart again, the reporter looked at me in amazement and said: "Then everything here was done by you and not by your father!" Well, I myself have never attempted to actively build my own profile but rather continued in my father's image. The end of my father's impressive epoch and the start in Stuttgart under my management are tightly interwoven. The Porsche mystique developed during my father's time but did not reach its climax until we produced the first of the unmistakable Porsche cars in Gmuend.

Question: Before we get to the subject matter, I would like to revert to the time when your father worked for Daimler, later Daimler-Benz in Untertuerkheim, where he had to deal intensively with supercharged engines.

Prof. Porsche: His development work was based on the work of Paul Daimler, who had conducted the first tests with supercharged engines as early as World War I. Supercharged engines were not yet ready for series production when my father came to Untertuerkheim. The SSK, for instance, which was given its finishing touches by my father, benefited from the experience Daimler-Benz had already gained.

Question: The supercharger, in fact, did not play a part in the development work of Porsche after the war ...

Prof. Porsche: That's not quite true. During the war we were contracted to develop the VW engine as a stationary unit. This unit had to

8

have a certain power output, also for applications in high altitudes, including high mountains, to serve as a generator. We took a normal VW engine and hooked it up to a Roots fan which gave it 45 to 50 hp. To me this concept was so interesting that I drove a VW with a supercharged engine at the time.

Question: And why did you not use this supercharged engine in the first 356 models from the very beginning?

Prof. Porsche: First of all, this supercharged unit was not fully developed; we had to make do with parts available to us during the war. However, Roots fans were available. With the 356 model, I took a different approach and improved its performance by radically reducing its weight rather than increasing engine power.

Question: Was this a principle your father taught you or was it born out of necessity?

Prof. Porsche: It's a basic principle in automotive engineering. The power-to-weight ratio determines the performance capability of a car. It is not the high hp count but rather the power-to-weight ratio that is taken as a measure of the performance potential of an automobile. A heavy car with a lot of hp may still have a poor power-to-weight ratio.

Question: But this term "power-to-weight ratio" that you have just emphasized, nowadays does not seem to play any role at all in advertising or even with normal drivers when it comes to discussing the quality of a car.

Prof. Porsche: Right. This is probably because the automotive industry directs its attention to what is important for advertising cars. And what layman would have a concrete idea of the definition of "power-to-weight ratio"? A technically-minded person would, but not the average consumer. This is why I think it's a mistake that the focus is always on maximum speed, although there are strong objections to this sales argument from many sides. And yet, maximum speed is a direct consequence of power-to-weight ratio. In other

words, when I have a car with sufficient surplus power (i. e., a very good power-to-weight ratio), its speed is bound to be high. Hence, a car with good accelerating power will automatically give me a high speed performance.

Question: The 356 is considered to be one of the major milestones in the history of sports cars. Do you think it was the product of a long thought process ("I am going to build myself a car I've always dreamed of") or how did it come about? Material and component procurement at the time was, after all, a big problem, shortly after the war. How did this ingenious concept originate?

Prof. Porsche: The design was already on the table, so to speak. When the design office was developing the Auto-Union race car I participated in every phase. We had some thoughts which were later reflected in the design of the VW. For example: The Auto-Union race car had a gas tank with a capacity of as much as 58 gallons located at the center of gravity of the car. Therefore, a full or empty tank didn't make any difference as far as weight distribution was concerned. Our competition did not have the same concept: At the beginning of a race, there was a greater load on the rear axle than at the end of the race, when the fuel tank was empty. This was not the case with our Auto-Union race car.

When we launched the Volkswagen project, there was one decisive criterion: Considering its scheduled price, the weight had to be low. Also, it was to be a four-seater. This, in turn, meant that, if I build a four-seater with very low weight, the payload is a much more significant factor than with a big Mercedes. To a heavy car like this, it makes no difference whether it carries two or three people, because its curb weight is already at 3,300 pounds. However, since the Volkswagen had to weigh less than 1,440 pounds, the distribution of the payload was of crucial importance. And it was this design consideration that led to the rear-engine car, with minimal difference between "full" and

9

"empty." Most of the time, a car like the VW is driven with only one passenger so that two persons are seated ahead of the center of gravity. Two additional passengers would then sit just behind the CG, which means that the weight distribution always remains the same. This Volkswagen experience served as the basis for our first sports car, with which we wanted to achieve the same effect as with the 911 later on, the rear-engine car, where the weight distribution at "full" and "empty" is always the same. By contrast, all other sports cars are fitted with a not-very-small engine at the front and the gas tank at the back. And in terms of weight distribution, it makes a big difference whether the gas tank is full or empty.

Question: Before we go back to the 356, I would like to bring up the subject of the Cisitalia, which I believe you conceived concurrently with your design studies on the 356. Was the Cisitalia your pet project?

Prof. Porsche: Yes, you might say so.

Question: Was this because of the engineering details that you had built in?

Prof. Porsche: Partly and it was for us a new start after the war. From 1939 to 1945, we were not allowed to do anything at all in the commercial and sports sectors. While our employees were occupied with the Volkswagen, our work primarily focused on the Kuebelwagen, the amphibious car, battle tank designs etc. And then the contract from Dusio came, bringing a sudden breath of fresh air for our company . . . With this new development of the Cisitalia and in spite of the then-valid 1.5-liter formula, my plans were to achieve the same performance values as those of the Auto-Union race car which, after all, had a 6-liter supercharged engine. The Auto-Union car first had a single-stage supercharger which was followed by a two-stage supercharger during the last racing years. By contrast, we had designed the 1.5-liter engine of the Cisitalia with a two-stage supercharger from the start.

Question: For instance, did you also design the Cisitalia with four-wheel drive at your customer's request?

Prof. Porsche: No, we were given a free hand at it.

Question: Was the four-wheel-drive concept technically a new area for you for such a fast car?

Prof. Porsche: Partly. For instance, we built the Volkswagen with four-wheel drive as a so-called commander's limousine. For the VW amphibious car, four-wheel drive was indispensable because the vehicle would otherwise not have been able to get out of the water or would have had to turn around and move up the embankment in reverse.

Question: What technical specialties of the Cisitalia influenced your later technical developments? Was there a situation much later in which you might have said: "We already did a detail design of this years ago?"

Prof. Porsche: You can even go further than that. In talks with gentlemen of our R & D Department, I will often say, "We had this on our drawing boards forty years ago, for instance the four-valve engine." At the time, this technology was not applied because it was more expensive than a two-valve design. So, the four-valve technology is really "old hat" to me. But today, this technology is once again of interest and a lot of effort is being put into improving fuel efficiency and reducing exhaust emissions. Thus, technical findings are again coming into their own, whereas a few years ago, this was not possible due to high costs.

Question: So, all the exciting innovations offered to us motorists are really nothing new?

Prof. Porsche: Actually, no.

Question: What was your father's assessment of your design layout for the Cisitalia?

Prof. Porsche: He had just come back from a POW camp und was ordered initially to stay in the French occupation zone of Austria. So I drove to Kitzbuehel with all my drawings in order to show him my designs. "I wouldn't have changed a line," was his verdict. I took it as an acknowledgement that my job was well done.

Question: In retrospect, it seems to me nearly inconceivable that, shortly after the war, it was possible to build an automobile like the 356 almost by hand in a small shed. No material, and all the logistic problems. How did it work with the first fifty Gmuend cars?

Prof. Porsche: We still had a number of development-standard Volkswagen parts in stock. There were engine blocks, crankshafts, connecting rods and many other important parts. But still, we lacked some important things which we then "organized," as we had learned during the war.

Question: Also abroad?

Prof. Porsche: Also abroad. I myself repeatedly crossed the German–Austrian border with Bosch spark plugs in my pockets.

Question: Were the first bodies made of aluminum? Was this a temporary solution?

Prof. Porsche No, I wanted it that way. I would have preferred it if the 356 had kept the aluminum body. The economic situation at the time didn't allow us to utilize aluminum. The aluminum sheets for the first cars came from Switzerland.

Question: Formed by hand? Who was able to do that then?

Prof. Porsche: Formed by hand and hammered on wood. We had an expert who was a specialist in his field. But his work habits were quite individualistic: As soon as he finished a body shell, he would go on a drinking binge. Then he would return, pound out the next body . . . and so it went on. He had already learned his craft with my father in Wiener-Neustadt at Austro-Daimler.

Question: Who did the styling and the design of the 356?

Prof. Porsche: I did.

Question: Was there a historical model involved?

Prof. Porsche: No, the form of the 356 originated from my own feel of a car. There were many elements and past experiences that came together. I always loved driving cars and owned an Alfa Romeo with Pininfarina body as well as a 3-liter BMW – just to name a couple. The Alfa Romeo with the Farina body conveyed to me a very special feel of driving. This had nothing to do with better road holding. It was the way the fenders were shaped that I actually had the feeling that I could see the wheels, which provided very good clearance marks. After the war, I had the opportunity to drive a small Cisitalia, a sports car built from Fiat parts. Front engine, rigid axle – a very manageable car in terms of its size. The only thing I did not like was that the engine was hidden under a huge hood and did not provide any clearance marks. From these perceptions the idea of the 356 body filtered through; how it should be done to my liking; the size should be the same as the Volkswagen or the Cisitalia sports car. And what's more, I was already thinking about designing a car, the front fenders of which would turn with the wheels . . . which was after all something that had existed before. But it would have been too sporty for a road car.

Question: Did you ever give any thought to Cd-values at the time? In fact did the term already exist?

Prof. Porsche: It sure did. We had already tested the Bernd Rosemeyer world-record-car in the wind tunnel, both in Friedrichshafen and in Berlin, at the DVL. We experimented a lot in order to get the best results. When dealing with the term Cd-value, people are still making mistakes. In addition to the Cd-value, one should also speak of the factor F, because the air drag is expressed by the Formula Cd $\times$ F, where F stands for surface area. With the factor F decreasing, the Cd factor may increase and still give you a lower value than for another car.

Question: And it was possible to scientifically define this relationship at that time?

11

Prof. Porsche: Yes, indeed. Since we did not have a wind tunnel in Gmuend, we tested the first 356 prototypes as follows: exactly as in a test in a real wind tunnel, we stuck threads on the whole body surface. Then we drove on a normal road and under a bridge from where we took pictures of all sides of the car, which was passing at a speed of 62 mph. Then we checked whether or not the threads were clinging to the body and in what areas we had to make improvements. This is how we improvised a wind tunnel in the health resort of Gmuend.

Question: When you started designing such a prototype, would you do a survey of prospective buyers to find out what kind of car should be built and what criteria it would have to meet? Was there something like market research at the time? Or did you go by the principle: "I'm going to build a car the way it appeals to me – hoping that it will appeal to others as well?"

Prof. Porsche: That has always been a delicate point in my later years. Marketing in today's sense of the word did not exist when I first started in this business. But when we started the Volkswagen, I pressed the point that we should build a product which could be sold worldwide. Not just a small car that couldn't even be driven from Stuttgart to Frankfurt because it would fall apart, or only half-occupied ... but as a roadworthy automobile even when fully occupied. For instance, cars exported to Latin American countries had to have the right track width, because of roads with only two paved tracks. Or another example: The door of the first VW would open in the driving direction. When I visited the United States with my father, we found that this forward location of the door catch was not accepted there. Not for legal or safety reasons, but because the customers did not like it. Especially the ladies didn't, because when they were getting in or out of the car with this door arrangement, one could see under their skirts.

So, we made a last-minute change and put the hinges in front – everything without any marketing department. The Volkswagen was also the first car which had a heating system from the very beginning. At that time, normal cars didn't have heating. The feet would get warm anyway, because the boards on the engine side were never sealed too well.

Question: The 356 was easy to service, which I am sure made it very attractive. Were you able to use VW tools or were there any special tools?

Prof. Porsche: Certainly not for the body and chassis. VW tools and equipment were available only for engine, transmission and front axle parts. But the good after-sales service had primarily been ensured by the fact that we were able to ask Volkswagen dealers worldwide whether they wanted to distribute our car. I had made that agreement with Nordhoff.

Question: Was it difficult to get VW dealers interested in the 356?

Prof. Porsche: Not at all.

Question: I understand the way you got the dealers sold on the first cars of this model was quite adventurous and unorthodox.

Prof. Porsche: Yes – the first were Petermax Mueller, Raffay in Hamburg (the father, of course), Fritz Hahn in Stuttgart and Gloeckler in Frankfurt. We gave them a demonstration of some of the first cars. They were all car buffs and there was no reason why they should not like this car, which really turned out very well? "But," we stressed, "you have to help us. Each one of you will order as many cars as can be sold in the first year. And then you give us an advanced payment on the last car that we deliver." In this way, we had created the financial basis required to even start an automobile factory.

This method of selling cars was a completely new approach at the time. Besides, our 356 was such a success at the Geneva Auto Show and inspired so much enthusiasm that we had no marketing difficulties whatsoever.

Question: Did you ever believe that your firm would become so large?

Prof. Porsche: No. We had begun very modestly and planned on about 500 cars. These 500 units of the 356 finally grew into about 80,000.

Question: One of the books written about you is entitled "A Dream becomes Reality." Was the 356 the fulfillment of a decade-long dream? Or was the 356 not quite loaded with this sentimentality?

Prof. Porsche: The realization of the dream was not so much the 356, but what I have done with the firm. The 911 was more "my car" than the 356. I finally had so much money that I could build any car I wanted to. With the 356, we had to rely on existing technical resources. In the case of the 911, we had an engine, transmission and front axle of our own development. Not one little screw is comparable to any mass-production part.

Question: What were the reasons for replacing the 356? Was it for pure technical reasons or was it because the market called for a new model?

Prof. Porsche: The 356 went through many stages over its life cycle. Engine power and volume were increased, starting from 1.1 liter and moving on to 1.3 and 1.6 liters. We developed the standard gear box into our own synchromesh transmission. We installed our own brakes, etc. The 356 was continually further developed, step by step. Finally, we had come to a stage where I had to say: "We have reached the end!" The last impetus that the 356 received was the four-camshaft engine, first with 1.5-liter, then with 2-liter displacement. But with that, we had reached the limit and I asked my people: "What is the 356 lacking? With a four-camshaft engine, it has enough power, but it is very loud. The trunk of the 356 is very small; there isn't even enough space for a few golf clubs ..." These were some of the typical remarks made by customers.

So, we started working on some new design layouts. Initially, we started to convert the 356 into a four-seater coupé, but quickly abandoned the idea — in line with the motto: "Cobbler, stick to your last!"

There were already enough four-seaters, so why should people buy a four-seater Porsche? We therefore stayed with the 2+2-seat principle, but also provided for some more roominess, smoother running etc. With that, the 911 had reached its starting point. There were also some concepts which suggested too big a step forward such that I decided to stop it right there. There was a trend to develop a four-seater after all — and if a four seater, it should have a full-size trunk.

Then I said: "Here is a styling concept from my oldest son, Ferdinand Alexander, and I would like to have it realized!" This design went to the body shop and when I saw the first attempts, I found that it had been altered again. It was too big and too long. I then made it perfectly clear: "If this doesn't work, we'll turn the whole thing over to the Reutter body factory for further processing." (In the meantime, we had to take over the Reutter company.) From then, our own design engineers became cooperative, because they realized that their ideas wouldn't go through. This is how the 911 began in its original form, which even then boasted as many as 120 hp. Today, its turbocharged engine is putting out more than 300 hp and, basically, the engines currently used in Group C vehicles are also offspring of the 911 engine, with even more horsepower. And so the 911 was another beginning, because we were at an end with the parts delivered by VW.

Question: The rear-engine principle was a very controversial concept a few years ago, as one can read in all archives. What is your personal position in this respect? Is the air-cooled 6-cylinder horizontally opposed engine a relic from a bygone great era of engine design?

Prof. Porsche: Now look — let me describe that situation by telling you a little story that we are currently experiencing. In our company, we've been working on four-wheel-drive designs for a long time and have always been hindered in going through with them. For instance, I had the idea of converting a VW Passat to four-wheel drive and putting it on the market through our sales organization – with the standard Passat engine. This was perhaps 12 years ago. The Volkswagenwerk did not allow me to go through with this concept. We then also wanted to use all-wheel drive on the VW Transporter, the Type 2 of VW. Again, the Volkswagenwerk rejected the idea – now they are building both concepts themselves.

Question: To Porsche design layouts?

Prof. Porsche: No, not to our drawings, but the principle is the same. We had built our prototypes the same way the factory in Wolfsburg does today. If you take a closer look at Audi's rally wins (initiated by Audi's Ferdinand Piëch with the Audi Quattro), past and present, you will find that some of the brainwork leading up to this success has its origins here in Zuffenhausen, partly at a time when Mr. Piëch was still here. Now, all of a sudden, some of the cars entered in rallies are superior to the Quattro and part of them are mid-engined models. That means, if taken to the extreme, we are not that far off with a 911, which in turn means that – for all the opposition – if you are looking for extreme rally capability, then the 911 with added front-wheel drive is the most modern car today. The successes of Peugeot and Lancia are teaching us that extreme performance is not necessarily achievable with a normal concept.

Question: What can be learned from this as far as regular, "down-to-earth" cars are concerned? Relatively little?

Prof. Porsche: Quite a few things. Four-wheel drive will give you better traction and road holding on wintry roads than two-wheel drive. But even with two-wheel drive, there are major differences: The winter performance of a two-wheel-drive car is poorest with front-mounted engine and rear-wheel drive. Next is the two-wheel-drive vehicle with front engine and front-wheel drive. Conditions are even better with rear engine and rear-wheel drive, because in this way, the load conditions for the drive train are most favorable also when going uphill. In other words, an engine with its weight at a location where the wheels need traction. It is for this reason, that the 911 concept is not bad at all for certain extreme cases.

Question: When reading Porsche chronicles, it strikes me that the 914 and 914/6 models seem to be somewhat neglected.

Prof. Porsche: The 914 was a consistent further development toward a mid-engine car. But there were two unfortunate factors: All 914 bodies were built by Karmann and therefore did not necessarily represent Porsche quality. This was one handicap. The second reason: The inexpensive 914 with VW engine was even called "VW Porsche," which was not exactly conducive to making customers accept it as a "genuine" Porsche. Thirdly, it can be said that the installation of a 4-cylinder engine and then also a 6-cylinder engine led to an engineering concept that was not very fortunate. My idea at the time was to build one standard car from the front end to the engine compartment partition, but to offer two different rear ends depending on the type of engine used. The design engineers tried to combine these two rear ends into one, with a few basic disadvantages in that there wasn't even enough space for a briefcase behind the seats – just to name one of these unfortunate circumstances.

By the way, I got a 914 with an 8-cylinder engine as a birthday present.

Question: The 911 was the first big break in your model policy. Then, the decision to build water-cooled front engines must have been even more incisive. This new engine concept initially caused a lot of confusion among Porsche fans ... The 928, for instance, did not have a good start.

Prof. Porsche: This is why the 911 hasn't been canceled up to now. Neither the 928 nor the 924 has been able to overtake the 911. We are still building two-and-a-half times as many 911s as 928s.

Question: The 924, which was not fully taken seriously as a Porsche, seems to have been some sort of "present" from VW, but the 928 must have been pushed through by someone . . .

Prof. Porsche: Yes, it was Professor Fuhrmann who did it.

Question: Did it take you a long time to get used to the idea that a Porsche could look so different?

Prof. Porsche: I didn't oppose the idea. As a matter of fact, as long as I was the only one in charge here, I've always tried to give my men a lot of latitude, because I believe that creativity should not be suppressed. If someone is convinced that the 928 should look like this and not differently, you shouldn't interfere too much, otherwise nothing will come out of it. And since the family decided on changing to an outside management, one must expect an outside management to take different views and pursue different intentions.

Question: Are you happy about the fact that, as a family business, you turned the management over to someone else?

Prof. Porsche: Every family expands. My father was alone. My sister and I were the next generation. The third generation already consists of eight children and the two of us and the fourth generation has as many as twenty-five descendants. The question then arises: How can a firm such as ours stay in one hand? The larger the executive body, the more difficulty it will have to function effectively.

Question: Speaking about family matters . . . In family-run businesses, there has always been a conflict between the successful father, on the one hand, and the ambitious son waiting for his great chance, on the other hand. Let's take the extravagant Bugatti family as an example. Jean Bugatti suffered under the dominating personality of his father, Ettore. Have you also had this experience?

Prof. Porsche: Yes, we also experienced the father-son conflict, but I also learned a lot from it. My father and I did a lot of traveling together. When I was alone with him, he was ready to listen to my critical comments in every respect. But when other people were present, this was not advisable. My father was too authoritarian to tolerate any critical remarks in the presence of others.

Question: What kind of behavioral patterns did you learn from your father, as an entrepreneur?

Prof. Porsche: Positive and negative things. My father was very authoritarian and stubborn. He would work at the drawing board until midnight when he wanted to solve a tricky problem. For myself, I took this as a lesson that this is not the right approach. If you spend a lot of time brooding over a problem and cannot come up with a positive result after a certain period of time, I think it is better to relax a little, take a walk or do something similar and then start afresh.

I considered this a good principle, even at the time when I was working with my father. I remember the time when we were discussing the rear-wheel suspension of the Volkswagen: There was a lot of brainracking and continual re-drawing, but nothing came out to his liking. Endless nights went by and one day he walks up to engineer Mickl who had been working on this design problem and says, "I've got the solution: It came to me in a dream this morning!" So, the solution came to him in a phase of relaxation. It has happened to me many, many times that I intentionally switch off and sleep on a problem if I can't arrive at a positive decision at the first go.

Question: Another subject I would like to discuss with you is "aesthetics in automotive engineering." The styling of an automobile always seems to reflect a little bit of the customer's sense of beauty. A car should not only be functional, but should also have a beautiful appearance.

Prof. Porsche: I think it has always been a philosophy of our company that function and beauty are inseparable. Beauty as an end in itself is out of place in automobile manufacturing. If a body styling detail is to be really satisfactory from an aesthetic point of view, it must be functionally justified.

In other words: A good Cd-value must exclude unaesthetic features. It is mostly due to the laws that you find unaesthetic details on a car today, such as the outside mirror. It is downright unaesthetic, causes a lot of air drag – but it's a requirement.

Question: ... and it's also useful.

Prof. Porsche: Certainly, but does it have to be so ugly, as is often the case? License plates are another case in point. The Italians are fortunate to have narrow and unobtrusive plates at the front, whereas we have to drive around with huge things, which certainly don't make the car any prettier. If the Italians are allowed to use such small license, plates, why can't we?

Question: Were automobiles built in the past more attractive and more fun to car fans?

Prof. Porsche: Mr. Kales of the Volkswagenwerk in Wolfsburg once said: "Nowadays, if you don't take a close look at the brand emblems of cars, you can't distinguish them any more."

It is Porsche's strong point that we avoid such uniformity. Of course, the difference in outward appearance between a sports car and a regular passenger car was greater in the past than it is today. Today, there are certain laws that bind the stylist. Here is an example: Today you have to test the windshield under winter conditions by letting it freeze up and allowing it to thaw to a certain percentage in so many minutes at minus 20 degrees. No lawmaker in former times ever thought about something

like that! Whoever thought of a heated windshield for the Mercedes-Benz SSK!? Motorcycles are not subject to such extreme regulations. They can get by with a lot of things that are unthinkable with automobiles. This is why so many expensive motorcycles are driven by sports car fans – as a compensation!

Question: What will a car look like in the year 2000?

Prof. Porsche: The automobile will of course have to become more beneficial to the environment, which also includes noise reduction. Small cars will be preferred because of increasingly overcrowded roads, particularly in industrialized countries. Smaller cars will one day give you the same performance as a mid-sized car today. I believe, though, that there will still be expensive and inexpensive cars. Peter Schutz would say that a mink coat is not any warmer than a normal wool coat, but even so, you would not be able to persuade the ladies not to wear mink coats.

Question: Last question, Professor: Will Porsche stay independent? Will it want to stay independent?

Prof. Porsche: We would like to, yes! I am not a prophet, of course. One can't say to what extent this will be possible or not. Sixty years ago, there were about 25 automakers in the United States – today there are only four left.

Question: ... and Ferrari had to take refuge with Fiat ...

Prof. Porsche: Ferrari's bread-and-butter is sports cars rather than mass-production cars. If Porsche were to merge with a large concern, then this concern would have to be very careful not to make a unique expenditure that didn't give it any profit. To live in the shadow of a giant just for advertising purposes and not to be able to be independent – this won't work in the long run.

The interview with Professor Ferry Porsche was conducted by Ingo Seiff.

6

1 Type 935 (1978), tank filler cap
2 Porsche Nr. 1 ("Sport 356/1"), before complete restoration

3 Ferry Porsche in "Nr. 1" on occasion of the Porsche-Parade, Nuerburgring 1981

4 Porsche-Parade Nuerburgring 1981
5 Type 356 A – 1600 GS Carrera (Speedster), 1958

6 Type 356 A – 1600 Speedster (1956)
7 Type 356 A – 1600 Speedster (1956)
8 Type 356 A – 1600 GS Carrera (Speedster) 1958

7

8

11

12

13

9–13 Four-seater prototype 695 (1962) with T-7-body and Carrera-2-engine. Later on the front section was kept for the type 911
14 Type 356 B cabriolet (1959)
15 Type 356 B ("Super 90") 1961

"IF I WERE A CAR, I'D BE A PORSCHE"

Question: Is America really such a paradise, a land of unlimited opportunity for Porsche? After all, the Carrera costs about $ 34,000 now.

Schutz: When you talk about unlimited – the only thing unlimited in this world is taxes. The dollar currently has a high exchange rate but at one time it was down to 1.70 deutschmarks – so we had losses in America. The favorable exchange rate allows us to make investments that have been overdue for years. But it's true: America does offer the greatest – short-term – possibility of reaching the necessary turnover. We plan to build "only" 50,000 cars in 1985. That includes three completely different lines – namely, the 4-, 6-, and 8-cylinder series. The cost of keeping all three of these series at technical peaks is considerable. For this reason we hope we'll be able to sell a greater number of cars.

Question: How does the typical American Porsche driver differ from one from the "Old World?" I had the impression that the Americans were completely different.

Schutz: I don't think so at all. Americans are different from Europeans – they live in another cultural environment. But the characteristics of our customers that attract them to Porsche are amazingly the same all over the world.

Question: Even though Americans can never drive their Porsche cars to the limit on their highways and interstates . . . like we can . . .

Schutz: That's not true. They have race tracks and organized club activities where they can do that. And to tell the truth: Who here drives his Porsche to the limit on the autobahns? In the first place, Porsches aren't made to be driven constantly at top speed on the autobahns. Porsche's top speed is a by-product of its accelerating power. If you drive a Porsche at 60 or 80 miles per hour and you know the car could easily go twice that fast, then you experience a very secure and comfortable drive. And it's just this margin that gives the Porsche owner the feeling that he's looking for. My opinion is that driving a Porsche to the limit is not the main point of Porsche enthusiasm.

Question: I know some British Porsche owners who make the trip from Dover to Calais on the weekend just to drive as fast as possible to Vienna because this way they can really "punish" their cars.

Schutz: When it comes to having a fling, why not do it on the Nuerburgring for 12 deutschmarks?

Question: They come to our autobahns to compare their power with other makes.

Schutz: I think that is an exception and not at all typical of our customers.

Question: Daimler-Benz and Porsche automobiles used to be connected with "built-in priority"; if they were behind you, get out of the way!

Schutz: I wasn't here then but I'd like to return to the topic of the Porsche's top speed. To drive very fast, straight ahead on the autobahn, you certainly don't need a Porsche. Any other car will do, costing a lot less than a Porsche. A Porsche is made to "enjoy," not to "use." Or, as Professor Porsche used to say, "It's great for a quick swing around the corner."

Question: The American market was the first to get the 928 S with the 32-valve engine. Was there a technical reason for this?

Schutz: Three years ago we decided not to develop any more engines based on leaded gasoline. In the past 10 to 15 years so many advances were made in the area of injection, ignition and combustion that there was hardly any difference in performance between an engine made for unleaded gasoline and a catalytic convertor, and the traditional engine made for leaded gasoline. For this reason we found it unjustifiable for a parallel development. That's why the 928 S 32-valve engine is the first Porsche engine designed exclusively for unleaded gasoline. It can only be offered in Europe when unleaded gas is widely available.

Question: You are an engineer. When you took over your position at Zuffenhausen how did you resolve the problem that, on the one hand, there was still the rear-drive concept with an air-cooled 6-cylinder horizontally opposed engine, and on the other hand the water-cooled engine in the front – besides, the 911's rear engine isn't the latest, technically speaking.

Schutz: I can't understand that type of question. It's like reproaching a restaurant owner for offering poultry, fish and meat all at the same time and asking him, "Can't you decide which is best?" Porsche builds technical works of art mainly for connoisseurs. It's impossible to say that this model or that is the best. It's all a matter of taste. It's the same when it comes to music. Some love guitar, others piano.

We now offer at the same time the 944 Turbo and the Carrera. They are about equal when it comes to road performance, acceleration and top speed. So, one could raise the objection when comparing these two cars, "Why?" You can drive them on the same roads, they have the same power, and yet you experience a totally different feeling when driving them. Different engine sounds, different handling. To return to the musical analogy: One person likes to hear a hit on the guitar, another prefers the same hit on the piano. The same song but still different. The same goes for the differences between the 944 Turbo and the Carrera.

That's why there's no use in comparing rear engined rear-drivers, on the one hand, and front-engined rear-drive models, on the other. The main thing is to fulfill our customers' expectations. And these expectations cover a whole range. We try, in our three series (4-, 6-, and 8-cylinder), to convey as many different driving sensations as possible using the technology on hand.

Question: There's an ongoing dispute among Porsche freaks about "true" Porsches and "false" Porsches. The universal consensus is that the 924 is no real Porsche, only the 911 is.

Schutz: I know even stricter standards: the only one and truly Porsche is the 356 . . . everything that came afterward was just second fiddle. This obsession produces strange effects. When the 356 Carrera, planned to have four cams, was offered in the U.S.A. with only one, there immediately appeared a T-shirt reading, "All real Carreras have four cams." I appreciate this dispute over what a real Porsche is or isn't. But to make it very clear: If the name PORSCHE appears on all the different models then it means that they were all designed, built, and offered by Porsche. For me that is the only real Porsche. A little bit less real doesn't exist.

Question: I've told friends about my experiences with the 944 and the Carrera. Hardly anyone was interested in the characteristics of the

4-cylinder engine, even though it's been a best-seller for a long time. Is it still considered a bread-and-butter car? It seems that the 911, on the other hand, is still the car freak's dream.

Schutz: You can apply the old Latin saying "So many heads, so many opinions," to this topic. A 911 enthusiast is crazy about his car, the 944 enthusiast about his. That's the way it should be. It would be stupid to build two completely different cars that extract the same emotions. To take another example from music: One loves Dixieland jazz, another Beethoven's symphonies. But I notice: You hang around with 911 owners quite a bit.

Of all the Porsche models the 911 seems to be the one to offer the most excitement for full fledged automobile enthusiasts. You can see it especially on the Porsche club scene. In the club races, on the slalom track, the 911 is the most fun. Porsche owners who organize clubs seem to make the 911 the focal point. Since I, too, am a 911 lover, I can understand that. Maybe your picture of the Porsche palette is a bit one-sided because of that.

Question: When I take the podium in Porsche club circles and defend the 944, confess that it is addicting, I don't have it easy...

Schutz: Then you're like a Catholic in the middle of Moslems.

Question: With all the noise coming from a 911 it's impossible to listen to music in peace. But in a 944 that's a different story.

Schutz: There you're wrong. In a 911 the machine makes the music. You just prefer a different kind of music.

Question: To continue our conversation on the same note, you'd get the impression that Porsche driving is like a religion – especially when it comes down to the preferences of a certain type.

Schutz: Our goal is to offer the full range of technical possibilities as well as driving sensations. Therefore, it's unthinkable to neglect any segment of our range of models.

Question: Before you came to Zuffenhausen there was talk of putting the 911 to sleep.

Schutz: Maybe that's the reason why I'm here.

Question: There was a time when it was heatedly discussed that maybe this car should finally disappear. The press files are full of stories about it.

Schutz: I talked about this many times with Professor Porsche. The discussion on the fate of the 911 weighed heavily on his mind. If I've brought anything to this company, then it is, I believe, that I've explained the Porsche philosophy, which has always been and always will be falsely interpreted. To understand it you have to consider the full range we offer.

Question: But I'm happy that there's the 944...

Schutz: Porsche wouldn't be Porsche without it. When I came to Zuffenhausen in 1981, the 944 was introduced. I made it clear to all the workers that, in this case, everything was essential. I said, "If we don't get the 4-cylinder series on its feet and make it a success then we're headed for some rough times here. The same goes for the 928."

Question: From previous interviews with you I've found out that you run the business with a very human touch, that you can motivate the workers. You supposedly once said that you weren't really an auto manager... Are you a seller of dreams?

Schutz: No.

Question: To own a Porsche is a dream for a *real* man.

Schutz: That's true – and also for a woman. I'm not *the* salesman in this firm. We all are.

Question: What's your secret to get the workers motivated? It must take more than just talk about yields and turnovers...

Schutz: Remarks about yields and turnovers won't motivate anyone. There's really no trick at all to motivating people, although countless books have been written on the subject. The basic thing is this: Wherever you find a positive working climate, whether in a business or on a team, you can almost bet that the following four questions have been clearly answered.

The first question: Why are we here? What are we supposed to be doing? What is the purpose of this business – its goal? Where do I fit in? What's my role in reaching this goal? The workers need to know why they are working here.

The second question which needs to be clearly answered: Can I do what's expected of me? And as feedback, how am I doing?

The third question is: What's in it for me? If I do what I'm supposed to do and do it well, what's my reward?

The fourth question: Who can I turn to if I have trouble and need help? If I can't do what's expected of me is there someone I can go to who will listen and be ready to help me?

If these four questions are constantly in front of all the workers and are always positively and clearly answered, then you'll have a team that's happy to go to work. Dr. Lange, our personnel director has a great example showing worker motivation. Three men on a construction site were each asked the same question, "What are you doing here?" The first one said, "I'm busting up rocks." The second one said, "I'm earning my money here." And the third one said, "I'm helping to build a cathedral." The differences between these three answers makes it clear: We have to motivate our workers so that not only do they believe, – in a broader sense – they actually are helping build a cathedral.

Question: This means that a lot of knowledge of human nature and psychology come into play.

Schutz: Knowledge of human nature, sure, but psychology is only necessary when dealing with workers who have emotional problems. What I'm talking about here is how to motivate mature, sensible people who work together with consideration for each other – how to get each one of those workers to operate at peak performance. You referred to me earlier as an engineer . . . that's irrelevant. Technical matters are the responsibility of Mr. Bott and his team. My job in this business is to see to it that firstly, the right people are employed; that secondly, these workers are so organized that they can reach their peak performance; and thirdly, that they are so motivated that they *want* to do only their best. When I can accomplish that, then my job is fulfilled. Above all, clarity must reign in the direction of our firm. In addition, I must recognize our customers' wishes and ideas and make sure that we as a company understand our customers better than we do ourselves. Only then can we meet their expectations. To make those targets clear and see to it that our workers are motivated, as I described above, that's my job. It has nothing to do with rear engines or water-cooled engines.

Question: What does your market research look like?

Schutz: The market research in this company is mainly done by the executive board, but also by all the workers here. It isn't market research in the usual sense of the word. It's the responsibility of every man and every woman in this business to know our customers thoroughly. When a company needs a department to get to know its own customers, then there's something wrong with the management.

The most important thing in this business is the customer. Every discussion about product planning in this house begins with him. The customer is always the starting point with us.

Question: You described the typical Porsche driver as an achiever, a man who has become something in life or who can afford something big, beautiful and expensive when he finds himself in the mid-life crisis.

Schutz: I don't like that word "man." Typical Porsche driver characteristics don't apply only to males and have nothing whatever to do with mid-life crisis. But it is true that Porsches are relatively expensive. That's why most Porsche buyers have successful careers (compared to others) – so they can afford a Porsche. And it has nothing to do with inclination. If 18-year-olds could afford a Porsche, then we'd have a gigantic portion of the market. Unfortunately, very few people in this age category can afford to buy one. There is no German term for the word "achiever."

We believe we know our customers so well that the word "achiever" could be applied to all of them worldwide. And they only seem to be risk takers. Basically, Porsche customers do their homework thoroughly. Outsiders have the wrong impression if they think Porsche fans are impulsive buyers. When a customer walks into the shop and orders a car he knows exactly what he wants. It usually takes many years of thinking before he decides on a Porsche.

Porsche buyers strive to be the best, like Martina Navratilova in tennis. Typical of the Porsche owners identification with their make is the activity involved. For instance you can tell this by the way they are involved with Porsche clubs. Maybe you could describe our customers best with this slogan: "If I were a car, I'd be a Porsche!" This striving for top-class performance, as embodied in a Porsche, also shows in our involvement in racing. As a company we have to continually portray ourselves in a way that the typical Porsche customer can identify with; that he would run the company the way we do. Or if he wants to get involved in racing, then it's best with a 956.

We don't need to win every race but the way we take part should be exemplary. We would never do something foolish for the sake of a quick success.

That would fit the Porsche image about as well as showing off would. If we were to behave differently, to show ourselves up, then I'd very soon have a pile of letters on my desk all saying, "That's not our style..."

Or, only as an example, if we were to make exaggerated changes to a Porsche model, like decorate a 928 S with chrome, or add air inlets and spoilers that weren't necessary, just for the sake of decoration... That might fit a Lamborghini – and by that, I don't mean to blast Lamborghini drivers – but it just doesn't fit Porsche style.

Question: From my many conversations with Porsche owners three emotional concepts kept resurfacing, which started me thinking. One American Porsche fan described his relationship with his Speedster as an obsession. Another said that owning and driving a Porsche was a religion or a philosophy of life. And in Germany a Targa driver spoke of a love relationship with his car. Do you find these declarations exaggerated?

Schutz: I think it's understandable – I can understand it well. But that someone "loves" his Porsche... I would like to explain the concept of "love." The best definition comes from an American scholar who had worked with the Indians for a long time and had taught them to read. When he was ready to say farewell, an old Indian woman called out to him, "I like me best, when I'm with you." That's what I think love is and it doesn't have anything to do with sex. Applied to my Porsche that means that I feel very good when I'm sitting in my favorite car. So I can understand that Porsche fan who loves his car. When I've had a pretty hectic day, which happens from time to time, I look forward to the journey home in my car – probably more so than some people look forward to a drink. I'm happy because when I'm in my Porsche I'm in surroundings which make me feel good.

Question: Porsche drivers used to be called "tough guys." Would that mean that Porsche cars are macho? In the London "Sunday Times" the 928 S was tagged as a "wife-beater."

Schutz: "Wife-beater" is a horrible description which I can't accept. If "tough" men drive Porsches, then "tough" women drive them, too.

In America the word "tough" has several meanings. In this case, I'd say "tough" was "cool." The characteristics of achievers, which we talked about earlier, are also found in Porsche-driving women. I would even say that women express the so-called Porsche personality quite distinctly. Whether they are career women or housewives, the way they manage their household, raise their children... they set high goals for themselves with marked individuality. A propos macho autos: Among the millions of machos among the men on this earth, the Porsche drivers are perhaps more macho-like than any other macho.

Question: Let's talk about racing. You supposedly once said, "It is fun, it's entertaining and motivating."

Schutz: I don't think I said it in those words. Instead, I'd say that racing is Porsche's calling card. It serves three purposes in this business:

1. Public relations and advertising. A Porsche success in an international race — which is a reflection of our technical know-how — is reported worldwide. 2. Racing makes an important contribution to further technology. We are able to carry out developments and innovations for a competition car at a pace and with such involvement that otherwise would not be possible. 3. When it comes to racing, there are some important things which are indispensable. For example, there's a deadline to be met regardless of working hours and holidays. The car must be ready for the race! Timing is of the utmost. A racing car must be a zero-faults-car. There are no excuses: The car has to be ready on time and it can't have any faults. This focus on achievement affects the entire company.

Question: What's going to happen with the TAG-Motor?

Schutz: We are only the firm accepting the order. What's going to happen next will depend on the client. If we are contracted to further develop this successful engine then we will do so with great involvement.

Question: Will Porsche return with its own team to the Formula 1?

Schutz: The only things certain in this world are death and taxes. Otherwise, anything is possible. But right now there are no plans to enter again.

Question: The turbo-engine principle is turning up everywhere, even in small cars. Do you think this trend will last?

Schutz: I don't agree with that statement totally. Turbocharging – like all other technical developments – can't be used just anywhere. It offers certain things but also has its disadvantages. Turbo engines are more complicated and therefore more costly to maintain, but they give you an increase in power unavailable any other way. We think that turbocharging has its place but there are other developments, such as the 4-valve technique, which need to be carried on.

Question: There's currently only one firm, namely Lancia, using supercharged engines in sedans. Has this ever been considered at Porsche?

Schutz: We're continually considering such technical possibilities and keeping ourselves in the picture as far as further developments go. Up to now we've decided that the supercharged variant just isn't attractive enough to add to the options at Porsche.

Question: To conclude, I'd like to pose two more provocative questions – why are Porsches becoming ever more powerful and ever more expensive? Isn't that a never-ending spiral?

Schutz: Ever more powerful? As far as I'm concerned a car can never have enough power! We're constantly making our cars more economical and better for the environment and at the same time improving the road performance. If these developments are available to us, why should we set a limit to driving fun and pleasure and better road performance?

As to "ever more expensive": The most expensive part of a Porsche is the wages and salaries. That applies not only to the designers but also to the builders. In addition to the scale wage, our employes receive bonuses, when the profits allow it. This way we really do have the best automobile makers in our firm. In the high-salary-land West Germany the price of a Porsche is due to the high proportion of wage costs. So it's unlikely that Porsche will be cheaper in the future. We also don't think about rationalizing here. Thank goodness we have customers who accept the price. As long as that's the case, we'll always build better instead of cheaper cars.

Question: Would Porsche, for financial reasons, be manufactured under license in another country, with strict quality control?

Schutz: At this time I don't think that is a worthwhile solution. It would be a very risky step to take. I don't think I'd dare do it. A Porsche is a Porsche because it's developed and produced by the Porsche staff here in West Germany.

Question: Do you already have robots?

Schutz: Yes. They bring the supplies and materials from the warehouse to the assembly line – which doesn't have any influence on the quality of our cars. We use robots in manufacturing only where they'd improve the quality of the working area. They clean the motor block when it's finished. That's done with a foul-smelling liquid. In the past, workers tasked with that job had to wear rubber overalls, rubber gloves and face masks. Today the robot does this difficult job, and better than a human ever could. We use robots to make the working environment more humane. We wouldn't use them to cut back on our work force or to make our cars cheaper. Maybe one day that will be a necessary step but it's not in our plans now. To sum up: robots, yes, when they help to improve the quality of the working environment and of our product.

Question: Since July 1985, a Mooney 201 has been flying around the world with an air-cooled 6-cylinder engine derived from the 911. Will airplane engine manufacturing enrich Porsche's palette in the future?

Schutz: A large portion of our customers are amateur pilots and we feel we should make these special Porsche buyers another enticing offer; I'm convinced that airplane engines could be an additional business for Porsche in the 1990s. Developing such an engine is a laborious and costly business that takes many years. We've made so many discoveries while working on the Mooney project that we're ready to apply some of them to current automobile engine developments.

Peter W. Schutz, President of Porsche AG, talked with Ingo Seiff.

HELMUTH BOTT

THE REAR-ENGINE / REAR-DRIVE PHILOSOPHY

During the first 100 years of automotive history, innumerable engineers of renown have attempted to find the optimal solution for transmitting engine power onto the driving wheels.

In accordance with the maxim, "horses pull with their front legs," which is often quoted even today, the first steam wagon to replace the horsedrawn cart also utilized front-wheel drive. The inventor, Nicholas J. Cugnot, had come up with a good solution in the year 1770 by placing the proper load on the front driving wheel of his three-wheeled vehicle. The steam boiler and both working cylinders were located ahead of the front axle. In contrast, the first automobiles, built by Carl Benz and Gottlieb Daimler, had their engines and driving wheels in the rear.

But even at this early stage, it is probably useful to define a few terms, because, according to our present definitions, those Daimler and Benz cars of the past actually featured mid-engines, or more precisely, underfloor mid-engines. And that puts us in the midst of technology, so we should first determine what various drive possibilities there are. Two things are important: the arrangement of the driving wheels and the location of the engine.

"Front-drive vehicles" have their engines and driving wheels in front, although the engine can be located in front of, on top of or behind the front driving axle.

"Standard construction" refers to vehicles that have an engine in front which, by means of a propeller shaft, drives the rear wheels.

"Rear-engine/Rear-drive vehicles" feature an engine located immediately in front of, behind or directly above the rear driving axle.

Over the past two decades, however, when the engine is located ahead of the rear driving axle it has come to be called a "mid-engine." During the days of the Auto Union racing car in the 1930s, the same system was referred to as a rear-engine car or as a rear-drive car.

And to add to the variety, today we also have four-wheel-drive vehicles, with engines in the front, the middle or the rear.

What are the advantages and disadvantages of these different concepts, and are there solid technical justifications for the different constructions? As is the case with most technical problems, there is no single solution. Use and application criteria, size and available space, styling and handling characteristics combine to produce an overall compromise – and every automobile is a compromise.

Especially under minimal load conditions, the location of the engine determines the weight distribution of the vehicle, and thus influences the handling characteristics.

"Front-drive vehicles" tend to feature good directional stability, good traction under winter

40

conditions, and trouble-free handling in curves, especially for average drivers. In extreme cases they tend to understeer and reach their limits fairly early in sports competition. As the payload increases the center of gravity shifts toward the rear, which can turn the advantages listed above into disadvantages.

The "standard layout" – front engine, rear-wheel drive – tends to feature good directional stability and balanced characteristics under normal conditions. In winter, sandbags in the trunk often have to compensate for insufficient load on the driving axle.

The Porsche Transaxle Principle, used in the 924, 944 and 928 series, constitutes a compromise between standard and rear-engine/rear-drive layout. Part of the drive train, the transmission, is separated from the front-mounted engine and located near the rear axle. This improves handling and road holding, particularly under winter conditions.

The "rear-engine/rear-drive vehicle" tends to have less directional stability and at the same time is more sensitive to wind than front-drive vehicles. This vehicle tends to oversteer in curves but has very good all-around characteristics under bad weather conditions, on mountain roads and in winter driving.

All inherent disadvantages – and this of course applies to the drive systems described above as well – can be compensated for by means of secondary measures and proper coordination of chassis and aerodynamics.

But to get back to the main topic. The rear-engine/rear-drive system has been utilized – in combination with a mid- or rear-mounted engine – in the best-known Porsche concepts: in the Auto Union racing car, the Volkswagen, in the Porsche types 356 and 911, as well as in all Porsche racing cars, from the 550 in 1952 on up to the 956 in 1982.

Does that mean that rear-engine/rear-drive has become a matter of philosophy, a sort of "Weltanschauung" at Porsche? Certainly not,

otherwise the modern Porsche 4- and 8-cylinder vehicles wouldn't have been equipped with the Transaxle system. What motivated Professor Porsche and his team to design the VW Beetle – with over 20 million built up to now, the most prolifically produced car in the world – with rear-engine/rear-drive?

First, there was the goal of designing an inexpensive, light, robust, economical and durable vehicle with plenty of payload. Inexpensive and light by cutting down on the elements used in the common standard construction of the day with its water-cooled front engine, for example by eliminating the cardan shaft and by integrating the differential into the transmission casing of the rear-mounted engine. Air cooling instead of water cooling: An engine with forced circulation cooling can be placed anywhere and is lighter than a water-cooled engine with its radiator system.

Torsion-bar springs and a stable body platform assembly with central tubular frame structure were designed to make the car robust and long-lived. The air-cooled 4-cylinder horizontally opposed engine was provided with an effective oil cooler, a feature usually reserved for high-performance engines. The rear-engine/rear-drive layout avoided the usual drive shaft connection to the steering axle, which is commonly subject to wear. Today the majority of all conventional cars – particularly in the lower mid-sized range – are front-drive vehicles. The usual justification for this is the car's easy handling, especially suited to the average driver.

But other conditions prevail when it comes to sports and racing cars. Although in the first few decades of the automobile age, several attempts were made to equip sports and racing cars with front drive, the standard concept prevailed. The decisive factor was the driver's ability to make the car more responsive in cornering with the rear-driven wheels. Driving wheel spin or wheel slip prevents optimal transmission of cornering forces, i. e., the car swerves. If this happens with front driving wheels, the car becomes unsteerable. But if the rear wheels of a rear-drive car skid, the experienced driver can compensate with the front wheels. This balancing act, steering with two axles, by maneuvering the steering axle and by giving gas to the driving axle produces faster lap times for the good driver, given equal weight and engine performance. This applies to the comparison of front-wheel drive with rear-wheel drive, although in the case of rear-wheel drive vehicles, the engine can also be located in front, in other words, in comparing front-drive with the conventional drive train concept.

Thus, with few exceptions which never proved terribly successful, all racing cars in the first five decades of automobile history were standard layouts: engine in front, drive in the rear. Until Professor Porsche and his team built their Auto Union race car and managed to win their first Grand Prix. That was on July 15th, 1934, at the Nuerburgring, with Hans Stuck Sr. at the wheel.

Despite the spectacular debut of the new rear-engine – or more precisely, the mid-engined concept – it took another 25 years for the rear-engine/rear-drive concept to prevail in race car constructions. Today there isn't a single formula racing car with an engine in front.

And that has nothing to do with "Weltanschauung" – it's simply a matter of competitiveness. Critical cornering with the engine in front and the drive in the rear can be further improved by adding additional load to the driving axle with a mid- or rear-mounted engine. Even at Indianapolis, where the front engine long endured because of the course's special characteristics, rear-engine/rear-drive has taken over completely. In addition to better handling in the curves, there is also more accelerating power and a more favorable brake response: With a greater load on the rear axle, brake power distribution can be more balanced.

What's the situation with sports cars? In 1948, the first vehicle to carry the name Porsche – the 356 – was a mid-engine car with rear-wheel drive, based on the principles of the Porsche Auto Union race car. The 356 lived up to expectations in terms of performance and handling, but for a sports car didn't offer adequate space for passengers and luggage. Thus only one mid-engine prototype was built; all its successors in the 356 series were rear-engined models, that is, transmission in front of the rear axle, engine behind the rear axle. In this way it was possible to make room for a large additional trunk behind the front seats, a trunk which, when necessary, could be transformed into seats for two additional passengers. Adequate weight distribution was achieved by keeping the 4-cylinder horizontally-opposed engine short, and by the use of light metals.

In its day, the Porsche 356 was the lightest and most economical sports car. The mid-engine 356 001 weighed 1,288 pounds, the later rear-engine coupé weighed 1,674 pounds, and the vehicles built in Zuffenhausen with a full steel body weighed between 1,784 and 1,828 pounds. With fuel consumption of 24 miles per gallon, and for those days outstanding acceleration and cruising speed values, the car was a solution that couldn't have been achieved with any other design principle.

In the early years there was still a lot to be learned and improved in regard to directional stability and critical range cornering, and discussions of the proper adjustment of the car's handling took up a lot of time. One anecdote from those days may serve to illustrate the point. There were a number of experienced experts whose suggestions were quite helpful. Among them were after-sales manager Hans Klauser, Huschke v. Hanstein, the racing driver and head of the racing department, and Richard von Frankenberg, a racing driver and editor of "Christophorus." He had discovered the military airfield in Malmsheim. It was at this field

42

that intensive experimentation went on in adjusting the chassis of our production vehicles. Richard loved the 356 and its strong tendency to oversteer, and he enjoyed power-sliding through the curves. He was convinced that there was a direct relationship between the car's angle of drift and its speed in the curves. The greater the angle, the higher the speed. While these discussions were going on, I had just concluded the preliminary work on the Porsche 356 A, and had discovered that, with less oversteer, and in particular with more emphasis on the front wheels in the curves, substantially higher cornering speeds could be achieved.

This of course didn't look nearly as spectacular, but the stop watch proved that it was faster. Richard wouldn't believe the theory at first, and wagered a bottle of champagne that he could drive the course faster with the old 356. The big event was held on a Saturday morning. We drove the two cars to Malmsheim, and it turned out that neither a stop watch nor a referee was necessary. The experimental car, with its less extreme tendency to oversteer, was considerably faster, and after five laps, I even managed to lap the "curve artist." This was due not solely to the higher critical range cornering speed, but primarily to the handling of the older vehicle, which broke away again and again, whereas the experimental car could be driven to the limit without problems. The result was the same when Richard and I switched cars and repeated the race. From then on he accepted the "understeering" newcomer.

The successor to the 356, the 911, has long since become the most prevalent Porsche, and has proved its value in all fields of racing. It has become the Rally and Grand Tourisme World Champion, and in its 935 form has also won the Le Mans 24 hours. Hardly any other vehicle concept has proved itself so thoroughly in so many different competitions over the years.

Over and over again, whenever it looked like the rear-engine/rear-drive car — which has become something of an outsider among mass production vehicles — could no longer fulfill new technical requirements or laws, solutions have been found which live up to all expectations. The pressure to build lightweight engines is strongest among rear-engine vehicles. Air-cooling also offers an obvious opportunity to save a few pounds.

Air-cooled high-performance engines are also in great demand for light sports, travel and business aircraft. Thus, it only made sense to develop an aircraft engine from the 911 rear-engine, which had been optimized repeatedly. The aircraft version received its approval from the Federal Aviation Authority in 1984.

This Porsche aircraft engine "PFM 3200" is more economical, lighter and, because of its simple operation, safer than its competitors. Its use in two different types of aircraft has fully lived up to all expectations, and it won't be long before this engine is included as standard equipment in a variety of aircraft, both as a front- and rear-mounted engine.

Porsche's car production features three different types, two with the transaxle principle mentioned above — engine in front, transmission and drive in the rear — and, even after decades, the good "rear-engine" car. This clearly indicates, I think, that our company philosophy is not bound to a single concept.

All our sports cars do have one thing in common, however: They feature rear-wheel drive, and up to now, we just can't imagine a Porsche sports car with front-wheel drive.

Time has not stood still, however, and, when it comes to rally vehicles, for example, a not-so-new concept has finally prevailed: four-wheel drive. But even here, the competition between the various concepts continues.

The possibility of unevenly distributing the torque between the front and rear axles, and combining the weight and torque distribution by means of engine placement, opens up new perspectives.

PAUL FRÈRE

PORSCHE 911:
THE LIVING LEGEND

The Porsche 911 is still one of the world's most popular and respected sports cars, even after more than 20 years of production, during which neither its form nor its technical features have been altered substantially. Continual advances in development by an enthusiastic team have kept the car fresh through all the years, and the ongoing success of the road and racing models have given it unprecedented prestige the world over. But the career of the 911 is by no means at an end: It is no secret that many new developments are underway, which will guarantee the 911 its "pole position" in sports car production.

The 911 is a perfect example of how sports car racing experience can contribute to the improvement of production line vehicles. But a car for everyday use has to meet requirements that have little to do with sport: comfort, elasticity, quiet running, endurance and environmental attributes. Porsche development engineers have recognized this fact.

The Porsche design office founded back in 1931 was responsible for such successful designs as the famed Auto Union Grand Prix car of the years 1934 to 1937. When design of the 911 began in 1963, Porsche could already look back on ten years of experience as an automobile factory. In those days it built the type 356 out of bodies fabricated by the Reutter company and mechanical elements produced mainly by Volkswagen. It was only the cylinder head and the double carburetor – which increased the performance of the Beetle engine from 24 to 40 horsepower – and the very streamlined body form developed by Porsche that provided for relatively sporty driving. Porsche continued to develop its own manufacturing facilities, and over the years, the 356 came to include fewer and fewer VW parts. Nonetheless, for the young company it was an ambitious undertaking to develop its own completely new sports car design, especially since the goals were set high: Using a 6-cylinder engine with only two liters of displacement, the car was supposed to hit speeds of at least 125 miles per hour, and to be more comfortable, roomier and quieter than the 356.

Following the death of his father in January 1951, Professor "Ferry" Porsche took over as head of the company. He remained faithful to a basic principle of the 356 he had developed: The 911 was outfitted with an air-cooled rear-mounted engine. In order to profit from experience with the 4-cylinder 356 engine, the 6-cylinder was originally conceived as an advanced development of the push-rod 4-cylinder. But because it was too noisy, and too large also Ferry Porsche finally decided on a camshaft engine. If he had not made that move back then, the 911 would surely not exist today.

44

Although Ferry Porsche wanted to make the 911 roomier than the 356, and to give it a larger trunk, he insisted that it be light and compact, and wouldn't allow his chief design engineer, Karl Rabe, a wheelbase of more than 86⅝ inches. Nonetheless, his son Ferdinand Alexander – now the owner of the firm Porsche Design – managed to give the 911 an elongated, streamlined form, which except for bumper alterations due to new legislation hasn't changed to this day and is still the epitome of elegance. Apart from the completely new 6-cylinder engine, the 911 differed from its predecessor in three major points. The twin trailing arm front axle with transverse torsion bars – a standard feature of all Porsche constructions since the Auto Union "P-Wagen" – was replaced by a shock absorber strut axle with longitudinal torsion bars. This not only allowed more freedom in the choice of axle geometry, it also created more trunk space. At the suggestion of the chief of development in those days, Hans Tomala, the Gemmer worm gear steering was replaced by a complicated rack-and-pinion steering gear. Instead of the swing axle, a semi-trailing arm axle was built into the rear. The car was also given a completely new 5-speed gearbox.

However, the innovative suspension by no means disposed of the handling problems that had created headaches with the 356. The relatively heavy 6-cylinder engine in the rear created a lot of trouble for the development engineers. Even as the new model was being introduced (at that time still called the 901: it wasn't re-designated the 911 until it was discovered that Peugeot held the rights for all 3-digit numbers with a zero in the middle), the handling was still unsatisfactory. Handling on straightaways was poor, and in the critical rpm range at moderate cornering speeds the understeer tendency suddenly switched to oversteer. As a quick remedy – by no means satisfactory for the technicians – 24 pounds of cast iron were simply packed into both ends of the front bumper, until the technicians could come up with a better solution. Improvements in handling followed step-by-step: closer production tolerances and a widening of the wheels from 4.5 to 5.5 inches. The biggest single step was taken as the 1969 model was introduced: The wheelbase was increased by 2¾ inches, to 89⅜ inches, by extending the trailing arms to the rear without changing the placement of the engine in the body. That shortened the rear overhang, shifting the weight distribution forward. In addition, two batteries were installed instead of one, as far forward as possible on either side of the trunk. For the 911 E and 911 S models the wheels were once again widened to 6 inches, and mounted with low profile 185/70 VR 15 tires. Further improvements came when Porsche decided to widen only the rear wheels by another inch, and to equip the "Turbo" version with super-low-profile tires on 16-inch diameter wheels.

The air-cooled, horizontally opposed 6-cylinder engine of the initial 911 version developed 130 horsepower at 6,100 rpm, with maximum torque of 174.81 Nm at 4,500 rpm. With a manufacturer-rated top speed of 132 mph, it was the fastest production line Porsche up to that time. It accelerated from 0 to 62 mph in 8.8 seconds and covered one mile from a standing start in 46.8 seconds: outstanding for a 2-liter sports car in those days. But only two years later, in July 1966, Porsche introduced an uprated version, the 911 S, whose 160 hp engine had profited from racing experience with the 6-cylinder. This engine offered considerably improved performance: a top speed of 140 mph, 0 to 62 mph in 6.8 seconds and only 27.6 seconds from a standstill – extraordinarily fast for the 2-liter class.

However, for really fast speed over longer stretches, the driver himself had to work hard: the engine didn't reach its maximum torque of 18.2 mkp until 5,200 rpm, and under that level little thrust could be expected. That necessitated constant shifting to keep the rpm between 5,000 and the maximum of 7,300, and the corresponding noise was not far from the maximum tolerable. As mentioned above, the handling also demanded ability and concentration on the part of the driver, because when the 911 S was introduced, it still had more or less the original chassis. Even the characteristic cast aluminum "Fox" wheels – which have since become something of a trademark of the top-of-the-line 911 S – were only 4.5 inches wide, with ordinary 82% profile radial tires.

An improved chassis was a precondition of yet higher engine performance. But how could more be extracted from the little 6-cylinder – which already developed more than 80 hp/liter – in the first place? Fuel injection was one possibility, which, introduced simultaneously with the improved 89⅜ inch wheelbase chassis, hiked the rating of the 911 S by 10 hp to 170, while the more elastic and quieter 911 E was rated at 140 hp. 85 hp/liter would have been the end of the line for the production-line 911 S if Ferry Porsche had not allowed so much room to play in the original development of the engine. Without any basic changes, the displacement could be expanded to 2.7 liters. No one even dreamed that the basic concept could be taken as high as 3.3 liters. "Otherwise," said Ferry Porsche, "we would have made it smaller and lighter right from the start. But today we're happy that the engine turned out to be so big."

Upping the displacement proceeded in stages: 2.2 liters for the 1970 model, 2.4 liters for the 1972 – which was built for regular fuel – and finally 2.7 liters for the "Carrera RS" which appeared in late 1972. During the first year of production, 1,036 of these lightweight versions were built. The first 911 Carrera – which boasted 210 hp on regular gasoline, only 8.5:1 compression and mechanical injection – was a significant step in the development of the 911. It evolved primarily to provide Porsche customers with a vehicle that, after preparation and

tuning in accordance with the regulations in each respective sports class, could take on all competitors on GT class circuit races or in rallies. This was the first 911 with spoilers front and rear (the famed "ducktail"), which substantially reduced the aerodynamic lift while improving the handling in fast cornering and in side-wind conditions. It was also the first 911 with broader rims (7 inches) in back than in front and correspondingly flared rear fenders – two characteristics which would later be adopted for all 911 models.

The 911 engines also became more elastic with increasing size, but the 2.7-liter Carrera surpassed all its predecessors in this respect: Its maximum torque of 26 mkp at 5,100 rpm was more than 40% higher than that of the 2-liter injection engine in the 1969 911 S, and almost 20% higher than in the 2.4-liter 911 S. For more than ten years this lightweight Carrera RS remained the fastest 911 without a turbocharger: Porsche's own ratings were a top speed of 150 mph, 0 to 62 mph in 5.8 seconds, and 25.4 seconds for a kilometer from a standing start. These values weren't just due to the engine, however: The car weighed just over 1,982 pounds (not counting fuel) and featured excellent body aerodynamics, built for the last time in 1973 with the small, more streamlined bumpers. Even the 230 hp, 3-liter Carrera RS – only 109 road versions of which were built the next year – wasn't any faster, probably because of its wider body and tires, constructed with an eye to the later turbo dimensions. Many experts regard the 2.7-liter Carrera RS as the best-looking 911 ever built. On into the 1980s, both of the lightweight "RS" models – even in private hands – remained highly competitive in international rallying, and 3-liter versions won the Monte Carlo Rally in 1978 and the Corsica Rally in 1980.

However, these two top models appeared on the market just as the oil crisis and increasingly stricter exhaust emission laws were combining to fundamentally alter the development goals of the auto industry. Porsche, too, had to offer cleaner exhaust, and fuel consumption became the topic of the day. The result was a new generation of less highly tuned engines with lower revs and the Bosch K-Jetronic continuous injection system, oriented more toward fuel consumption than engine performance. To compensate for the reduced horsepower-per-liter rating, the displacement of all the engines was increased to 2.7 liters. In 1976 the 2.7-liter Carrera (the successor to the Carrera RS which was built until late 1975 with a normal body and full luxury equipment) was replaced by the Carrera 3-liter with K-Jetronic injection and 200 instead of 210 hp. In 1978, when the 2.7 and 3-liter models were replaced by the single model 911 SC, the horsepower rating dropped to 180.

Porsche may have been hoping that traditional 911 buyers would switch to the 928, which had just been introduced. That was not the case, however, and Porsche was soon forced to give 911 fans what they wanted: more horsepower. As of 1981, the 911 was finally being offered again with more than 200 horsepower. Today, the horsepower rating of the Carrera 3.2-liter is already up to 231. But the car's performance is more economical than ever before, thanks to the full electronic "Motronic" system, which precisely regulates the ignition and fuel injection in accordance with all of the factors that can influence combustion. Despite more extras as standard equipment, substantially more comfort, better elasticity and considerably less noise, the current Carrera — despite 330 pounds of additional weight — almost matches the acceleration values of the unforgettable Carrera 2.7 RS, and is even faster, with a top speed of more than 153 mph.

Porsche was the first company to successfully enter vehicles with exhaust turbochargers in major international races. Expanding this successful development into production-line models was a logical step. But just as the development of a turbocharged 911 was completed, the oil crisis began creating uncertainty. A lot of credit is due to the head of the company at that time, Professor Ernst Fuhrmann, who had the courage to begin production of this car with dragster-like acceleration, a top speed of 156 mph, but relatively high fuel consumption. Another decisive factor was that the 911 Turbo (referred to internally as the 930 Turbo) was intended to serve as the basis for a racing car developed from the 911 — the type 935 — with which Porsche wanted to compete in the World Championship of Makes. In its original form — which went into production in late 1974 — the 3-liter 911 Turbo, which didn't yet have an intercooler, developed 260 hp at only 5,500 rpm, with maximum torque of 35 mkp at 4,500 rpm. This necessitated a new transmission, because even the 915 transmission developed for the 2.4 liter normally-aspirated engines wasn't able to meet the requirements. The new transmission had only four gears instead of five, in order to save space, but also because it just wasn't necessary with such high torque. The chassis was modified to match the higher performance, but also to meet sport classification requirements: Improved anti-dive geometry, a wider front track and a $3^{59}/_{64}$ inch wider track in the rear, as well as improved steering characterize the Turbo chassis, which features 7-inch wheels in front, 8-inch wheels in the rear.

Starting with the second year of production, the Turbo was also equipped solely with super-low-profile tires on 16-inch rims. As of 1978 the turbo engine was increased to 3.3 liters, which together with the addition of an intercooler, hiked its rating to 300 hp. In keeping with the policy of continual improvements, the maximum torque was raised from 42 to the present 44 mkp. The top speed rose to 162 mph, and with an elapsed time of only 24 seconds for one kilometer from a standstill as of early 1985 the 911 Turbo is the fastest production-line automobile in this acceleration discipline. In

47

accordance with this level of performance, the brake system was improved by employing the type 917 brakes developed for racing use.

Naturally, over the course of 20 years, development of the Porsche 911 has not been limited to the engine and the chassis. Increasing engine performance demanded – apart from the turbo – a completely new transmission, and a sturdier clutch. The brakes had to be adapted to the higher performance values, and were eventually equipped with a servo-system. In order to save weight and cut down on corrosion, many parts of the chassis formerly made of sheet steel have been replaced by aluminum components. One spectacular step toward fully eliminating corrosion was taken in 1976, when the entire body shell was first made of hot galvanized sheet steel. Even today, no other manufacturer has carried anti-corrosion measures this far. In terms of form and construction, the basic frame has remained practically unmodified, with the exception of the shifting of the rear wheel arches when the wheelbase of the 1969 models was extended, and the bumper modifications to meet legislative requirements in the U. S. The same is true of the basic dimensions of the engine: a 3.2-liter Carrera engine could easily be built into a 911 of the original series, and vice-versa. A lot of effort has also gone into increasing comfort. Accessories have become increasingly luxurious, the seats have been improved several times, and the heating and ventilation system has been made more and more effective. The optional air-conditioning system, which wasn't offered at all in the beginning, has also been improved continually.

Although the Coupé has always been the most popular body form, the "Targa," which first appeared in 1966, quickly won many admirers. The roll bar, integrated as a stylistic element, was a Porsche innovation that was soon copied by many others, and the word "Targa" evolved into the generic term for convertibles with roll bars.

The Targa was born of the supposition that, for safety reasons, American legislation would soon do away with the conventional form of the convertible. Even American manufacturers began phasing out their production of convertibles. But the expected law never came to pass, and when it was realized that the type 928 could not serve as a successor to the 911, Porsche decided to intensify further development of the 911. The cabriolet began rolling from the production line in 1982 and became an overnight success. Especially remarkable is the stability of its top, which allows very high speeds when closed without bunching up, and the relatively low noise level by convertible standards.

Almost simultaneously with the premiere of the 911 (at that time still referred to as the 901) at the 1963 Frankfurt Auto Show, Porsche was preparing a car intended to compete in the upcoming 1965 Monte Carlo Rally. Driven by test driver Herbert Linge and test engineer Peter Falk – two names closely associated with the history of Porsche – the car finished in fifth place. Soon other engines developed from the 901 for racing use were being built into the Porsche 904 racing car and competed in a number of events. With their Weber carburetors, these engines developed 210 hp, guaranteeing the reliability of the 160 hp engine of the 911 S introduced in 1966.

Porsche first concentrated on rally competition and as early as 1966 Guenther Klass, with a car differing only slightly from the 911 series, won the European Rally Championship in the GT class. 1967 brought the first circuit races competition. The small, 2-liter car won the Targa Florio (driven by Bernard Cahier, the well-known journalist, and three-time Olympic and world champion skier Jean-Claude Killy), the 12-hour Sebring race, the Daytona 24-hours and the 1000-kilometer race at the Nuerburgring to capture the overall title in the GT class. The Sportomatic transmission (a semiautomatic with a torque converter and no clutch) also had to prove itself first in competition before being offered for sale. With this transmission an extremely lightweight 911 – the 911 R, of which only 20 were built – won the 84-hour "Marathon de la Route" at the Nuerburgring in 1967. This series of successes – most of them chalked up by independent drivers – continued in the following year. In 1968 a 911 took the overall win in the GT class in the famous 24-Hours of Le Mans, a victory that has been repeated many times since. Every increase in displacement in the production series also produced more performance for the competition models, and over the years the 911 had practically no serious competition in the classes for homologated vehicles.

Factory-sponsored 911s competed in most international rallies only until 1970, but private drivers continued to exploit the car's abilities with great success until, as of 1981 – four-wheel drive became almost compulsory for overall victory.

With only one exception, the 911 has won every major rally at least once; it took the Monte Carlo Rally four times: in 1968, 1969 and 1970 as a works car, and in 1978 under the French private driver Jean-Pierre Nicolas. As late as 1980 a 911 prepared by the Almeras brothers and driven by Jean-Luc Thérier won the Corsica Rally against a phalanx of works teams. The exception – the one the 911 never won – is the Safari Rally in Kenya. Works teams participated in that mud and dust-choked flight across the African continent three times, finishing second each time. The last try was in 1978, after Porsche had long since withdrawn from rallying, but made the long trip to Africa just for this event. I can't imagine that's really the end of that story.

The high point in the 911's sports career came in the 1970s, as the international sports commission opened the World Championship of Makes – as of 1976 – to homologated vehicles based on production-line cars. The 911 enjoyed unique prerequisites for racing development within the framework of the regulations. With one, and later two, turbochargers, the performance rating of the Porsche 935 (the designation stands for "930 – Group 5"), with a displacement of 2.85 liters, rose from 590 to 630 hp in only two years – and the engine was still very similar to the production-line version. The 935 brought the House of Porsche two World Championship titles. After that, Porsche withdrew from Group 5 for all practical purposes, successfully leaving the defense of the world title to its customers, who had purchased more than 30 units of the 935 in the meantime. 1979 produced the greatest success of the 911-based 935, when a car prepared by the Kremer brothers in Cologne beat all competitors – including the much lighter and more streamlined racing prototypes – to take the overall win in the 24-hours of Le Mans.

Not since the end of the World War II, when prototypes were first allowed to participate in this most famous of all European races, had a car based on a production series managed to win this test, which is especially brutal for the engines. But in 1979, four racing versions based on the 911 took the first four places, including a 934 in fourth place that differed only slightly from the normal production-line model. The 3-liter engine of the winning car produced almost 700 hp, but in the short races making up the German Championship, 3.2-liter engines were used, with a turbocharger rating of 1.7 bar and more than 800 hp.

The 911 still has many years ahead of it and at Porsche there is no intention of sacrificing its outstanding characteristics to environmental concerns. The 911s that meet even the latest restrictions will be just as fast and lively as today's 3.2-liter Carrera. The shelves of the racing department are packed with plenty of developments just waiting to go into production. Nor will the Turbo retreat from its leading position.

49

The direction 911 developments could take is indicated by the prototype displayed at the 1983 International Auto Show, the "Group B" Porsche, type 959. It is yet another car, destined for sports competition for the first time in 1986, based on the 911. Once again few changes have been made to the basic design, and the 911's horizontally opposed 6-cylinder engine is mounted in the rear. But unlike the conventional 911/930 engine, the 959's engine features 4-valve cylinder heads. Two turbos provide the new car with a 400 hp rating, 600 for the racing version. The prime characteristic of this car is its permanent but variable four-wheel-drive system, in which the torque is split between the rear and front axles by means of electronic sensors, and automatically regulated by means of a hydraulic power source in such a way that the moment the rear wheels begin to spin the superfluous torque is automatically transferred to the front axle. Other features are double-wishbone suspension front and rear, a six-speed transmission and hydraulic valves which don't have to be adjusted. Future designs might also be influenced by such features as the front cowling with integrated bumper, the low front fenders and integrated rear spoiler. How many of these developments will find their way into future 911 models remains to be seen. It is fairly certain, for instance, that not all 911s will feature four-wheel drive.

In order to gain more experience with four-wheel drive, in the second half of 1983, Porsche used the 911 Carrera — whose 3.2-liter engine remained practically unmodified — as the basis for the design of three cars with four-wheel drive that participated with factory support in the Paris–Dakar 1984 desert rally. These cars featured double-wishbone suspension, enormous ground clearance of 11 inches and two fuel tanks with a total capacity of 69 gallons. For Porsche this rally ended with an overall victory — by the Metge-Lemoine team — and all three vehicles completed the murderous, 7,500-mile course without serious technical problems. The cars didn't yet have the variable torque distribution system; they were equipped with a traditional limited slip differential. That success could not be repeated the next year, however, with insufficiently tested forerunners of the 959 that were not properly adapted to the driving conditions in Africa.

Despite continuous development work, the Porsche 911/930 is objectively not the perfect automobile. But many of its idiosyncrasies, which would be chalked up as defects in other cars, serve to enhance the fascination of the 911. No 911 fan would want to miss the music created when the accelerator is jammed to the floor. The primary function of the 911 is not to transport passengers in greatest possible comfort from A to B. Comfort in the 911 is adequate, but secondary to the fun of driving. For, in contrast to many modern cars that need only to be steered, the 911 must be driven consciously. Extracting all it can give under the proper circumstances is a genuine challenge, and no other automobile reacts so well to genuine driving ability. Much of what could be criticized in the 911 is simply part of its unique character. And the popularity of that character is demonstrated by the faithfulness of the fans who, when one head of the company wanted to discontinue the 911, simply would not let the car die.

PAUL HENSLER / WOLFGANG EYB

THE NEW PORSCHES: 924, 928, 944

The technical aspects of future Porsche models have always been a subject under consideration. The repeated tightening of American exhaust emission standards and the onset of emission regulations in other industrial countries influenced automotive industry development trends worldwide. Most strongly affected was engine technology, especially since major efforts to reduce fuel consumption and vehicle noise were being initiated. In the 1960s, for example, the 911-engine boasted up to 80 hp/liter. The realization that the new exhaust emission standards could be met only with lower specific performance ratings led to the development of larger-volume, low-speed engines.

This theory was also discussed at Porsche. How could a 911 engine of the future be adapted to the modified requirements? For a while there was little optimism. A large-volume engine – 5 to 8 liters of displacement were being considered – could no longer be air-cooled, and a water-cooled engine could not be mounted in the rear. The only alternative left was a front-mounted water-cooled engine, a truly alien concept for Porsche engineers of the time. If the engine is up front, as much weight as possible has to be placed over the rear axle, which is logically the driving axle in such a concept.

That was how the transaxle concept evolved – engine in front, transmission on the rear driving axle. The first practical studies were applied to the 928, which was to be newly designed. A 5-liter, V-8 aluminum engine was proposed. Since this power plant was supposed to lie under a flat hood, the valve and valve-gear arrangement was selected in such a way that the engine remained squat, and as many peripheral components as possible could be placed within the open V.

While intensive development work proceeded on this fully new type, Porsche was simultaneously developing yet another car, as the successor to the mid-engined 914 sports car. In this case, the 2-liter, in-line 4-cylinder engine – also to be mounted in front – was to serve as the basis for further model developments. What the engineers considered proper for the 928 also applied to the somewhat smaller 914 successor. Thus the development parameters for this type were also set, once again as a transaxle concept.

The development phases were very short, as, first, an existing type had to be replaced; second, the 928 development experience could be applied, and, third, for reasons of cost, essential components, even if partially modified, were to be adopted from volume production.

The study phase began in 1972, prototypes were built and tested, and as of spring 1974, the acquisition of production tooling got started. Then, in the spring of 1975, it was decided that the 914 successor would be built and distributed by Porsche itself, but the production site selected was the Neckarsulm plant, about 25 miles from Stuttgart-Zuffenhausen. The automakers in Neckarsulm are motivated by the same Swabian spirit of inventiveness as the Porsche team in Stuttgart.

Here, the 924, as it was to be called from then on, was in the right hands. In the early autumn of 1975 construction of the first vehicles began. In January 1976 the planned production series got started, and with the initiation of the U.S. version in April 1976, the assembly lines were really rolling. There were months in which up to 2,500 vehicles passed through Point 8, the final inspection station.

Let's stay with the 924 for the time being, since the 928 was still in the testing and tool-making stage, anyway. What did the 924 have to offer knowledgeable buyers in 1976?

A 2-liter, 4-cylinder in-line engine with K-Jetronic injection. This Audi engine modified by Porsche developed 125 hp. The original clean-exhaust U.S. version offered 110 hp, as of February 1977, 115. Transaxle design with a four-speed transmission on the rear axle, and as of 1977 also with a three-speed automatic.

Also remarkable was the very low drag coefficient of 0.36, although at that time not so much attention was paid to this factor. The product of the frontal area times the drag coefficient $(0.36 \times 1.76\,\mathrm{m}^2 = 0.634)$ was the lowest among all production-line road vehicles at that time. It is no wonder that for more than ten years, this model, always with the same engine performance, remained very popular in Europe, and particularly in West Germany. The special fascination of this car is its top speed of over 125 mph on West German autobahns, but extremely low fuel consumption. It was not surprising that customers began demanding a five-speed transmission, which was made available as of summer 1978.

For the chassis, a McPherson strut axle was selected for the front, a semi-trailing arm axle for the rear. These constructions were well known from the 911 and 914 types, and could be quickly adapted to the new requirements. The use of many production parts – some unchanged, some modified – made it possible to keep costs within limits and to minimize development risks. The front axle was equipped with coil springs, arranged centrically around the McPherson struts. The wheel suspension featured a wishbone affixed to the body and to the engine mounting, to which the steering assembly was also attached. A rack-and-pinion steering system was chosen, connected to the steering wheel by means of a three-point levered safety steering column.

The rear-axle, semi-trailing arms are attached to a transverse tube which also support the torsion bars. The complete rear-axle is insulated from the body by means of rubber buffers, in order to reduce vibration. The dual-circuit brake system with vacuum booster features floating caliper disc brakes on the front axle and drum brakes on the rear axle.

As a result of the increased performance of the 924 turbo engine and the 944 engine, further developments focused on the chassis, in particular to adapt the brakes to the higher requirements. The new models featured disc brakes on the rear-axle, with in-board drum brakes for the handbrake – a design that has proved its value during many years of use in the type 911.

The body styling was largely determined by the desire for low drag, for the interior roominess of the 911, and for the largest possible rear trunk. Other characteristic features are the integrated bumpers, retractable headlights and a partially concealed windshield wiper assembly. The trunk space under the hinged hatch-back window can be enlarged to a volume unusual for a sports car by folding down the rear seat backs. The body shell – just as in the 911 –

is made of hot galvanized sheet steel, and it was possible to offer a six-year anti-corrosion warranty. Based on favorable customer experience, the warranty was later extended to seven years.

Powerful engines are simply part of the Porsche image. In this case, it could only be a turbocharged version. In early 1979 the 924 Turbo appeared with 170 hp, and as of 1980, the U.S. version with 143 hp. This car featured impressive performance statistics, including acceleration from 0 to 100 km/h in 7.8 seconds (0–60 mph in 9.2 secs.), and a top speed of 225 km/h (132 mph). At Porsche it is taken for granted that, when top speeds are increased, the tires, chassis and brakes are modified to meet the new and tougher demands. The Turbo was equipped with VR tires, 15-inch wheels with five lugs and internally vented disc brakes front and rear. Two unmistakable exterior characteristics were the air-intake slits over the bumper and the hood scoop.

Increasingly stricter emission and fuel consumption legislation in the U.S. accelerated the development of even more fuel-efficient and cleaner-exhaust engines. In 1981, for example, the Turbo engine was equipped with a full electronic ignition system. Besides reducing emissions and fuel consumption, this feature alone also served to increase performance to 177 hp (154 hp for the U.S. version).

It has become a matter of tradition in the Porsche engine department that great attention is paid to the further development of turbocharged engines. Boost pressure control by means of a bypass valve was the first step taken from racing to production-line vehicles in the case of the 911 Turbo. That was followed by full electronic ignition that operated as a function of boost pressure.

The next racing feature to be included in the production-line vehicles was turbocharger air cooling. A 210 hp turbo engine with an intercooler was chosen. The cool-air hood scoop intake and the flared wheel arches have become distinguishing characteristics of this car. In order to comply with homologation requirements, the series was projected for 400 vehicles and given the sales designation 924 Carrera GT. It boasts 0–62 mph acceleration in only 6.9 seconds and a top speed of 150 mph.

But even that wasn't enough. A further evolution of this model was brought out in May of 1981 – the 245-hp 924 Carrera GTS, well-suited for motor sport events.

The year is 1981, and the 928 has been in production since 1977. Energy market developments had motivated us engineers to limit the engine to 4.5 liters of displacement. An even smaller 3.9-liter version was also tried out in prototypes. At about the same time, the realization was growing that the 911-engine continued to offer new potential for meeting increasingly restrictive emission and noise legislation. Thus, an end to its production was still a long way off. As a result, the 928 didn't have to function as a successor, but could be offered as an additional model.

The V-8 engine featured a block made of a special aluminum-silicon alloy that made it possible for the iron or chrome-plated pistons to be seated directly in the cylinders, which had been galvanically treated. This solution had been used with great success in the 911 for several years. A K-Jetronic injection system guaranteed the proper fuel-air mixture, and the two camshafts, arranged directly above two hydraulic bucket tappets, were driven by a single cogged belt. 240 hp (220 hp in the U.S. version) was a good performance rating for the beginning. The compression ratio of 8.5:1 was set for regular gas. As in the 924, the engine was linked by means of a sturdy transaxle tube – in which the shaft rotating at engine rpm was suspended – with the newly-developed five-speed manual transmission, or a three-speed automatic.

The high-performance engine demanded a corresponding chassis. For the front, a double-

53

control-arm axle was chosen. It has the advantage of combining optimal kinetic energy properties with minimal height. Combined with the rack-and-pinion hydro-steering, the caster offset of 40 mm provides the desired roadholding and good straight-line performance. The negative scrub radius of 16 mm largely compensates for under or oversteer, for instance, when braking on roads of different friction coefficients. The control arms are made of cast aluminum. A coil spring is attached to the shock absorber, which is mounted on the lower control arm. Camber and caster action can be adjusted by means of cams on the lower control arm.

In order to obtain good lane-changing response and cornering, the steering kinematics were chosen in such a way that, when the shocks jounce, the front wheels toe out. In addition, the elasticity of the steering system – from the screwed up steering arm on the steering knuckle to the rubber-mounted steering gear on up to a flexible steering coupling – was adjusted in such a way that in terms of kinematics as well as driving comfort optimal conditions were achieved.

Porsche broke new ground in order to prevent oversteer when the throttle was released in fast curves. By means of elasto-kinematic effects, the rear wheels were made to toe in when the throttle is released or when braking during cornering. After a long period of testing, a relatively simple concept was finally decided on, known as the "Weissach Axle," featuring double control arms. The upper control arm is a simple transverse support. The lower control arm is attached to the body structure via a control lever in the front and to the rear-axle crossmember via a spring strut in the rear.

The kinematics and defined elasticity of the rocker arm and the spring strut are adjusted in such a way that when decelerating the wheels toe in. This achieved more neutral handling, which is insensitive to a change in load. The rear axle is suspended – much like the front axle – by coil spring struts attached to the body via properly matched rubber shock mounts. Sliding caliper brakes were used on the front and rear axles and in later models floating caliper brakes were substituted in front.

Anti-lock braking has been offered (the Bosch 2-B) since 1983 and was subjected to rigorous testing before its introduction. The specific tests – tailored to the handling dynamics of a sports car – led to a new shifting logic, which has since benefited conventional vehicles, and 225/50 VR 15 tires were chosen for all four wheels. Working in close cooperation with the tire companies, it was possible to achieve especially good lateral force characteristics as a function of slip angle and a good aligning torque.

It was soon realized that this car would benefit from more torque and higher maximum performance. In 1980, a larger displacement version – the 4.7-liter 928 S was introduced on the market. Higher compression (10:1) necessitated the use of premium fuel, but together with the increase in displacement it led to a remarkable 300 hp rating. The car thus had a top speed of over 155 mph and accelerated from 0 to 62 mph in 6.6 seconds. Spoilers front and back improved the drag and drift values. In the U.S. this engine, offered with L-Jetronic injection and oxygen sensor, and including a three-way catalytic converter, developed 234 hp.

For the development, production and workshop departments it is always a major advantage when certain assembly groups are used in as many different models as possible. Porsche's first successful use of digital engine electronics for the injection and ignition systems was in the type 944, to which we'll return a bit later.

The 928 U.S. version already featured electronic injection with oxygen sensor. Now, in the form of the 928 S, the "rest of the world" was to get the newest of the new. A thermal wire instrument was used to measure the air volume (in contrast to the conventional flap

54

measurement), and the firing point was optimally determined fully electronically for each point. Because of the low flow resistance of the thermal wire – compared to the flap – it was possible to increase performance to 310 hp.

While improvements and additional wishes were continually being added, for example, the four-speed automatic, the engine builders were drawing up new plans. Why did the low-emission engines equipped with catalytic converters necessarily have to have lower performance ratings than the European versions? Or, to put it another way, shouldn't it be possible to achieve superior performance even when converter technology is used?

Excellently suited to this goal is 4-valve technology, which makes it possible to place the spark plug in the center of each cylinder's four valves, providing optimal combustion. In addition, two intake valves per cylinder make for better volumetric efficiency. The result is higher performance per liter of displacement, with lower fuel consumption and exhaust emissions.

In late 1984 the 928 S-32-valve was introduced on the U.S. market. This engine, now with five liters of displacement, is offered only with a catalytic converter and boasts 292 hp or 288 hp for the U.S. version respectively. It reaches maximum torque of 410 Nm (302 lb.-ft.) at only 2,700 rpm. The engine has always been the heart of any sports car. When a newly developed power plant is built into an existing model, the exterior appearance should also call attention to this fact. This was the premise under which the 944 evolved.

As mentioned above, development costs, production planning and potential customer problems can be substantially reduced when the same basic concepts are applied to various types of engines. For example, when a 4-cylinder version is produced on the basis of the V-8 928, few parts are exactly the same in both versions, but many parts or components are similar or even identical in terms of material. An 8-cylinder camshaft will never be the same as a 4-cylinder camshaft, but the materials, processing, heat treatment and dimensions of the cams and bearings can be identical, and that is a tremendous advantage.

Back in 1977 it was decided to develop the 944-engine on the basis of the 928. The same bore of 100 mm was used, which meant 2.5-liter displacement for the 4-cylinder. But these relatively large cylinders caused rough engine running. In order to make up for this disadvantage, the 944 incorporates a system of two balancer shafts counter-rotating at twice the engine speed. This technique gives the 4-cylinder engine vibration-free performance. The use of the most modern injection and ignition electronics made it possible to develop an extremely high-torque engine which gives the 944 a hp rating of 163 (143 in the U.S. version) and a top speed of 220 km/h (137 mph for the U.S. version). The sporty styling and the impressive driving characteristics resulted in a new model, the 944, which has been well-received. By the end of 1984, the dashboard, center console and door panels had been completely revised, adding to the unique appearance of the 944. In addition, technical improvements were made in the heating, ventilation, air-conditioning and electrical systems.

Because U.S. emissions regulations now serve as the basis for new legislation in West Germany and other West European countries, the catalytic converter is being introduced in these countries as well. Porsche has ten years of experience in this field. For a long time now, about 50 per cent of all Porsche vehicles have been equipped with regulated three-way converters. The resulting experience and know-how in regard to new engine technology have made higher performance in converter-equipped vehicles possible, especially since unleaded, higher octane fuels can be utilized.

The Porsche philosophy for the future is: low-emission engines that meet U.S. requirements boast the same high performance as those not subject to such strict exhaust legislation. Since the spring of 1985, Porsche has been offering the 944 Turbo worldwide. With or without the regulated converter, the engine has the same performance rating: 220 hp (217 hp U.S. version). This is made possible by modern electronic knock and boost-pressure control, intensive charge air cooling and progressive catalytic converter design. In addition, fuel octane differences have no effect on this engine.

The 944 Turbo features almost the same impressive performance characteristics as the 911. And the similarity of these two vehicles in terms of dimensions and weight explains the successful development of the transaxle principle. The "monoculture" era has truly come to an end. There is no longer any question that sports car designs with front-mounted engines and transmissions on the rear driving axle can be successful.

This is impressively demonstrated by the 944 and the 928 S, and, especially in comparison with the rear-engine 911, by the 944 Turbo.

IGRIN
OLY
V. MERL
JOEST RACING
LIQUI MOLY
LM
Wir halten Autos fit
SACHS
Turbolader
KKK

16 Type 956, with Derek Bell at the wheel, Kyalami 1.000 kms (1983)
17 Type 917 K, driven by Gijs van Lennep, Spa-Francorchamps 1.000 kms, 1971
18 Type 956, with Japanese driver Takahashi at the wheel, Fuji 1.000 kms, 1983

19 In front: Type 917 K, driven by Hans Herrmann, Brands Hatch 1.000 kms (1970)
20 Nuerburgring, German Championship 1978, Volkert Merl in "Karussell", driving a 935

21 Type 917/20 (test model with extended wheelbase) during test runs on the Weissach skid-pad; Herbert Müller at the wheel (1973)
22 Le Mans 24-hours 1984. French driver Alain de Cadenet piloting a 956

23 Type 908/3 Turbo driven by Herbert Müller, Nuerburgring 1.000-kms 1975
24 Daytona 24-hours 1985; Al Holbert at the wheel of type 962
25 Type 917 K at Laguna Seca, on occasion of the 9. Annual Historic Automobile Races 1982

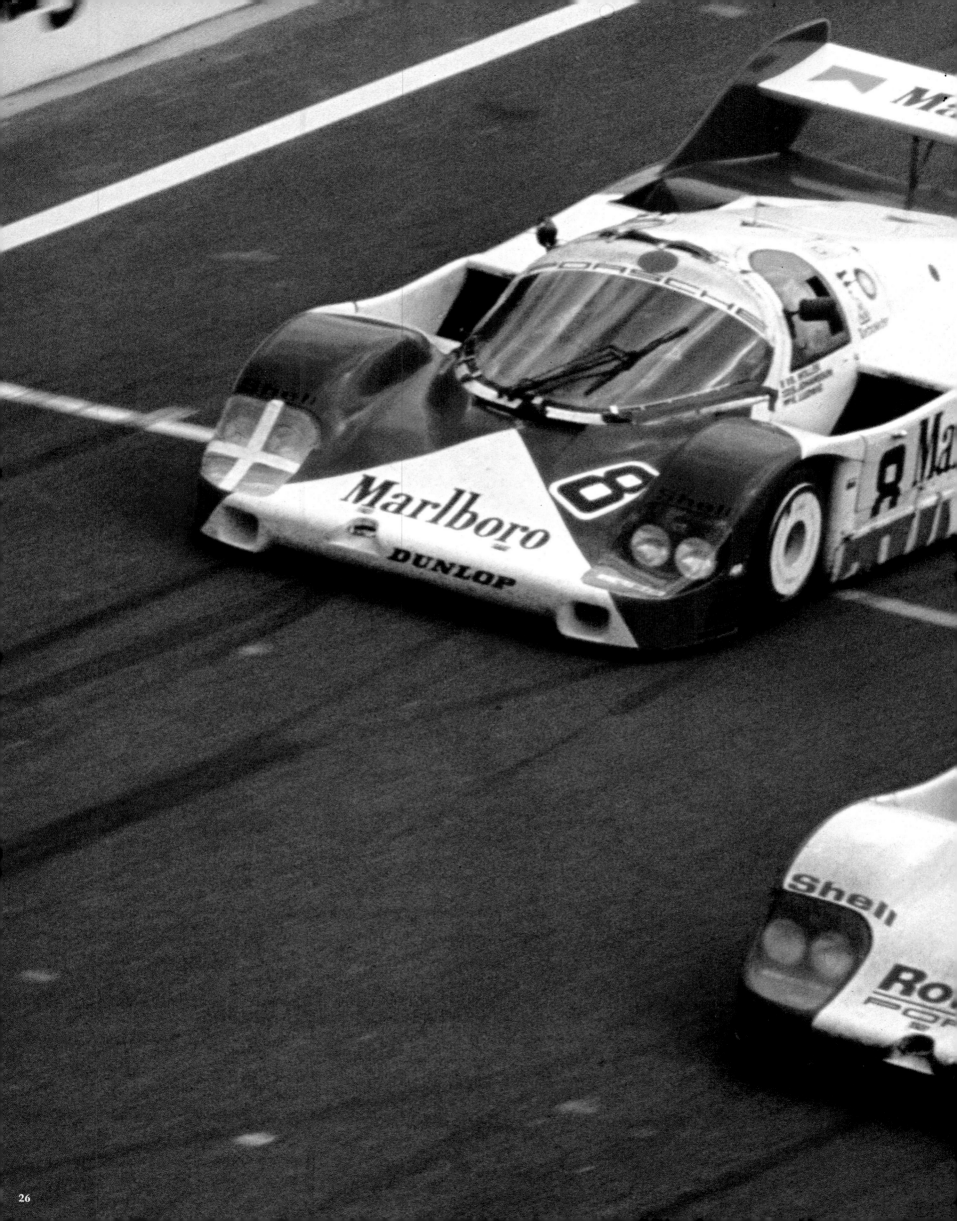

26 Le Mans 1983, last lap: Al Holbert takes his winning Rothmans Porsche 956 across the line for the last time, passing the 956 of Ludwig/Johansson/Wollek
27 IMSA GP Miami 1985; in front: Bob Wollek at the wheel of a type 962. On third position is Al Holbert in his 962. Second is a Chevrolet March

28 Le Mans 24-hours 1974; a 911 Carrera RSR Turbo 2,1 liter in the Mulsanne section
29 Le Mans 24-hours, 1983; Stefan Bellof driving a Rothmans Porsche 956. That car retired in lap 281, due to engine trouble

30 Left: Type 934: Right: Rolf Stommelen at the wheel of his 936, Nuerburgring 500 kms (1975)
31 Type 936/78 during test runs for Le Mans 24-hours 1978. The runs took place on Paul-Ricard circuit (South France). Jacky Ickx is the driver
32 Formula-1-World Champion 1984, Niki Lauda, at Dijon (French GP 1984) in his McLaren with TAG-engine

33 Brands Hatch 1.000 kms 1983; German driver Dieter Schornstein at the wheel of a 956
34 Le Mans 24-hours 1981; Hurley Haywood driving a 936/78, at the beginning of the notorious Hunaudières straight

LOTHAR BOSCHEN

THE PORSCHE MODEL LINE FROM 1945–1985

Germany left the turbulent 20s without looking back. During Hitler's "Thousand-Year Reich," industry and science received state support on a scale that had never been equaled before – that is, if they served the goals of the political leaders. In this climate, Professor Ferdinand Porsche worked very successfully for the European automobile industry. But the professor could only see his future in forming his own independent company. In 1931, he was entered in the Stuttgart register of commerce as "Dr. Ing. h. c. Ferdinand Porsche GmbH." Purpose of business: design and consulting for engine and automobile production.

Thanks to the seemingly inexhaustible supply of ideas from Porsche and his team, interesting orders filled the books from the first day on: Wanderer, Zuendapp, NSU, Auto Union, Daimler. These industries and the government would become the biggest customers in the years to come. Porsche's work at that time principally consisted of design studies for the German Army and work on the famous "Volkswagen," the impact of which is still felt today. The "people's car" didn't start running until after World War II, but the beloved "Beetle" greatly influenced the Porsche product from the beginning.

The war and its aftermath did not spare the Porsche company. The team received orders to move to Gmuend in Kaernten, Austria, in November 1944. When the almost 70-year-old Professor Porsche was arrested by the French on questionable charges in July 1945, and later sent to prison for several months, his son Ferdinand, "Ferry," took over as company director. Ferry again brought up the idea of building a two-seater, open sports car – a "Porsche" – based on the Volkswagen.

The first design of the forebear of all Porsche automobiles was made in mid-1947. This documented the beginning of a new make of automobile whose name, "Porsche," is the embodiment of sports car for young and old worldwide.

The Porsche 356 (the model number is identical with the design number) was built from 1948 to 1965. The first 50 of these models were produced in exile in Gmuend. These cars today, if any are available, are almost unaffordable rarities.

The 356 model range began with Coupé and Cabriolet versions boasting 1.1-liter, 4-cylinder engines with 40 hp. They could reach a maximum speed of more than 81 mph and cost between 10,000 and 12,000 deutschmarks. Even Ferry Porsche didn't think that he'd be able to sell more than 500 of these cars. This was a more than pleasing miscalculation, as we well know today.

Great interest from foreign buyers poured badly needed funds into Porsche's empty tills.

A decisive step forward, both for the technicians and the buyers, was involvement in motor car racing. As the last 356 from the Gmuend series was being delivered in February 1951, the Porsche team decided to accept the invitation to participate in the 24-hour race in Le Mans, France. After overcoming many snags before and during training, the long distance race ended successfully for the Swabian engineers and the French driving duo: victory for the Porsche 356 with aluminum body and improved aerodynamics.

A new automobile market was rising and this increased the sales of the winning sports cars which were now being produced in Stuttgart-Zuffenhausen; the move from Gmuend began in early 1950. By the end of 1951, annual production volume far surpassed the once contemplated 500 cars. But Professor Porsche didn't live to see the great success in Le Mans, or the establishment of the "Porsche" product on the market. He died January 30, 1951.

Growing competition in the manufacture of standard cars and also in the racing field forced Porsche to come up with ever-new answers. One of these: In 1953, the first racing car not evolving from a standard one – the 550 (1500 RS) model – was produced for sale to customers. The Porsche 356 series reached its technical peak with the "Carrera" – a 356C with a four-camshaft engine of 2-liter capacity and 130 hp. Top speed: 125 mph. At the time this model was first offered in 1963, its successor was already in the starting blocks. But first, a few more words on the traditional model 356, before moving on to the 911 series.

When the Federal Republic of Germany won the world soccer championship in 1954, the five-thousandth Porsche 356 left the factory. More than 100 dealers worldwide handled the still very young brand of sports car. Porsche clubs were springing up everywhere, which still today organize flights and excursions for group tours to view the factory in Stuttgart. Some of the club members would take this opportunity to take home their previously ordered Porsche. From 1955 to 1958, a desirable collector's item rolled off the production lines: the 356A Speedster – a stripped-down version of the Cabrio with a fold-back top, which unfortunately was sold almost exclusively in the U.S.A. The Speedster had a 1.1-liter, 4-cylinder engine with a choice of either 60 or 75 hp. Unrestored Speedsters in very good original condition were sold for more than 50,000 deutschmarks in 1984.

After 17 years of production, the last car of the 356 series, a C-model Cabriolet, left the factory. 76,302 Porsche sports cars in Coupé, Cabriolet, Speedster, Roadster, Hardtop and Convertible versions were built and then sold all around the globe. The slogan, "Porsche – driving in its finest form," became a solid concept. A new Porsche was revealed to the public in 1963 at the International Motor Show in Frankfurt am Main. The 911, which was originally designated 901, but had to be changed due to objections raised by a French automobile firm, had an air-cooled 6-cylinder engine. It had a 2-liter capacity which produced 130 hp and helped the Coupé perform with a maximum speed of a little over 125 mph.

Drivers hooked on the 356 were quick to oppose the new and fashionable Porsche model. They argued that it wouldn't be a real Porsche sports car anymore, neither its shape nor its technology was appealing, and it was too expensive. This was a reaction the Porsche company could count on in the following years whenever a new model was introduced that differed greatly from its predecessors.

But the 24,000 deutschmarks cost of the Porsche 911 seemed to be too high for some of those willing to make the switch to the newer model. Bowing to their wishes, Porsche was quick to produce a more affordable version of the 911, the Porsche 912. It was equipped almost identically to the top model, but it had the old 4-cylinder engine with 90 hp. Although it was supposedly in demand by just as many customers as the 911, the 912 remained in the shadow of its big brother. The 912 series went out of production after being offered in the U.S.A. for several years. According to Porsche, the best way to promote a new car and to quickly overcome its growing pains is to enter it in races and rallies. The debut of the 911 was no exception in comparison to its predecessors. In 1965, just a few months after being put on the market, the rear-engine standard car went through purgatory in the Monte Carlo Rally. The reward: victory for Porsche engineers Herbert Linge and Peter Falk!

Just as the successful victory of the 356-Alu in Le Mans in 1951 boosted sales, the Monte Carlo result set the 911 rolling. Six months after the rally win, Porsche presented its next hit: the first standard safety Cabriolet in the world, the "911 Targa." This Targa (Italian for shield) is a Cabriolet with a skillfully designed integrated roll bar. Among the existing variety, there is a Targa with a removable central hard or soft roof section, and another with a separable flexible rear window. For technical reasons, this last option will soon be canceled.

Rising performance standards in ordinary automobiles forced Porsche to continually improve their quality, and additionally, to increase the cubic capacity of the 911 series. This increased cubic capacity ranged from 2.0-liter, progressing through 2.2, 2.4, 2.7, and 3.0-liter to the 3.2-liter capacity of the present 1985 model. The air-cooled, horizontally opposed, 6-cylinder engine can handle any power range from 110 to 231 hp. The inimitable roar still fascinates schoolboys as well as sportsmen, as it has throughout the decades.

Those in the know, who are "in," or want to be, and naturally those who can afford it, buy the Porsche 911. To satisfy the special demands frequently made by Porsche customers, the company introduced "Besonderes fuer Besondere" – "Special things for special people." For example, a Carrera version of the basic model was available starting in 1972 with 2.7-liter engine (210 hp, 150 mph), and from 1975 Porsche came out with a 3-liter version with 200 hp and 144 mph.

The first Carrera version of the 911 unintentionally launched a trend that has been copied a thousand times over: the rear spoiler, called a "Birzel" within the Porsche company.

Racing experience once again led Porsche to incorporate the results obtained from the Turbo version of the 917 into production cars. The 917/10 Spyder demonstrated that an exhaust turbocharger was practical. Ten years later this way of increasing power output was quite usual, even in once traditional cars. The 911-Turbo (internally referred to as model 930) came on the market in 1974 with 260 hp from 3 liters, which was the optimal capacity during this period. Three years later, the capacity would be expanded to 3.3 liters and the output raised to an even 300 hp.

The maximum speed obtainable separated the men from boys. This Porsche, because of its enormous power, required a firm, expert hand – or better, hands. Perhaps because of this, and in spite of a sales price that reached over 110,000 deutschmarks by the end of 1984, the 911 became nominally the strongest, and best-selling car.

The first worldwide oil crisis of 1973/74 caused the automobile manufacturers to worry. The Porsche company, with 50% of its sales in the U.S., distinctly felt the purchase cutback. And similar to the Volkswagen plant, which waited too long to come up with a successful model, the Porsche 911 stagnated.

What seemed to be bad news from Wolfsburg turned out to be surprisingly helpful to the Stuttgart team. The Porsche engineers in Weissach had developed a sports car for the Volkswagen plant (which had practically stopped production overnight). Without further ado, Porsche bought back its own idea and presented it in 1975 as the Porsche 924. The technical concept behind the 2+2-seater consistently breaks with the practiced tradition of automotive design within Porsche: The 924 has a water-cooled 4-cylinder VW engine installed under the front hood, and the transmission, together with the differential, is mounted on the rear axle. The engine and transmission are connected by a rigid tube. The engineers call this system the "transaxle."

Even the 924 received a negative reaction from the Porsche fans: "This sports car is not worth the Porsche brand; it's too much like a Volkswagen." Although the engineers in Weissach made efforts to rid the 924 of the VW-image in the following years, it still remains, no matter how well-built, a VW-Coupé in the eyes of most Porsche enthusiasts.

The 924 is popular with women because of its softly rounded form. It is economical, reliable and also fast (125 hp, 125 mph), and has found an increasing circle of new customers. (The 924 with the VW engine will be discontinued in 1986 and fitted with a downgraded version of the 944 engine, which will give the 924 a fresh impetus.) In just a short period of time the 924, followed by the 924-Turbo three years later, is a highly competitive product on the U.S. auto market.

However, the Japanese automobile manufacturers put up a strong fight and were able to restrain the 924's upswing. Around this time rumors were rampant that the management planned to delete the time-honored and renowned 911 from their model line. Further technical developments were neglected. The 911 thus aged quicker than normal and sales as well as output figures rapidly declined, almost to the margin of profitability.

The Porsche 928 (in 1977), which was intended as an alternative to the classic rear-engine sports car, suffered during its debut

under the disadvantages that it was hastily put on the market and that its design concept missed the requirements of the market.

Like the model 924, the 928 was built on the transaxle system (4.5-liter capacity, V-8 aluminum engine, 240 hp), and, especially in the electronics area, was not fully developed. Performance was not impressive and the fuel consumption was too high. The 928, as well as the 928S (4.7-liter, 300 hp), which was introduced in 1979, both acquired a negative image until 1982, when Porsche reduced the 928 line to one model.

It was then the 928S with 310 hp, which was still powered by the 4.7-liter engine. With the introduction of the 5-liter version, the fast Sport-Coupé technically reached its peak. The proven V-8 engine had four-valve cylinder heads, a modified air intake system (LH-Jet-ronic), and a catalytic converter. The first presentation of the 928S-32v came out with U.S. specifications by the end of 1984. American customers have to be content with only 288 hp. In Germany the 928S/32 valve can be seen on exhibit at the International Motor Show in 1985.

An American turned Germany's famous sports car factory around. Peter W. Schutz, an American born in Berlin, took over as President of Porsche AG on January 1, 1981. A respected energetic prototype of a sales manager, Schutz quickly grasped that the positive image of the Porsche 911 should not be underrated. An earlier concept from the past became reality and Porsche was able to exhibit their forgotten old-timer in the IAA 1981 as a full convertible.

Shortly before that the 944 made its debut. Production was then headed by Dr. Ernst Fuhrmann, Schutz's predecessor. The "944" is an optically and technically revitalized model of the 924, which finally satisfied the critical Porsche customers. The revised 4-cylinder in-line engine and halved V-8 power plant from the Porsche 928 had a 2.5-liter capacity. For improved smooth running of the 600-cc cylinders, two balancer shafts were installed. This is a high-torque engine, which enables the 944 to perform at a maximum speed of 137 mph. Average fuel consumption is approximately 21 miles per gallon. At an initial sales price of under 40,000 deutschmarks the 944 was an immediate success in Europe and overseas. A Porsche worthy of the company's slogan: "Driving in its finest form." Following the trend of increased automobile production capacity, the Sedans made in Ingolstadt, Munich and Untertuerkheim equaled and even surpassed the 944 in a short time. The engineers in Zuffenhausen accepted this challenge and successfully developed the 944 Turbo, which went on sale at the beginning of 1985.

Long months of debate among politicians over a final decision on the installation of catalytic converters set back the production of this Porsche model by six months. Nevertheless, the offered model is something worth seeing: a barely noticeable renovated interior and exterior – also available in the naturally aspirated 944 model –, plus a complete technical revision which led to a turbocharged 2.5-liter 4-cylinder engine with 220 hp – with or without catalytic converter. With a top speed of about 152 mph and average fuel consumption of 19 to 21 miles per gallon with premium gasoline, this series became an alternative to the 911. The attempt to join the 911 ranks is clearly evident from its 72,000 deutschmark price tag.

Porsche's new boss gave the green light for the gradual renovation of the beleaguered 911. The Porsche fan clubs expressed a sigh of relief, and to show their appreciation, ordered more Porsche 911's, many more than in the past. The 911 first received its name "Carrera" at the International Motor Show in 1983, with a 3.2-liter rebored 6-cylinder engine. With 230 hp, the Coupé, Cabriolet and the Targa reach a maximum speed of almost 156 mph. Twenty years of development lie between the first 911 with its 2-liter 6-cylinder, 130 hp and about 125 mph, and the 911-Carrera.

A facelift along with interesting technology is in store for the future of the 911: For instance, an electronically controlled all-wheel drive, anti-lock braking system (ABS), lowered body, and modern engine technology, just to name a few of the modification plans.

Porsche's economic situation has never been so good as in the beginning of the 80s. Americans, with their favorable exchange rate, are buying more than half of the Porsches manufactured. Production lines are running to the limit; the work force is growing continually, and Weissach, the development center where the sports car dreams begin, has grown to a firm with more than 2,000 employees.

The non-stop activity of the motor-racing scene worldwide will see to it that in the next years to come – as in the early 70s – Porsche will be on top of advancing technology. Porsche driving means more than just owning such a car, it also means identifying oneself with all the consequences of the product – whatever the cost.

HELMUTH BOTT

WEISSACH – THE PORSCHE THINK-TANK

The names Weissach and Porsche have been linked ever since the initial construction phase of the test site (a circular area of over 650 feet in diameter) was inaugurated in 1962. With the extension of the test tracks and the installation of the first factory building on Flachter Markung in the 60s, the first associates came to Weissach. A testing staff of over 400 then moved into the R & D Center to open up the workshops, offices, test stands and laboratories.

In 1974, the remaining R & D departments, most importantly the engineering design staff groups, were relocated from Stuttgart. A team of about 800 now having been assembled, the complete "Weissach Think-Tank" was ready to get down to business.

However, Porsche had already been a "think office" long before there were Porsche cars. The Porsche Engineering Design Office, founded in the winter of 1930/31, initially carried the following letterhead on its official documents:

F. Porsche, Ltd.
Neutral Design and Consulting Office
for Manufacturers of Automobiles, Aircraft,
Engines and Their Parts in the Gasoline,
Crude Oil and Electrical Fields.

A telling testimony to the many-faceted plans and possibilities of an engineering team that initially consisted of hardly a dozen people and had to make do with rented space in Stutt-

gart for seven years before the company (by then numbering almost 200 employees) could move into its own factory at Zuffenhausen. This was in the early summer of 1938; at the same time, the equipment arrived that was needed for producing test components and building prototypes in conjunction with Reutter, the nearby body manufacturers.

The wide scope with which the enterprise was founded was vindicated by what the "first generation" of Porsche engineers designed and developed during the first 15 years: passenger, sports and racing cars, cross-country vehicles, amphibious vehicles, tractors, trucks and defense projects, not forgetting aircraft engines, boat engines and heavy-duty diesel engines, as well as hydraulic turbines and wind-driven power stations. These projects were developed with varying degrees of intensity. The best-known fruits of this period's labor were the Auto Union racing car, the Volkswagen and the VW's military offshoots, the "Kuebelwagen" and the amphibious car.

Even when vehicle production commenced at Zuffenhausen in 1950, development was not restricted to the company's own products. A contract signed by Professor Nordhoff assured the Volkswagen factory of a large part of Porsche's R & D capacity, at the same time guaranteeing that the engineers at Porsche had sufficient work to get on with. Besides the many racing and other vehicles, no less than eight possible "Beetle" successors were developed at Porsche, but because the Volkswagen Type I was still selling well, they never came into production.

Since the contract between the Volkswagen works and Porsche was limited to a displacement of up to two liters, a project involving air and water-cooled 6-cylinder engines for Studebaker in the U.S.A. was developed on the side. Additionally, a "tractor family" was created. Initially called "Allgaier-System Porsche" and later, "Porsche-Diesel," it was a widespread success.

A large number of concepts were also developed in the field of military technology and many of them were carried through to the production preparation phase. The best-known Porsche project, the Leopard battle tank and its subsequent variants, kept a substantial part of the ordnance department busy. For a private client, the same team designed a series of construction machines.

During the postwar reconstruction years however, the Porsche R & D team concentrated on working on its own products. The important step from the 356 (originally fitted out with a large number of Volkswagen components) to the independent 911 was the main concern of this period, and a considerable number of Porsche buyers and admirers still regard that particular vehicle as the Porsche to end all Porsches.

The young production company's image was determined mainly by the charisma of its products and the success of its racing cars. No less than 36 different types of racing vehicles were built and entered in races between 1950 and 1970.

The change from Zuffenhausen to Weissach at the outset of the 70s was seamless; it's the dimensions that have become different. The original "think-office with a workshop" has

turned into a "think-tank." In the decade between 1974 and 1985, the team has expanded from 800 to 2,000, and it's still growing. Installations have been expanded, completed, and adapted to the many tasks that are set.

One series of models and a 50-million deutschmark annual budget for research and development of production and racing cars have turned into *three* series of models and an annual budget of over 250 million deutschmarks. Additionally, the initial 25-million deutschmarks turnover in contract development work in this field is now at over 100 million deutschmarks.

So what makes Weissach so special?

Is Weissach really a "think-tank"? And if it is, what does that term mean? If you take it to literally mean the production and development of ideas, you are doing present-day Weissach an injustice. In the initial decades, the "Porsche Design and Consulting Office" sold mainly ideas, drawings, calculations and designs, i.e. software. This was apparent not only in the scope of training and activities of its staff, but also in the fact that prototype construction and testing were realized principally with the aid of other firms. Today, the majority of the R & D team is involved in practical application of the continuing abundant flow of ideas. The R & D workshop dialogue among design engineers, test engineers and skilled workers that is so important for realizing projects takes place within the company's walls.

Model makers and casters, prototype builders, saddlers and materials engineers (to name but a few) all participate in the development process, guaranteeing satisfactory results in conjunction with the engineers and technologists of the production departments. The constant dialogue with hundreds of engineers and scientists from all over the world during the development of commissions from abroad is also of great importance.

The variety of projects, the need to compromise and at the same time the need to come to grips with deadlines and overheads (and not giving up when faced with the apparently insoluble problems that sometimes crop up) is what makes Weissach special. The ability to improvise is especially important during the R & D phase, and project groups have been learning to do it marvelously. This is most apparent when they cooperate with other teams who lack this training. Motivation and commitment (qualities that have become rare nowadays) are very apparent in the Porsche R & D team; it's obviously important how interesting and challenging the tasks imposed are.

It is absolutely impossible to describe all the projects and fascinating tasks that the team at Weissach is engaged in. Also, contractual stipulations in most contract orders prevent us from going into detail. We can, however, present an outline.

Forty percent of our contract order volume consists of engine development. In the spring of 1985, for instance, no fewer than twenty-two projects between 50 and 1,000 hp were being developed on the drawing boards and test stands.

Research and development projects often begin with a 1-cylinder engine, which is especially suitable for the testing of different combustion chambers. In these, the combustion process and the resulting efficiency of different concepts can be evaluated and further developed.

Porsche is especially in demand in the field of lightweight and high-performance engine construction and development, also in turbo engines, in catalytic converter technology, in conversion to modern fuel injection systems and (much more frequently in recent years) in developing and improving racing engines. The TAG Formula 1 engine is our best-known project. In its first year on the track, it was able to win 12 out of 16 races. With its aid, McLaren drivers Niki Lauda and Alain Prost finished 1–2 in the World Championship 1984 ratings.

Among the engines currently being developed, there are 3-, 4-, 5- and 6-cylinder in-line engines; 4-, 6- and 8-cylinder V-engines and 2-, 4- and 6-cylinder horizontally opposed engines, not forgetting Diesel engines.

Another area which R & D is concentrating on is AWD technology. In this field, a dozen projects are already in the works, including front and rear engines, center differentials and various torque proportioning systems, propeller shafts, the transaxle concept between the front and rear axles, and various limited slip differentials for the rear axle. Here too, there are high-performance variants like the Porsche 959 with more than 400 hp on the one hand, and commercial vehicles, station wagons, coupés and mid-sized cars on the other.

In the field of transmission development, Porsche has been a favorite consulting partner for many years. Besides their own developments, they are constantly working on several contract development orders ranging from power-shift automatic transmissions to six-speed manual transmissions.

There are many projects underway, such as truck and bus development as well as several studies and development contracts for electric vehicles.

Parallel to developing its own new aircraft engine, Weissach is busy working on several contract orders in aeronautics. Its development of a new interior styling for the Airbus A 310 became well known. Years ago, a 911 engine was adapted for use in the English "Airship" company's dirigibles. In the meantime there is a turbo version, and the small series of these airships is equipped exclusively with engines that are not only developed but also built at Weissach.

Weissach engineers are also creatively involved in the field of motorcycle development. Important commissions so far include various tests, conversion from chain to cardan drive, performance improvement, the construction of an entire family of motorcycles for a renowned manufacturer, as well as the testing of a motor bike.

It's public knowledge how manifold the roster of Weissach's R & D clients is. There is a major contract for a Russian mid-size car, there are consultancy agreements with a North African state, there are studies and R & D projects for American vehicle producers and the Japanese industry, there are R & D contracts for all German and most other European motor companies, there are contracts from Germany's Federal Ministry of Research and Technology as well as the Federal Environmental Agency.

One of these research projects for Germany's Federal Environmental Agency was particularly interesting. With six motorcycles of differing European makes, the technical possibilities of noise reduction were examined and then employed in modified series bikes. Improvements of 2 to 7 dB were attained without any change in motor construction, i.e. mainly by changing the intake and exhaust systems and the differential gear ratios. At the same time, maximum performance and torque curve were improved in all test objects.

In another research project for the same client, a motorcycle was conceived in cooperation with German motorcycle manufacturer BMW. It was quieter by 7 dB without any reduction in performance but actually with an improved torque curve in the medium speed range.

The development of a family of Porsche aircraft engines mentioned in another chapter of this book is worthy of note when considering the Weissach "think-tank." Doing without the great experience of the well-known aircraft engine builders, Porsche engineers within four years developed an aircraft engine that offers distinct improvements in all the important areas, thereby setting new standards. The following are the most significant advantages of this new engine system (PFM 3200):

1. Increased flight safety due to single lever control. With only one lever the pilot works the throttle and the propeller pitch. The fuel-air mixture formation for all conditions is automatic. The pilot is relieved of a part of his work. He can concentrate on flying, and improper operation of the motor is rendered impossible.

2. Increased fuel economy due to the use of automobile fuel instead of aircraft fuel and due to the use of forced-air cooling, which renders fuel-air mixture enrichment for engine cooling unnecessary. Optimal consumption is achieved by an excellent ignition and injection system and good combustion chamber design.

3. Advantageous aerodynamics due to better design of engine cowling, leading to improved flying performance with the same engine performance or lower consumption with equal flying performance.

4. Greatly reduced exterior noise due to lower number of propeller revolutions and highly effective exhaust muffling.

5. Markedly reduced interior noise (and reduced vibration) due to the measures described in item 4 in conjunction with carefully calculated and innovative engine mounting.

6. Reliability due to the main components having been proved 300,000 times in the 911 automobile engine.

7. Possibility of clockwise and counterclockwise rotation due to an additional intermediate gear and reversing capability.

This aircraft engine is intended to be the first of a series of modern aircraft piston engines; especially the later versions with modern exhaust turbocharger technology might be able to provide an impetus in the construction of new and progressive sports planes. These are certainly hallmarks of superior technology in an area outside of automobiles. But Porsche is also setting new standards in the automobile field with the superior technology of the 959.

Porsche engineers have never doubted the

fact that concentrated racing development could at the same time be important for future developments as a whole. Measures taken to achieve high specific performance are also applicable to maximum economy, and an advantageous power-to-weight ratio is also good for production-line vehicles.

New knowledge about handling, light-weight construction, aerodynamics and other areas also applies to production-line vehicles. The Porsche 959 was conceived as base vehicle for a high-performance sports version of the so-called Group B. Group B regulations call for a series of at least 200 vehicles that have to be built within one year.

Could there be a better set of conditions for producing a car of the future than these? That's why correspondingly high aims were set for this project in all facets of automobile technology. Thus, the cultivated, suited-for-everyday-use racing engine of the 959 today has four-valve cylinder-heads, hydraulic tappets, an electronic system for ignition and fuel injection control, and a new turbo technology with a double carburetor system.

The drive train has a widely spaced six-gear transmission and AWD in the transaxle concept, with electronically controlled torque dis-tribution. Both in the front and rear, the chassis is provided with double-wishbone axles (borrowed from racing car construction), four-piston brake calipers on each wheel and an anti-lock braking system that is ideally suited for AWD. Ground clearance can be either manually controlled or regulated by a cruise control system. Shock absorber stiffness can also be set manually or automatically regulated as a function of speed. The hollow-spoke safety wheels, made of magnesium and also taken from racing technology, are equipped with an electronic inflation pressure control system.

The 959's durable body, made of a combination of steel, aluminum and fiber-reinforced plastic, presents interesting options for new manufacturing processes. Meticulously crafted aerodynamics with special attention to under-body design show that low air drag without simultaneous lift is something that can also be achieved in a production-line vehicle.

I'm sure the future will present increasingly greater challenges to our research and development people. Combining the efforts of experienced builders and developers with those of young and creative engineers is a tradition at Weissach and at the same time a prerequisite for facing future challenges.

HEINZ HORRMANN

INTO THE FUTURE WITH THE PORSCHE 959

The caravan at the palace park in Versailles was sent off along the 8,500-mile route from Paris to Dakar with fireworks, fanfares and thousands of good wishes. On this cold and misty first morning of the New Year 1985, the near-hysterical jubilation of the French also embraced the participants in the seventh Paris–Dakar Rally: the rich and the beautiful, the clever ones with a nose for the sensational public relations value of the event, the fanatics who often sacrifice everything just to take part, and the cool professionals. Three of the latter had received a two-fold order: to attempt to repeat the Porsche victory of the preceding year, and to carry out the most vigorous test drive imaginable. Jacky Ickx, Jochen Mass and René Metge were driving red-white-and-blue 959 prototypes, the sports car of the future.

As usual, Porsche had not spared any expense or extravagance. In accordance with Porsche custom, the cars provided for this test of technology were masterpieces, outfitted with new elements other manufacturers could only dream of. This time, only the power plants were the same as the year before: the normally-aspirated engine of the 911 Carrera, because the innovative 959 twin-turbo engine hadn't been sufficiently tested for the requirements of such a brutal endurance run. "If our primary consideration had been only overall victory we would

have played it safe," argued Porsche's chief of research and development, Helmuth Bott. "We would have entered the improved version of last year's car. But a thorough test was more important than our role as favorites."

When the remaining entries prepared for the finale after ten days of wild desert driving, the Group B Porsches sponsored by the Rothmans cigarette company were nowhere to be seen. While racing to catch up, Jochen Mass had flipped his car, Hollywood style. Jacky Ickx had run into a sand-obscured boulder at a speed of 110 mph, and Metge demolished his oil line during a spin-out. This rally will thus go down as one of the few total flops in the long motor sport history of the company. But there was no mood of defeat in the development department. The engineers were unperturbed. It was only to be expected that problems would arise with prototype models, and a lot of time had also been lost as a result of a long labor dispute. When the now famous king pins repeatedly broke during the initial legs of the rally, the drivers, pressed for time, lost their feeling of superiority and risked more than anticipated. But because recognized defects are eliminated in the final product, this test without victory had greatly helped to cut the development time.

As a rule, seven years are calculated for the development of a new car, from the initial

99

design layout to the production line. But the evolution of Porsche's supercar took only two years! Unimaginable! A few critics – the usual know-it-alls – complained that the vehicle was "only" the expected further development of the 911, which is, of course, nonsense. Actually, the idea for the Car of the Future was born just a few months before the 1983 Frankfurt Auto Show. Right from the beginning there was a conscious attempt to give the "new popular sport instrument" as it was officially referred to, lines similar to those of the successful Porsche rear-engine type. At first, the development specialists in Weissach experimented with a styling study that would be an eye-catcher at the 1983 jubilee exhibition. The intention was to discuss production of a small series after the auto show. As it is usual within a dynamic management board opinions on the project varied greatly. There was necessarily a discussion of the huge effort involved, of the enormous costs and of the difficulty in later having to justify to customers the high final price of several hundred thousand marks.

The Group B class newly created by the sport moguls – for which a minimum production of 200 vehicles is required for homologation – naturally demands a lot of manual labor and an inconceivable financial strain on a small company. Producing the required quantity brings with it a dependence on affluent private buyers, some of whom want to drive the car on public roads, others in races. But even at a price of 450,000 deutschmarks – gigantic at first glance – some 100 million deutschmarks in development costs are not going to be covered. That was clear right from the start. And that was the reason for the long period of debate. The argument that finally won out and got the project started was the plan to make this 959 a technological wonder of the future, with solutions that are destined for upcoming generations of vehicles. Financing is also easier to obtain for such a car – a futuristic prototype and sports car

in one. After the final go-ahead, the designers and technicians in Weissach quickly conjured up a car that can simply do everything. A reflection of the automotive potential of our century, if you will.

These are the outstanding elements, the technical characteristics of this unique sports car. The roof, front and side body elements and the fenders are made of the lightest material available: aramide fiber plastic, with the same tensile strength as steel, but eight times lighter. Parts that could be used from the 911 – such as the flooring, the inner paneling and the doors were made of aluminum. Thus it was possible to achieve a low final weight of 2,420 pounds. For stylistic and aerodynamic reasons, the spoilers were integrated into the body. The drip molding used on the 911 was eliminated. This was also the first time that a car body was assembled with this kind of combination: steel for the parts demanding great tensile strength, aluminum for parts which could be made lighter, and Kevlar plastic parts, for which new tooling had to be set up. This is a future-oriented experiment that will certainly turn up in larger series within a few years.

The engine is the heart and pride of the 959. The 2.85-liter, 6-cylinder version features digital electronics – and advanced development of the engines found in Formula 1 and Group C vehicles. The engine itself still has air-cooled cylinders, but the cylinder heads are water-cooled. Hydraulic valve regulation and contactless ignition electronics also contribute to making the engine easy to service and repair. The power plant with 400 base horsepower is a variation that lies between a pure racing engine and a highway version. The Porsche engineers' long experience with turbos provided yet another technical feature: two electronically controlled turbochargers. Using just one large turbo provides very high performance at high engine speeds. One small turbo gives better results at lower revs, but the performance is limited at higher levels. So Porsche's engine specialists utilized two small turbochargers, one behind the other in series. The first kicks in at relatively low engine speed, and reacts very quickly to changes in acceleration. Only when high performance is required does the second turbocharger kick in fully, providing a sufficiently large flow for the combustion mixture. This system offers definite fuel consumption advantages in comparison with Lancia's very good technical combination of a turbocharger plus compressor, which is utilized in the rally competition car, the Delta S 4.

The completely new form of multi-variable four-wheel drive caused the technicians a lot of headaches, but the problems were finally solved. The on-board electronics make it possible at the push of a button to distribute the drive power variably between the front and rear wheels, depending on road conditions, but also in accordance with the driver's individual wishes. In addition, the mid and rear-axle differential can be locked for driving under very extreme conditions. That all sounds like it's the most natural development in the world. In fact, however, the infinitely variable system represents a tremendous step forward over the permanent 50:50 four-wheel-drive system of the Audi Quattro or even of the four-wheel-drive 911 SC, which won the 1984 Paris–Dakar rally. For different sports events and everyday driving, the variable system exploits the additional dynamic advantages of front-wheel drive (pulling) and of rear-wheel drive for conscious oversteering under competitive conditions by ordering the drive power wherever it is most needed at any particular moment.

At Porsche the simple rule that only the best will do also applies to the chassis. The wishbones, front and rear, are equipped with two shock absorbers each – in other words, a total of eight – of which four are made of aluminum and, by means of electronic controls, provide the regulation of ride stiffness. Two different types of adjustment are possible. One is automatic, dependent on speed. It ensures that the shocks remain soft and comfortable in city traffic and stop-and-go situations. At increasing speeds the controls shift through numerous stages of stiffness, electronically adjusted. And finally, when the driver accelerates over 110 miles per hour, extreme stiffness is adjusted automatically – for reasons of safety.

Adjustment can also be made manually by means of a switch in the cockpit. Three different stages are possible: soft, medium and hard. To raise or lower the chassis, the all-purpose 959 doesn't require a trip to the garage like a normal car. Flat sports cars with low ground clearance are known to run aground often with their spoilers or the middle of the undercarriage, and they face insurmountable problems with inclined garage driveways. On the other hand, "long-legged" ground clearance for everyday use has aerodynamic drawbacks and the higher center of gravity is a definite disadvantage when cornering. The 959's cleverly devised shock absorbers also make it possible for the driver to electronically raise the chassis when he faces difficult or swampy terrain, for example, or when pulling up to a curb. At high speeds the car is then automatically returned to the lowest clearance position.

Investing a large share of the development work in active and passive safety elements reflects the traditional thinking of the engineers in Zuffenhausen, and the "Weltanschauung" of many fans. That certainly includes the four-wheel-drive concept, and the extra-large brakes with an improved, racing-tested anti-lock braking system – both features, of course, are not exclusive to Porsche. But in addition, the 959 features safety tires (as standard equipment), tires that hold the car on course even when they lose air. The 959 also has automatic air pressure indicators, so the driver is warned immediately if one of the tires begins to lose pressure. The control system also applies to the hollow spokes of the centrally-locked wheels: Cracks in the metal are registered just as reliably as leaks in the tires. Both systems are already used in the Porsche 956, where they have proved their value.

Of course, there will be many customers who gladly accept the advantages, but who are far less interested in technical details than in exterior appearance and accessories. These considerations were also major points of discussion. In comparison with the 911, drag was reduced by giving the 959 softer, rounded lines and by completely encasing the underbody. In fact, this is probably the form the 911 of the future will take on. In contrast to their otherwise rather sober image, the Swabians have outdone themselves when it comes to accessories and the interior. They realized that many buyers regard technical details as fascinating, but expect solid, ingenious and valuable accessories and comfort to match. For weight reasons, the competition version of the 959 is stripped down and simple, but the highway version is equipped with every imaginable luxury. Soft, fragrant leather has been used for the seats, elegant instruments and consoles are integrated and the exclusive upholstery and soft carpets have been painstakingly matched to the body paint. It goes without saying that the heating, ventilation and air conditioning systems are electronically controlled.

Thus it comes as no surprise that customers enthusiastically embraced this luxurious Car of the Future even before the first model was completed, and even though it costs as much as a bungalow in the suburbs. Months before the premiere at the '85 International Auto Show, Helmuth Bott summed up: "General interest and demand were so great, we could have sold many more than the 130 comfortable roadgoing models." (20 cars in the series were pro-

duced as pure competition vehicles with minimal weight and maximum performance; another 50 were built as lighter street models also suitable for sports events.) That is not always the case for small-series homologation models. Audi, for instance, counted on similar demand for the short Sport Quattro, but after more than a year, only 50 had been sold. Porsche's experience was very different, even back in the 1960s with the 911 RS. That small series sold faster than it could be built.

Even if the incredibly short development phase constitutes an absolute industry record, a lot can still change in two years. New findings and improvements overtake the tried-and-true. For example, in the initial phase of the 959, the topics of environmental technology and emission reduction were relatively insignificant. But once environmental protection and air pollution reduction became dominant issues, Bott and his team realized that a car of the future simply had to feature a complete emission control system. In the midst of development, Bott's crew jumped on the bandwagon and came up with a catalytic converter that almost totally cleans the exhaust of the 959. Adjustments were also made to the electronic regulation of the four-wheel-drive system, which was originally designed primarily with the sports driver in mind. Over a number of months, the Weissach engineers altered the system in favor of customers who wanted to drive the car on public streets and highways.

Additional improvements are still being made even as series production proceeds. The philosophy behind this Porsche, for which the future has already begun, is the evolution of a vehicle into which everything worth striving for has been built. Everything that inventiveness and today's technical know-how make possible.

FROM COUP TO COUP

As an amateur painter, Hans Mezger's models are French impressionists Edouard Manet, Claude Monet and Paul Cézanne. As a design engineer, he has found no one to emulate: "I have met many people with a conception similar to mine, but there aren't really any models."

The man from Porsche does have a certain admiration for McLaren boss Ron Dennis: "Dennis got Niki Lauda back, he talked Porsche into building a Formula 1 engine (something quite a few people had tried without success before him), and he was able to secure Mansour Ojjeh's financial backing."

When the Briton Dennis commissioned a Formula 1 engine at Porsche in the fall of 1981, it was time for painting and music aficionado Mezger to give up his private interests. The only time George Gershwin's "Rhapsody in Blue" still emanated from the designer's cassette deck was early in the morning or late in the evening, when he drove the 21 miles between his home in Ludwigsburg-Freiberg and the Porsche think-tank at Weissach.

The easel and oils in his old farmhouse gathered dust. In those days, creativity was called for only in a large, soberly furnished open-office that Mezger shares with 100 other development engineers. His design philosophy is as sober as the environment. "Ideas you can have anywhere; it's at the drawing board that they get their polish," says the designer, whose aim lies in structural elements that are as simple as possible. They rarely succeed on the first try. "The first layout is usually far too complicated," is what he has learned by experience.

After three decades of professional activity, Mezger is one of Porsche's veterans. He can be considered part of the inventory, for Porsche history is closely linked to the 56-year old Swabian's strokes of designing genius.

As a young man, he didn't limit himself to engine development, but also designed underbodies. Mezger's first serious challenge was a prototype with the internal designation "Ollon-Villars," which wasn't really a pure bred Porsche. The wheel carriers and the small 13-inch cast rims that were then coming into fashion came from Lotus stock.

Today, the designer justifies himself by saying there wasn't enough time. Gerhard Mitter had just suffered a bitter defeat at Monte Bordone, and the people at Porsche quickly decided to build a new prototype. Mitter himself supplied the wheel carriers and rims, Mezger designed a tubular frame, and 14 days later, Mitter entered at Ollon-Villars with the new Porsche. He was again beaten by Ludovico Scarfiotti in his Ferrari Dino, but Mezger's concept was to be the cornerstone for Porsche's first proper racing car, the 910.

In the following ten years, Mezger was responsible both for racing engine and racing chassis development. His next coup was the Porsche 917. "A big one," its creator remembers. Between 1969 and 1971, Porsche won the World Championship of Makes three times and, subsequently, the American Can-Am racing series twice. In its most powerful version, the supercharged 917-30 finally mustered 1,100 hp. Its superiority was so overwhelming that the

Americans gave it the boot by changing the rules.

This is what Hans Mezger says about the triumphal progress of his child prodigy, the 917:

"The air-cooled 12-cylinder engine of the 917 did indeed set new standards: Its 1,100 hp turbo version is still considered the most powerful automotive engine of all. (In 1976, legendary engineer Professor Eberan von Ebenhorst called it the glittering apex of 100 years of worldwide engine development in a speech commemorating the 100th anniversary of the SI engine.)

The 917 racing car's dominance in long-distance races and in the American Can-Am series could only be halted by changing the rules. The Porsche 917 could be entered as a works car solely for five years, from 1969 to 1971 at the World Championships of Makes, and from 1971 to 1973 at the Can-Am races. But that was time enough to make it one of the most successful racing cars of post-war history.

"In its 917 Can-Am engine, Porsche had for the first time employed the exhaust turbocharger, developing it to a maturity enabling it to be used in road races. Due to its unsatisfactory response characteristic, this supercharger system had up till then been unsuitable for races featuring a lot of curves. Turbo engines had so far only been used in Indianapolis cars. They raced on simple oval tracks, where the problem of turbo lag was not so important.

"The decision reached in 1972 in favor of the exhaust turbocharger for the 917 Can-Am vehicle was not to remain without consequences: Porsche did pioneering work in the application of automobile turbo technology. The new technology became the focal point of Porsche's engine development. And so, the idea for a production-line vehicle with an exhaust turbocharger, the 911 Turbo, arose. Weissach's engineers joined those leading the field in exhaust turbochargers."

From 1975 on, Mezger was busy not only with his own engine projects, but also with contract developments, and he concentrated more and more on engine design. The most important prerequisite for his job is "logical and analytical thought." A dash of creativity and the search for possible new solutions are what continually spur Mezger on. But, he certainly doesn't want to be regarded as your typical Swabian eccentric. "Being eccentric puzzle solvers isn't enough in what we're doing; we have to turn our ideas into functioning hardware," the development engineer hastens to explain.

"That Porsche," which is what he likes to call his employer, knows what his design engineer's work is worth. Mezger's official title is "manager of advanced engineering."

Says Hans Mezger on the subject of Porsche's racing engines: "In the 35 years since Porsche began its own automobile production at Stuttgart-Zuffenhausen in 1950, there have been, strictly speaking, four pure bred racing engines: The 4-cylinder 547/587 Carrera engine in the Fifties, the 8-cylinder 753/771 for Formula 1 and long-distance races in the early Sixties, the 917 12-cylinder engine in the late Sixties and, finally, the V-6 Formula 1. This list, however, would be incomplete without mentioning a production-line engine that some people at first considered too much of an effort: The air-cooled 6-cylinder horizontally opposed 911 engine. The 911 engines or those derived from it were on the production-line and employed in racing from 1964 on. Among the 911 versions are successful developments like the 935 stock racing car engines and those for the 936 sports racer, which has won at Le Mans more than once.

The 1980 Indianapolis engine was derived from the 911 type, as was the 630 hp engine of the Group C racing cars, which is in the World Championship works entries. Even the air-cooled 3-liter, 8-cylinder 908 engine is a development based on the 911. To sum up, it's thanks to the many-sided 911 production powerplant that

Porsche has been able to participate in international racing in a way that no other automaker has managed to do."

For the designer with an eye for beauty, who has wandered through more museums during stopovers in London than he cares to mention, the Formula 1 challenge was like the severing of the Gordian knot.

"Constructing the Fomula 1 engine wasn't just another project. A development of that sort is something that hadn't been done in a long time, not even at Porsche," explains Mezger, who for the first time was faced with the no-holds-barred task of designing a new engine that had only one purpose: to win.

However, the project wasn't completely without constraints. The pressure of contract work was high on the small development staff; "The client was told of every step and of every mistake." Also, the reputation of the company was closely linked to this particular project.

The difficulties of the 1981 Formula 1 turbo were analyzed painstakingly by Mezger and his engineers: "It got too hot and consumed too much." Mezger knew what he had to do: "The engine's cooling mustn't be laid out like that of a 1.5-liter, but like that of a racing engine that happens to perform at 800 hp." Aim number two: The TAG-Porsche Formula 1 was to be small and compact. Today, Mezger still gets excited about it: "Until then, Porsche never had a crankshaft as small as the one in our Formula 1 engine."

In 1984, Niki Lauda and Alain Prost proved what Mezger's masterpiece was capable of. In the space of one season, the Porsche turbo powered a McLaren to victory twelve times, something no other engine had so far been able to do.

It was probably thanks to the Porsche engineers' reputation of being in the forefront in the field of exhaust turbochargers that in November 1981 McLaren International commissioned Porsche to begin development of a Formula 1 turbo engine. And Porsche, which hadn't been represented in Formula racing for almost twenty years, took up the challenge. The project received the designation 2,623. In May 1982, Technique d'Avantgarde (TAG) provided the financial backing. In December 1982, the engine ran for the first time under its own power on one of the Weissach test stands. The development went ahead according to plan. In early July 1983, Niki Lauda tested the engine on the Weissach test track in the original Formula 1 chassis.

According to an "optimum plan" decided on by the client and Porsche, racing was to begin as early as the second half of the 1983 season. And development went ahead so quickly that participation in the last four races was possible. On August 26, 1983, the engine made its first public appearance in the Dutch Grand Prix' Friday training at Zandvoort. Two further races were necessary to fuse the McLaren chassis and the "TAG turbo engine – made by Porsche," which is what it was officially called. In the last race of the 1983 season, the South African Grand Prix at Kyalami on October 15th, the full potential of the McLaren/Lauda/Porsche combination became apparent: Seemingly without effort, Niki Lauda advanced to second place, and it was only an electrical failure five laps before the finish that prevented the first possible Grand Prix victory.

Porsche's powerful competitors had been warned. But no one could know that the 1984 season was to be an unprecedented triumph to drivers Niki Lauda and Alain Prost, the McLaren team and the Porsche company. On March 25th, Alain Prost came in first in the 1984 season's first Grand Prix at Rio de Janeiro, thus gaining the first Grand Prix victory for the Formula 1 engine developed at Weissach. "Maybe it was just luck," the people at Porsche thought; "Just a coincidence," the competitors mused. But in the next race, the South African Grand Prix at Kyalami on April 7th, 1984, a double victory was scored, with Niki Lauda coming in

105

first. Now people started talking about dominance because Alain Prost had to start the race 26th and last, due to having switched to the backup car in the preliminary lap. And at the end of the race only Lauda and Prost remained in the same lap.

When Alain Prost and Niki Lauda came in first and second respectively in the Portuguese Grand Prix at Estoril on October 21, 1984, a season of superlatives drew to a close. Niki Lauda became world champion with 72 points, Alain Prost finished second with 71.5. McLaren won twelve out of sixteen Grand Prix competitions (the record till then had been eight) and gathered 143,5 world championship points (120 had been the previous record).

After an absence of more than twenty years, Porsche had made an impressive comeback to the Grand Prix scene. One of the most coveted titles in racing, the Formula 1 World Championship, had been won on the first try.

The V-6 Formula 1 engine was a milestone in SI engine technology. The development center at Weissach had demonstrated its capabilities to the public at large and proved that contract orders are handled just as conscientiously as Porsche's own projects. Development of the type 2,623 Formula 1 engine is without a doubt, a milestone in Porsche's illustrious history of engine development.

Naturally, success bred envy – even in the home camp. Clients McLaren and TAG were upset by the free publicity that Porsche and Mezger were getting everywhere. Whenever possible, Ron Dennis hastens to emphasize the TAG turbo was really a result of his designer John Barnard's stipulations. "We certainly didn't need Barnard to convince us not to build a horizontally opposed engine for Formula 1,"

replies Mezger, who regularly attended Formula-1-races to gather information on the latest technology long before the McLaren contract.

Gaining victories is something Mezger's TAG turbo hasn't forgotten how to do in 1985. But the competition has been on its toes, and at least as far as training is concerned, it is already superior to McLaren. "It's easier to build a powerful qualification engine than to develop a racing unit that is also able to win races; that's something that requires a little more thought," Mezger emphasizes.

In his Formula 1 development work, he sees many parallels to the production line. "We learn from Formula 1, but at the same time, the Formula 1 project profits from the production line," Mezger explains. "In electronics, for instance, and in experiments with ceramic materials. Mind you, our engine isn't yet made entirely of ceramics."

We're in the middle of the Formula 1 season, but at Weissach, work on winter projects is still in progress. "We haven't managed everything," Mezger confesses. His contract prevents him from being more precise, but it does seem he has one or two things up his sleeve. The turbo's responsiveness is to be further improved and its water injection brought up to racing standard.

There is nothing more unpleasant for an engineer than being forbidden to chat about his tricks and amusements. TAG and McLaren have sealed Mezger's lips with an especially impregnable variety of tape. When questioned about the performance of his ward, a little gap does appear in the tape, permitting the following pronouncement: "If I look at our competitors' figures and assume Prost to drive equally fast, I can only say we have at least as much performance – but so far I don't know of anyone driving around with 1,000 hp."

REINHARD SEIFFERT

PORSCHE IN FORMULA 1

Presenting the builders of racing cars and engines with new and interesting challenges is the real intent of formula racing. You have to keep that in mind: What's at stake in the final analysis is not the greater glory of specific manufacturers, sponsors, team chiefs or entire nations. The idea is to promote technical achievement, and simultaneously, to give the best drivers a chance to show what they can do.

Of course, Grand Prix sport has never been entirely free of advertising gimmicks, of national and personal hubris, a fact which is easily explained: In Formula-1-racing, outstanding achievement is demanded and delivered; every success or failure occurs before the eyes of masses of spectators. That was just as true back in 1934 – when the Auto Union Grand Prix car designed by Porsche won three events in its first year of competition – as in 1984, when Niki Lauda narrowly edged Alain Prost – both driving McLarens with TAG-engines, which Porsche designed and built under contract to the Technique d'Avant Garde company – to win the Formula-1-World Championship.

The motivation behind it all differed only slightly: In 1934 it was the hope of bringing new racing renown to Germany and in 1984 it were ambitious team managers, sponsors and drivers who hoped to get an edge on the competition by exploiting Porsche's design know-how.

Porsche's role was the same in both cases: to produce successful technology.

Starting with the fifth development contract, which the young design office ever received – entered in the files as No. 22 – there is a continuous line of development leading to the TAG engine. This continuity is personified by the head of the House of Porsche: Ferry Porsche played a key role in the design of the "P-Wagen" (Porsche Car) for Auto Union in 1934, and fifty years later served as the grey eminence behind the fourth Grand Prix project in Porsche history.

There was also that summer day in 1980 when, for the first time in many years, the Auto Union racing car, which had been restored by Audi NSU, once again vented its unmistakable compressor roar at the test track in Weissach. The start signal was given by Robert Eberan von Eberhorst – before the war the chief racing engineer at Auto Union – and at the wheel was Porsche's head of development, Helmuth Bott.

Whereas on the McLaren-TAG project Porsche was responsible only for the engine, in 1932 and 1933 Porsche designed the entire car. The same was true in 1946 and 1947 with the Cisitalia development contract and with Porsche's own Formula 1 racing car in 1961 and 1962. Today, conformity more or less rules when it comes to racing chassis, which is not to say that there couldn't be improvements. But back in the early 1930s, Porsche dared a step that not until 30 years later would become a standard of racing car design: In the P-Wagen, the engine was placed behind the driver's seat, in front of the rear axle. That created a favorable center of gravity near the middle of the car, and increased the load on the drive wheels.

Today, that is one of the ABCs of racing car technology, and it is astounding to note that even with that construction, the tremendous engine power of the Auto Union car was hard to tame.

Ferry Porsche reports that there was dissatisfaction with the initial 4.5-liter engine and its 400 hp. The engine displacement was increased to 6 liters, and soon it was 600 hp: "Given a car that weighed less than 1,760 pounds, that was a fantastic power-to-weight ratio, no matter what standards it is measured by or what period of racing car history it is compared with." It was impossible to fully exploit the engine's capacity at the start: "There weren't any extra-wide tires in those days. If you weren't careful, the wheels spun out and smoked."

This performance potential demanded corresponding drive train technology. Ferry Porsche had noticed that, when accelerating through curves, it was usually the inside rear wheel that broke out and began to smoke. "Since we had had good experience in touring cars with limited slip differentials, I suggested to my father that we try one out." He agreed: "You might have hit the nail on the head." The ZF company produced the right kind of differential, and for several months the Auto Union cars clearly dominated the Mercedes in accelerating out of the curves – until in Untertuerkheim they finally figured out what the secret was.

Today the limited slip differential has also become a standard feature, but the performance of the formula racing cars long lagged far behind the Auto Union's 600 hp, until new formulas halved the displacement of supercharged engines to three liters, and finally quartered it to 1.5 liters. Hans Stuck Sr., since his first major successes in his debut year of 1934 the star driver at Auto Union, sometimes mounted twin tires on his rear wheels in order to get the engine performance onto the track – the forerunner of today's slicks. It was also Stuck who set the first world records in the Auto Union Grand Prix car. Stuck's successor was Bernd Rosemeyer as top driver – he died in that tragic accident which called into question the practice of using road racing cars to go after records.

At that time, in early 1938, Porsche's contract with Auto Union expired, and a new one was signed with Daimler-Benz, which foresaw, among other things, the design of a special world record car, the T 80, designed to bring the absolute speed record to Germany. Then the war seemed to put an end to all racing car developments, but something very unusual happened: Under the most primitive conditions, in the Kaernten substitute quarters in Gmuend, a Grand Prix project was put together in 1947, one that is considered sensational even today. Built in accordance with the 1.5 liter formula, the Cisitalia Grand Prix was a logical successor to the Auto Union, and at the same time, an anticipation of a future that was a long time in coming. In today's terms it was absolute high technology, that car built in the wooden huts, new right down to the last nuts and bolts: a water-cooled, horizontally-opposed 12-cylinder engine with a mechanical charger, designed for 385 hp at under 10,000 rpm and for mid-car placement in a lattice-tubular chassis with independent wheel suspension, featuring a five-speed, quick-shift transmission and a mechanism to switch into four-wheel drive.

Commenting on this car in 1985, Professor Ferry Porsche said: "We had projected very high engine performance, and on the basis of our 1-cylinder tests we were convinced, that we could attain it. But with the narrow racing tires available in those days, we couldn't get the engine

108

performance onto the track using only the rear axle. There was also another factor involved: According to all our calculations, we could beat Bernd Rosemeyer's Auto Union record for one kilometer from a standing start – which was of great importance then – only by utilizing four-wheel drive. Thus, the Cisitalia was ahead of its time not just because of the mid-engine placement, but also because of the four-wheel drive."

It was to take more than 15 years for the mid-mounted engine to prevail in racing car construction. If contractor Piero Dusio's credit hadn't been cut off by his partner company, Fiat, an early parallel to the TAG relationship might have emerged. As it was, Grand Prix technology took a different course, the pre-war supercharged cars were forgotten, and the great normally-aspirated engine era of the Maseratis, Mercedes-Benz and Ferraris dawned. That was followed, as a result of continual reductions in engine displacement, by the age of the "midgets," the ultra-light racing cars, and thus the mid-engine concept.

It was this development that led to sports car maker Porsche's first and only venture onto the Grand Prix scene. Prior to that, and later, it was always the development company Porsche which fulfilled contracts on this scene, and always in brilliant form. The interlude in the early 1960s can't be compared to a planned entry – it arose coincidentally from that fact that the technology of Porsche's racing cars was almost identical to that of the Formula 2 cars, and Formula 2 evolved into Formula 1.

In 1957, Porsche racing drivers and racing engineers in Zuffenhausen realized that the Spyder 550 A perfectly fit the regulations governing Formula 2 – it was only necessary to cover the headlights and the passenger seat. It was in such a car that Edgar Barth won the Formula 2 event at the Nuerburgring – the Grand Prix of Germany. Based on this success, racing engineer Hild and racing director Huschke v. Hanstein got their boss, Ferry Porsche, to

agree to a special budget for the 1958 season in order to carry out a Formula 2 conversion: a no-longer-new Spyder was equipped with a flat front cowling without headlights, and a seat in the middle. In this car, still very much a sports car, the great French driver Jean Behra won the Formula 2 race in Reims. Behra later died in an accident at the Berlin Avus circuit, at the wheel of a Behra-Porsche Formula 2 car he had developed himself. At the Nuerburgring, Edgar Barth in the middle-seat Spyder finished sixth overall and second in the Formula 2 class, just behind a young man by the name of Bruce McLaren, driving a Cooper. The modest venture had produced astonishing success.

As a result, young Porsche engineers, including Helmuth Bott and Hans Mezger looked into the possibility of building a single-seater with exposed wheels, based on the Spyder RS. Thus, under the Spyder model number 718, the first true formula racing car to carry the name Porsche evolved. It corresponded to Formula 2 regulations, but the racing fans at Porsche knew full well that with a good mid-engine Formula 2 car they stood a good chance even against the heavier Formula 1 vehicles, most of them still with front-mounted engines. In addition, the FIA had decided to make the Formula 2 class into the new Formula 1, as of 1961. Thus, starting in 1960, Formula 2 could serve as a true predecessor of the Formula 1 to come.

Even in 1959, the 1.5-liter Formula 2 cars were eligible to start in the 2.5-liter Formula 1 events. At Porsche the enthusiasts figured they might at least do well in the Monaco Grand Prix, a circuit rich in curves. But first there was one obstacle to be overcome: When the Porsche foremen Herbert Linge and Hubert Mimler, both with racing experience, unveiled the car at the Malmsheim airfield (there still wasn't a test track in Weissach) for Ferry Porsche, the boss set one clear condition: They had to beat a time of 9 minutes, 30 seconds at the Nuerburgring. The best racing lap in Formula 2 was 9:48.2, the best unofficial Porsche time was 9:42, driven by Edgar Barth. Young Wolfgang v. Trips was brought in to drive the new car – and he clocked 9:29.8. He was allowed to start in Monte Carlo, qualified in grid position number twelve, and careened off the course in the second lap of the race.

That didn't mean a thing – the Porsche technicians and racing director Huschke v. Hanstein were optimistic. Joakim Bonnier drove several successful races in England against Cooper and Lotus, and v. Hanstein was negotiating with Stirling Moss for the 1960 Formula 2 season – with an eye on the 1961 Formula 1. Was Moss – who had once gained world renown together with Fangio for Mercedes – destined to play a leading role with Porsche? Moss was given a Formula 2 car in the colors of his Scottish Rob Walker Team, and on April 30th, 1960, Moss, Bonnier, and Graham Hill finished a picture-perfect 1-2-3 at Aintree, ahead of Cooper. Hans Herrmann (Moss had been injured in a Lotus accident), Joakim Bonnier, Graham Hill and the American newcomer Dan Gurney placed 2nd, 3rd, 4th and 5th at the Stuttgart Solitude circuit. The victory on Porsche's hometown track went to none other than Wolfgang v. Trips driving a Ferrari. Trips had signed on as a works driver in Maranello. Ferrari didn't start at the Nuerburgring... Trips drove one of the five Porsches, finishing second behind Joakim Bonnier and thus contributing to Porsche's victory in the Formula 2 Championship of Makes ahead of Cooper.

Formula 2 then became Formula 1, but the Trips-Ferrari combination had already demonstrated that Formula 1 was tougher competition. 1961 did not produce much success. Despite Moss's departure, Porsche fielded excellent drivers with Bonnier, Herrmann and Gurney, but the cars didn't live up to expectations. The re-worked type 787 with a Kugel-Fischer fuel injection system was developed, but it didn't prove to be an improvement on the

718. Nonetheless, Dan Gurney gathered enough points to capture third place in the world championship standings, together with Moss.

The people at Porsche saw the mediocre results as a challenge: They continued to develop the 1.5-liter, horizontally-opposed 8-cylinder engine, which had reached the drawing-board stage in 1960. Simultaneously, the 4-cylinder was pushed to 170 hp, and then, with Bosch fuel injection, to 190 hp, and a new car with a lattice-tubular frame was built. The slim, low-slung vehicle was given the type number 904, and became the first and, to date, only fully competitive Grand Prix car produced by Porsche. Competitive, but not dominant, for the new V-8 engines from Coventry Climax and BRM were equal in performance, and the new monocoque Lotus proved to be a high-quality design with development potential. Porsche won one of seven Grand Prix events – the 1982 French Grand Prix, captured by Dan Gurney. The Zuffenhausen company also finished well in five other races.

But that wasn't enough for Ferry Porsche – he knew that the Grand Prix arena demanded investment too high for the parallel development of sports racing and formula cars. His decision to stop work on the 804 single-seater proved to be correct. Formula 1 continued to develop in a direction that demanded technical specialization, and didn't allow the close identity to series production that Porsche strove for. Porsche concentrated on sports car racing, and launched off on a series of major successes that has lasted for two decades. The return to the technology of Formula 1 was to be made in a much different, typically Porsche fashion.

That return was preceded by an episode that really shouldn't be forgotten. The work and commitment of the 1979/80 season were devoted not to a Formula-1-car, but to a single-seater with exposed wheels, whose 2.7-liter, horizontally-opposed 6-cylinder turbocharged

Porsche engine developed no less than 630 hp. This performance did not suit the responsible sports officials, however: When the American Interscope team wanted to enter the well-tested car in the 1980 USAC series, in particular, in the Indianapolis 500, a drastic reduction of the permissible boost pressure was quickly ordained, thereby eliminating this technological advance. The driver foreseen for the winged car was the experienced Danny Ongais ("Danny on the Gas"), who had to go shopping for another vehicle.

Thus, an Indy victory is missing from the list of successful Porsche constructions, but the World Championship in the 1984 Formula 1 had been sewn up long before the last event in Portugal. Not for the manufacturer Porsche, but for an engine "Made by Porsche," and for the McLaren-TAG Formula 1 cars, into which the engine was built. The winning driver wasn't decided until the last lap at Estoril, however. Alain Prost won the race, but, incredibly, Niki Lauda fought his way up from eleventh place to second, and beat Prost by half a point to capture the title.

It was also Niki Lauda who, during the initial testing phase of the new engine the previous year, several times demonstrated its superior performance. But at that time the engine and car were still not optimally attuned to each other. In 1984 they were – and the competition had to acknowledge that it didn't stand much of a chance against the British-Arab-German combination. Mutual congratulations were in order for Mansour Ojjeh, the determined chief of "Technique d'Avant Garde," McLaren team chief Ron Dennis, chassis designer John Barnard and Porsche's Hans Mezger.

In accordance with the contracts, the name Porsche remained in the background, even if the reporters did tend to talk about the "McLaren-Porsche." As with the Auto Union racing car in the 1930s, a "P" in the type designation "TAG Turbo P 01" was a strong clue to the origin, and a

closer look turned up the name "Porsche" on the engine.

Also obvious was the presence in the McLaren pits of racing technicians from Weissach, led by Hans Mezger, who as a young engineer in the 1960s had contributed to the development of the 1.5-liter, 8-cylinder Porsche Formula-1-car. And as director of development at Weissach, Helmuth Bott was able to contribute previous experience, in addition to his tremendous accumulation of know-how.

This time it was a 1.5-liter turbocharged V-6 which turned out to be the favorite during the initial studies. For the first time, not a horizontally-opposed engine – the V-shaped angle of 80 degrees and the narrow crankcase enable better aerodynamic placement in a single-seater. "A V-8 was also under discussion," says Hans Mezger, "since at 800 to 1000 hp the larger number of cylinders could be an advantage. But we were certain that we could achieve the rpm for the planned horsepower rating with 6 cylinders. And if the rating had risen too high, the regulations might have been changed. We were relieved that the performance limitation was made in the form of a restriction on fuel consumption."

It was certain right from the beginning that there was performance to spare in the 6-cylinder, particularly as Swabian engineers tend to understatement. And that they were capable of dealing with fuel consumption restrictions had already been proved in Group C competition, where the 956 is not only the fastest, but also the most economical car. Intimate knowledge of the various possibilities of exactly controlling combustion and consumption by means of fuel injection and electronic ignition is a key to the secret of success in Group C and in Formula-1-racing.

The mechanical and thermal robustness of the graceful TAG-engine was evident right from the start, apart from the fact that it also weighed much less than the competition. Porsche's engineers have done their homework not just well, but perfectly: superior knowledge of the material properties of aluminum, magnesium and titanium alloys, computer-optimized tensile strength and an absolute command of thermal relationships. In addition, they could depend on their familiarity with turbo technology. What others have not managed even after years of endeavor was accomplished seemingly without effort: quick response to pressure on the gas pedal, loss-free buildup and reduction of the charging pressure. The TAG-engine assured once and for all the dominance of the turbo in Formula 1, and initiated a new wave of hectic engine developments. Porsche has thus made its presence known with brilliance in the Grand Prix racing of the 1980s. Even if the media continue to speculate about its imminence, an entry into the Formula 1 arena as a manufacturer is just not compatible with Porsche's philosophy to date: Factory sports have to serve the interests of serial development, whereas outside contracts can lead to more far-flung fields of endeavor. All in accordance with the motto: We accomplish the impossible immediately, miracles take a little longer.

THE PORSCHE BARON REMINISCES

Brescia, Italy April 1940. Although the World War II had already been in progress for seven months, the Italian motor sports enthusiasts prepared for the Mille Miglia. This was one of the last classic road races. All the renowned international race car drivers were at the start on April 28. Since Italy was not yet at war, friend and foe met each other on neutral ground in Lombardy. They met for a peaceful competition behind the wheels of fast sports cars. French and British race car drivers shook hands with their German competitors and even Nazi uniforms were seen mingling among the spectators – meanwhile, 500 miles northwest, troops of the German Wehrmacht were preparing to march into France.

The German colors were represented in the 1940 Mille Miglia by five streamlined BMWs based on the type 328. One of these cars, driven by Baron Fritz Huschke v. Hanstein (born in 1911), with Walter Baeumer as co-driver, won the race. Hanstein (Porsche's racing manager since 1952) won the 1,600 cc-GT-class again 18 years later in a classic Italian road race – the Targa Florio in Sicily – with Italian co-driver Baron Antonio Pucci. The same Porsche team was also victorious in the 2,600-cc-class in 1959.

While from 1952 on v. Hanstein went to the starting line as public relations manager and chief of race and sports car entries for Porsche. In 1940 at the Mille Miglia he was still a wealthy private driver. As a student, he had already participated in and won numerous motorcycle events, both cross-country and on tracks. Eventually, he switched over to four-wheeled vehicles and for years represented the firms Adler and Hanomag, achieving great success both in rallies and long-distance races. In addition, he also won the 1938 German Hill Climb Championship and had a contract as an up and coming driver before the outbreak of World War II – for the Auto Union Silver Arrows.

Turbulent years lay between the victories of Mille Miglia, Targa Florio and many other race successes in Europe and abroad. As a result of the war, the v. Hanstein family lost all their property and possessions in the Soviet-occupied part of Germany, including Europe's largest seed-producing farm and the thousand-year-old Hanstein Castle in the Werra Valley. Huschke v. Hanstein fled to the part of Germany occupied by the Western Allies. A single rucksack was all he took with him.

He later started a new career with help from the family income of his wife, Ursula. He began the restructuring of the family business and – as sales manager from 1949 to 1951 – successfully introduced Vespa-motor scooters in Germany. He again became active in the racing scene, but only in a limited way at first. BMW engines which had been buried during the war were dug up and installed in made-up chassis which were passed off as self-built makes. Hanstein's first races (in a self-built VW) were only possible because he traded ham, peas and potatoes for spare parts and swapped poultry for gas ration coupons. On the day of the currency reform (June 20, 1948), a race took place at the "Karls-ruhe Triangle" – a section of the autobahn. This race would not have been possible without the "barter system." Hanstein risked his life to earn his first solid deutschmarks. It wasn't long until word got around among the circle of sports car drivers, that Mr. Porsche (Jr.) was developing a new sports car in Gmuend (Austria)... There-fore, it was not surprising when newspapers reported in 1949 the new beginning of the Porsche firm in Stuttgart-Zuffenhausen. It was also reported that the 356 cars were to be intro-duced. This was the sign of a new turning point in the varied and changing life of Fritz Huschke v. Hanstein. As he remembers it:

I had already met Ferry Porsche before the war; I met him on occasion in the pits at the Grand Prix races. Because of my contract as junior driver with the Auto Union (which could not be fulfilled due to a hurt shoulder-joint fol-lowing an accident), we sometimes would get into conversations. I had been a Porsche admirer even before the World War II. And it was in 1949 at the Geneva Auto Exhibition where the first 356 models were introduced that gave me the initiative. This event, which was reported in great detail by the press, made me decide to depart my old job. I climbed into my old rickety DKW and drove to Zuffenhausen.

The firm of Porsche was at that time still a tiny business. The "old" Professor Porsche, his son Ferry and Professor Albert Prinzing (com-mercial business manager) resided in a modest wooden barracks. Production took place in an old factory building that was rented from the Reutter firm. The so-called race section was

located behind a curtain and two clothes closets which had an area about the size of a normal living room... Unauthorized personnel were not allowed a glimpse inside the room. An increase of 5 hp was being coaxed out of the 40 hp "beetle"-engine – which at that time was a sensation. Work at the old Porsche-factory was not yet possible because it had been turned into a hospital for epidemic cases. It later served as a maintenance shop for American vehicles. My coming to work for the Porsche firm came about in an unorthodox way. The firm's public rela-tions mentor, Professor Prinzing, was looking for quick effective ways of selling the new 356 models to the right people. The group of buyers he wanted to reach would have to be – which was a correct assumption on his part – com-prised of members of the higher nobles, high society and rich sports car enthusiasts. In other words, a clientele that required expert advice and careful cultivation.

Dr. Karl Feuereisen (formerly Auto-Union-race manager and VW's head of sales in Wolfs-burg at that time) recommended me for this delicate job, for which there was no really accu-rate description: Porsche's business contact for princes and counts, area coordinator for the dealers, public relations man, welcoming com-mittee, race manager... Porsche offered me a salary of 1,500 deutschmarks a month which, for a newcomer like me, was a lot of money. This also threatened to bring the salary struc-ture of Porsche into confusion. Head of finance Hans Kern had misgivings: "He's only costing us money... and he's supposed to bring a turn-over at the same time! His trips would create expenses..." I was firmly convinced that the money spent would be brought back in. Inciden-tally, it was already a common practice for other auto firms to employ former race car drivers to introduce new models to exclusive customers! I can still remember when the legendary Mer-cedes-Benz race car driver Otto Merz (winner of the first Grand Prix race at the Nuerburgring in

1927), presented my family the new Mercedes supercharged cars.

This was the way we also wanted to work for Porsche. All very modest, very personal and somewhat bohemian, but it had to be good for the image. Porsche could fall back on the VW dealer network. We were of the opinion that every Porsche buyer at that time also owned at least one Beetle, one of the few available models on the market.

Porsche has also been a synonym for automobile sports from the beginning. The prince's heir of Fuerstenberg scored a victory in the 1950 Midsummer Night Rally with his 356. A year later, the French team Veuillet/Mouche caused a sensation with the factory's first car entry. They achieved a class victory at Le Mans 24 hours with a 356 Alu.

The story of international auto racing after the war virtually goes hand in hand with the Porsche successes. It would take too long to list the thousands of victories. Only one thing quickly became clear to us: The advertising benefits of the Porsche victories could not be bought with money! Even if there was no available budget for large-scale advertising campaigns, we wanted to at least turn our sport successes into favorable publicity, which – in my opinion – occurred. With this concept, I ran into Ferry Porsche's open doors.

We pushed Porsche's racing activities forward with a minimum of expenditures in the 50s and 60s. Organization and logistics were a combination of Swabian precision and a lot of "chutzpah." Every mark was strictly budgeted and turned over twice. It was completely unthinkable for – which is normal today – big transporter convoys to travel from race to race. It was normal for us to drive the race cars to the competitions ourselves. When we finally got the opportunity – thanks to the efforts of Porsche and VW importer Max Hoffmann – in 1953 to participate in races in the U.S.A., we drove in the same way to Hamburg, got aboard

the ship and, upon arrival in New York, unloaded the cars ourselves and drove then through the city to Max Hoffmann's garage!

The most prominent member of our small Porsche expedition was Karl Kling – winner of the 1952 Carrera Panamericana in a Mercedes Benz. We borrowed him from the Mercedes-Benz people in Untertuerkheim. While I went through the customs and immigration procedures without a hitch, Karl Kling, on that Friday afternoon, was detained by the American immigration authorities. He had to spend the weekend with twenty others who were detained in a cell on Ellis Island. Nothing could be done during the weekend, despite efforts of our embassy in Washington and the consulate in New York. Max Hoffmann had arranged for a big party that coming Monday. We were to be introduced to the press and auto dealers, with Karl Kling as the most important guest. But he was still behind bars on Monday! It was left up to me to do the honors.

It was that evening that Karl Kling could join us as a "free man." We never found out why he was detained and why he was released without comment. A wonderful side story with a lot of human touch: An American millionairess read about Karl's misfortune in the newspaper. She offered to marry him so he could be released . . .

Porsche's first race entry, which took place in Albany, Georgia, got tremendous press coverage, partly due to the fact that we were the first German race drivers in the U.S.A. after the war. We were not particularly successful. For instance, my Spyder's fuel pump went on strike. But our biggest adventure was still to come: The Carrera Panamericana, a murderous six-day road race through Mexico that covered 1,912 miles, from the northern to the southern border. Our Porsches were transported on semi-trailers to the start at Ciudad Juarez, near El Paso.

Practicing took place in rented cars in order to go easy on our cars that were to be driven in competition. In the meantime, Hans Herrmann, our second driver, arrived from Stuttgart. We worked together for the first time with our sponsor, Fletcher Aviation of Pasadena. They had installed our Porsche engines in their light jeeps. There were 197 competitors at the start of the race on November 19, 1953. Eighteen thousand soldiers barricaded the course and were ordered to shoot all cows, chickens, cats and dogs that roamed about on the road.

While Karl Kling had to withdraw due to a technical defect, Hans Herrmann finished third overall and achieved a class victory in Tuxtla Gutierrez. Ferrari drivers Umberto Maglioli and Phil Hill finished first and second overall. They sped through Mexico with an average speed of 173.7 km/h (107.96 mph). Max Hoffmann credited the increase of more than 1,000 Porsche sales in the U.S.A., to Hans Herrmann's class victory and third place finish overall.

In the meantime, my role as multi-purpose trouble-shooter for Porsche grew: I was the race manager, public relations and press release chief, and photographer at the same time. When I had time in between, I participated in the races. It would take too long to mention each and every victory I had in the Bahamas, Switzerland, Daytona, Monza and Venezuela, Mont Ventoux and the "Grand Prix" in Japan in 1963. The Japanese Grand Prix was anything but a Grand Prix, as we Europeans know it to be. It was a handicap race, but one which was very important for our firm, because it meant getting a foothold on the Japanese market.

I won this handicap race – heavy race cars against small cars with extremely good power-to-weight ratios. I also received as first prize, besides a long string of pearls and the standard silver bowl, a two-year unlimited supply of Coca-Cola! I took two world and three class records in 1965 with the so-called Berg-Spyder. And in 1973, at the age of 62, I ended my career in sports on the VW factory circuit in Ehra Lessien (Lower Saxony). I ended with two international class- and two world records.

Porsche's entry into Formula 2 was initially fairly uncomplicated in that we only had to move the seat and the steering to the center of the car. The 1.5-liter engine in the Formula 2 Porsche developed about 150 hp. Because of these favorable conditions, it was possible for us with a relative minimum of effort, to participate successfully in the Formula 2.

We made so-called "cheap deals" in order to acquire the services of famous drivers like Sterling Moss. We loaned out our Porsche car to the British race manager, Rob Walker, under the condition that the driver would be Stirling Moss. I made it clear to him – "You get the car, but you provide the upkeep." And then I said to Moss: "You can keep all the prize money that you win, but you won't receive a penny from us."

Porsche was very successful in the Formula 2: 1957 – first place (Edgar Barth), German Grand Prix; 1958 – first place (Jean Behra), Reims Grand Prix; 1959 – first place (Fraser Jones), in Capetown; 1960 – first place (Stirling Moss), in Aintree, and also first place (Joakim Bonnier), German Grand Prix. Count Wolfgang Berghe von Trips took second place. The successes in the Formula 2 were splendid publicity for Porsche. However, racing sports became stricter and more professional. Nevertheless, eccentrics like the Dutch driver Carel de Beaufort, kept their place in the racing circle. This 200-pound driver brought his Formula 2 car for inspection to Zuffenhausen regularly (with the help of a trailer pulled by a strong American car). He brought with him 500 bottles of Dutch beer for the Porsche mechanics.

Porsche's entry in the Formula 1 was difficult and full of risks. But the whole nation urged us to participate, and in an opportune moment, we were able to convince Ferry Porsche. He was until then hesitant because of the high costs involved. It was Hans Mezger (responsible today for the TAG-Porsche engine in the McLaren Formula 1 car), who developed

116

the 8-cylinder engine for the Formula 1. We had a very good competitive engine, but it needed more time to be perfected. There was also the matter of capital to help us through the barren periods.

The Hanstein principle: "Hand in hand, and without money," which was still practical for the Formula 2 did not work for the Formula 1. With a lot of luck, we won the 1962 Reims Grand Prix with driver Dan Gurney. At the same time, we realized that the competition was getting much stronger. This meant that we either had to spend more of our own money, or the money of a sponsor, for the Formula 1, or work together with an English team.

Ferry Porsche then made his decision: "We better stop now, and turn our attention to the capabilities of the customers' cars!" Nowadays, big teams of engineers work for the racing section. But in comparison, in the past, only engineer Wilhelm Hild and four mechanics were responsible for Porsche's Formula 1 car. Weissach still did not exist, and the available development capacity was needed for series production, most of all for the model 911, which had to be carefully prepared.

I catch myself more and more often sentimentally looking back 20 years to the racing seasons. I believe that we had more fun and more style during that period. Before every start of the Italian Grand Prix, for example, Count Johnny Lurani, the famous and elegant former race driver, would invite drivers and friends to dinner in his castle near the Monza circuit. Everybody dressed in their finest and dined in style. In contrast, today's "matadors" move around with their doctors and masseurs from race to race and crawl into their trailers. It was formerly the "gentlemen" drivers who went to the start. At least most of them belonged in this category, even if they drove for money. Hans

Stuck Sr. and Caracciola didn't drive for free, but they were still "gentlemen" drivers who earned money on the side. Today, most of the drivers are big money makers, they are not gentlemen drivers...

I also often become sentimental when I remember how it felt to be in constant close contact with the fast Porsche cars, then as always a special feeling of being alive, a savoir-vivre. Those were the times, when I flew to Jordan to get King Hussein acquainted with his new Berg-Spyder, and compete against him in the race! After the end of the race, King Hussein invited me to go water skiing in the Gulf of Aqaba.

Or when I asked Prince Rainier of Monaco: "Would Your Highness take the Porsche for a test drive once?" And then we had to take these rare specimens out of the small series... Or when my friend Prince Berthil — second to former Swedish King Gustav — received his first Porsche in the early 50s, and I had to personally deliver the car... Or the present Swedish King Carl Gustaf, as a 14-year-old crown prince, was allowed to drive his first rounds with a Porsche in a closed part of an airfield... Or as an eyewitness, when Juan Manuel Fangio (one year before Fidel Castro took over Havana), was kidnapped in Cuba in 1958. I immediately called the DPA (German Press Agency) in Frankfurt to make sure they got the red-hot news first.

Fritz Huschke v. Hanstein retired from his position as multi-functional manager in 1968, and now serves the company in other areas. He holds honorary posts in German and international racing sports: He is, among other things, the sports president of the AVD (Automobile Club of Germany) and vice-president of the International Automobile Sport Federation (FISA).

JUDITH JACKSON

A WOMAN'S THOUGHTS ABOUT MALE PORSCHE DRIVERS

When a driver climbs into a Porsche, he climbs into a man's world. A world created by men with men in mind. A macho world with no concessions for the faint-hearted. A masculine world, redolent of race tracks and blind bends, Le Mans and the Mulsanne straightaway. If you are a woman, they may let you drive one, now and then. If you are very good and kind, they will even let you own one. But when the key is turned and the garage doors are shut, the Porsche reverts to what it always was. A man's machine.

Look at the Porsches as they flash past you – silver gray or fiery red, pristine white or mysterious black – streaking to some ever-so-important appointment in a distant place. Not for the Porsche, the slow lane. It's natural habitat is the outside lane, flirting with the Armco barrier, jousting with Mercedes and Ferrari, and grumbling with that unmistakable Porsche sound at some slower upstart in front.

They tried to tame it once. The 914 was the first Porsche offered at a price which ordinary mortals could aspire to. A car which looked as though it would almost feel at home in the supermarket parking lot or taking the children to school. But it wasn't a roaring success. Despite its mid-engine tucked away behind the seats and its amazing capacity for luggage, it always looked slightly ashamed of itself. Of course, the men who drove it tried to convince you that it was a real Porsche and that the engine had come from the velvety silence of Stuttgart and not the roar of Volkswagen at Wolfsburg.

There was nothing wrong with its performance – the 914/6 even had a real Porsche engine and did plenty of miles an hour – at least 125 if you tried. But even with wide wheels and fat tires, Porsche men knew it wasn't the real thing. The genuine Porsche man probably regards the 911 as his ultimate automobile. Purposeful, firm to the seat and demanding to be driven well, the 911 gives nothing away. Indeed, until recently, heated seats would have been considered very out of character in a car which is designed for *real* men. The four-spoke leather steering wheel and a gear lever which shrinks with each succeeding model year declare to the world that the 911 driver is a man to be reckoned with. Even if his seat is upholstered in black leather to match his jacket, or in pinstriped flannel to match his suit – even if his quadrophonic speakers play the latest rock – even if his bronzed torso is laden with gold medallions to impress his admiring public, the cognoscenti look at the car. *They* know that it is one of the fastest production cars in the world and with a turbocharger under the hood, 160 mph and 0–60 in 5.4 seconds, are as nothing to this car. The car can perform, but can the driver?

The gentler, rounded lines of the 928, proclaim a gentler, more distinguished man. He can afford the extra second it takes from 0–60. The subtle blend of luxury and performance, as they say in the advertisements, tells you a great deal about this man. Less flashy than his 911 counterparts – more likely to cherish a woman than to try and impress her with his checkbook.

Porsche drivers are undeniably a special breed. To own a Porsche, to tax it, run it, service and maintain it, and above all insure it, spells affluence. The sort of man who drives a Porsche does not mind your knowing that he has money to spend – or that he works for someone who does, and who values him sufficiently to put him in a Porsche. No one can ignore the stylish presence of such a car, but nevertheless some Porsche owners seek to put their personal stamp onto it.

In Britain registration numbers can be obtained which spell out the owners initials. Its a lengthy and costly business but the effort clearly appeals to many Porsche owners. (In Britain, such numbers are called 'vanity' numbers, for obvious reasons. They are intended to tell the rest of the world that you regard yourself as someone special – as though owning a Porsche was not enough. Their greatest disadvantage is that they are likely to tell the rest of the world a lot about your whereabouts and are easy for people to memorize should you, by any unfortunate chance, be found to break a speed limit or two.) It is hard to be totally anonymous in a Porsche, but I find further self-advertisement deplorably vulgar.

As the sun comes out, the Porsche driver is the first to remove his targa top or drop the hood on his cabriolet. Drivers of more mundane open cars are aware of the hazards this creates. A sudden shower can soak the seats, leaving you to arrive at your destination in a moist condition. Passing truck drivers are happy to use your car as a waste-paper basket, or worse, an ash-tray, with lamentable results. If we owned a Porsche we would hardly take it out of the garage, far less invite its desecration. Not so the 911 driver. With the targa stowed away and a nubile blonde at his side, her hair being blown into painful knots by the wind, he zooms away from the traffic lights – with the appropriate amount of tire squeal intended to attract your attention.

In many countries, Porsche has become a cult. Owners clubs meet in all corners of the world to swap stories of bravado and excitement, all the varying degrees of accuracy. Passing Porsches flash their headlights at each other as drivers used to do in the days of the boyish frog-eyed Sprite. But the Porsche is a *man's* car. Such behavior may be acceptable in an adolescent, but indignified in a man. As St. Paul said in the Bible, "When I became a man, I gave up childish ways." And so should those privileged to drive a Porsche. As if further acknowledgement was necessary of their status as men of discernment, such men also flaunt their Porsche belts, sunglasses and watches. Not for them the mark of Gucci or Tissot. Only Porsche will do. They even give their girlfriends handbags which sport discreet Porsche badges and, horror of horrors, wear jackets emblazoned with the Porsche shield. Is nothing sacred? Their aim is apparently to create as great an impression in the city center as they do on the highway. And if their driving technique is not the best at least they will not frighten themselves while cutting a dash in the company parking lot or outside the golf club.

I very much doubt if all Porsche owners know and appreciate the pedigree of the cars they drive. Do they really understand how much research and development, on and off the race track, has contributed to the excellence of the car they treat in such a cavalier fashion? Motor sport success has been paramount in the development of Porsche road cars. When Ferrari appeared to be unbeatable, Porsche spent a

119

small fortune in money, men and time, to develop cars that would win. They did, and they keep on doing so. Probably more than any other make, Porsche road cars have benefited from racing technology. But I suspect that not a lot of Porsche owners know that.

Sometimes it seems that Porsches are produced primarily for the sheer pleasure of the men who plan them, design them, build them and ultimately race them. Their eyes light up when they talk of their cars, and Porsche, to its eternal credit, would rather keep the company alive by producing high-tech designs and fashionable artifacts, than debase the coinage by building a mass-produced car which would be within the reach of a wider audience. That would mean a lowering of standards, which would be unacceptable. Standards are high at Porsche, even if those of Porsche owners do not always match them.

The eminent American motoring writer Ken Purdy, when writing about Porsche – a make of which he was particularly fond – once said:

"Most of the machines we use today, are stamped out by the thousands and hardly touched by human hands in the process. The Porsche is an exception, a kind of survivor from the days of craftsmanship, slowly and carefully put together by people who would rather do it right than do it fast." What he should also have said, was that a Porsche deserves to be driven by people who do it right *and* do it fast.

Regrettably, this is not always the case. A sad fact about male drivers is that they are usually reluctant to confess their inadequacies behind the wheel. It is easier to blame the car. But it is sad to hear a man explain away an accident by blaming the car, particularly when that car is a Porsche and you know that it has probably not only saved his life on several occasions but will also go around bends from here to eternity without putting a tire wrong, or giving the driver a moment's anxiety. Of course, if you put your hand between the shark's jaws, you have only yourself to blame if the shark bites it off. A Porsche will have a similar reaction. Too often the car is driven by someone who has no conception of the nature of the car he is driving. It is a status symbol, not a precision instrument which deserves skill and understanding.

I particularly dislike those drivers who risk life and limb – often other people's – in an effort to prevent someone from overtaking them. They appear to think that there is some stigma attached to allowing another driver to be in front of them – it is almost as though their virility is being threatened. And if that driver is a woman, no maneuver is too drastic to prove their supremacy! "My Porsche is faster than your BMW/Mercedes/Lotus/Ferrari" is a game we can all play. But it is pointless, dangerous and undignified. And Porsches have a right to their dignity.

To say that Porsche owners put their cars before all else, is no exaggeration. One such, announcing his forthcoming marriage, wrote to his friends saying that instead of wedding presents for his home, he would prefer donations toward buying his next Porsche. What his future wife's reaction was is not recorded. Had it been me I would have battered him with a plug spanner. It isn't that I have anything against Porsche, you understand. On the contrary. I believe the company and the cars to be of the highest caliber. It's just the men who drive the cars who drive me mad.

35 Type 911 Carrera (1984)
36 Type 911 SC Cabriolet (1983)
37 Different tuner versions, based on the 911 Carrera (1984)
38 Type 911 Carrera Cabriolet (1983)

39 Type 911 Carrera (1974) and
40 Type 911 Carrera (1977), participating at a safety training, organized by Porsche Club Berlin, on Gatow airfield (1984)

41 Type 911 SC (1983)
42 Type 911 Turbo 3,0 liter (1978) paying a visit to the Daimler-Benz trial track
43 Type 959 during test runs at Hockenheim motodrome (1985)
44 Type 959 ("X-ray photograph"), 1985

45 A 911 SCR (1978), tuned by a privat company. Engine has been bored up to 3,2 liter, with 217 hp
46 Prototype 959, with 3,2-liter-production engine, participating at the rally Paris–Dakar 1985; Jacky Ickx is the driver

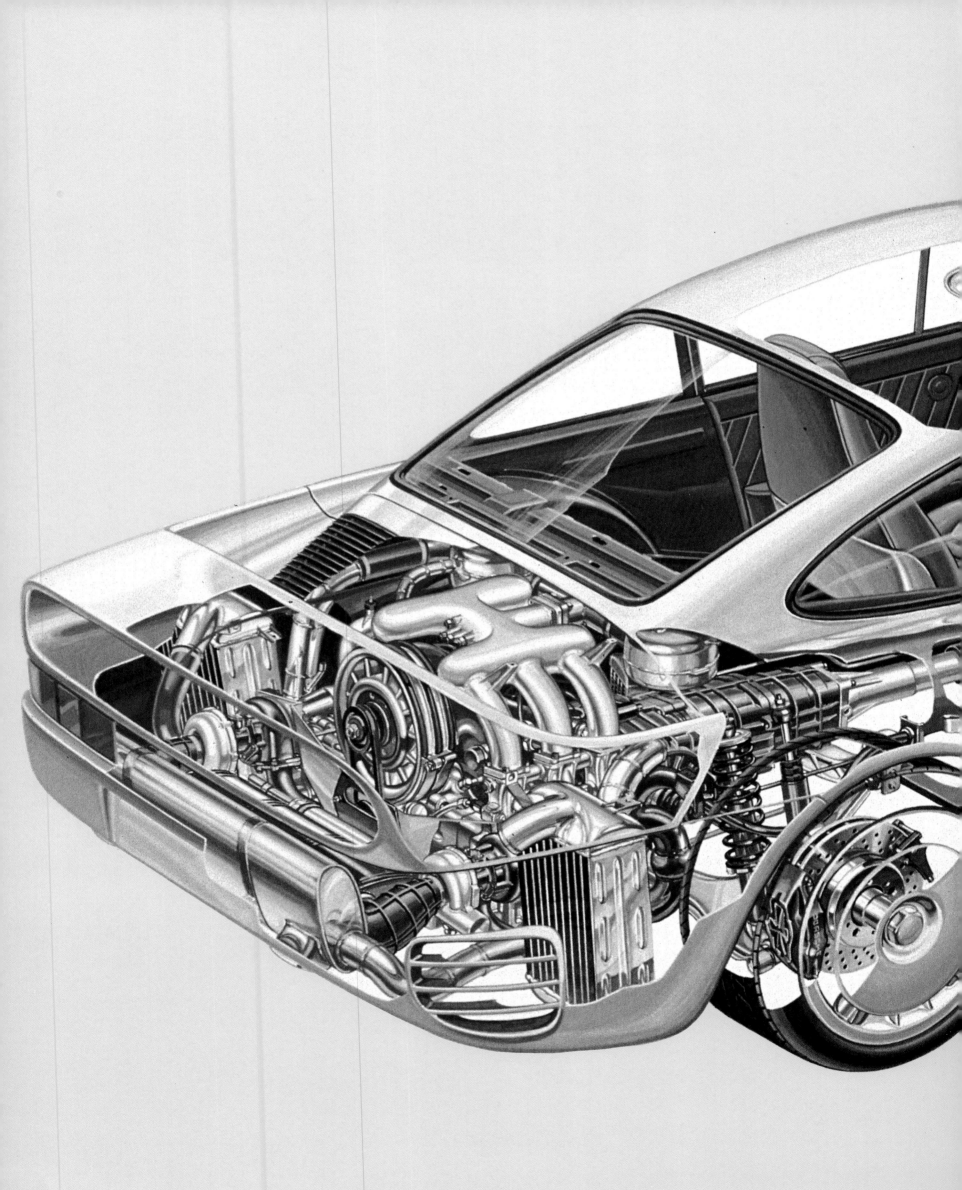

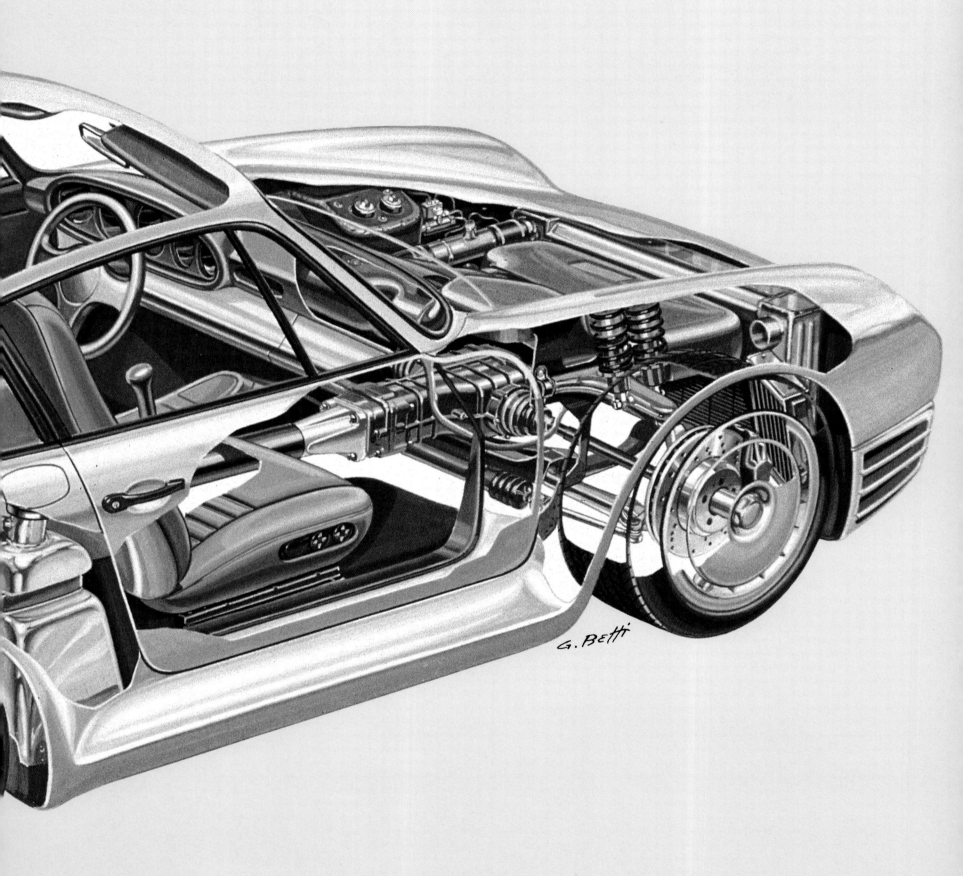

G. Betti

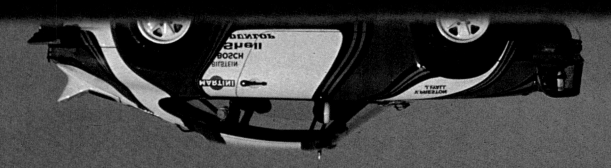

49

50

53

54

47 Two cars type 911 SC-3,0 ("Safari") at Weissach, before being shipped to the East-African-Safari 1978
48 Type 924 (1984)
49–51 Type 928 S 32-valves (front section view, rear-view, engine) 1985
52 A power-sliding 928 S (1983)

53 Type 928 S "Race", with French driver Boutinaud at the wheel, Silverstone 1.000 kms (1983)
54 Type 924 (1984)

55 Type 944 above Lago Maggiore (Italy) 1984
56 Type 944 Turbo, test running (1985)
57 Type 944 Turbo ("X-ray photograph") 1985
58 Type 944 on foot of the Kaiser Castle Hohenzollern, near Hechingen (1984)

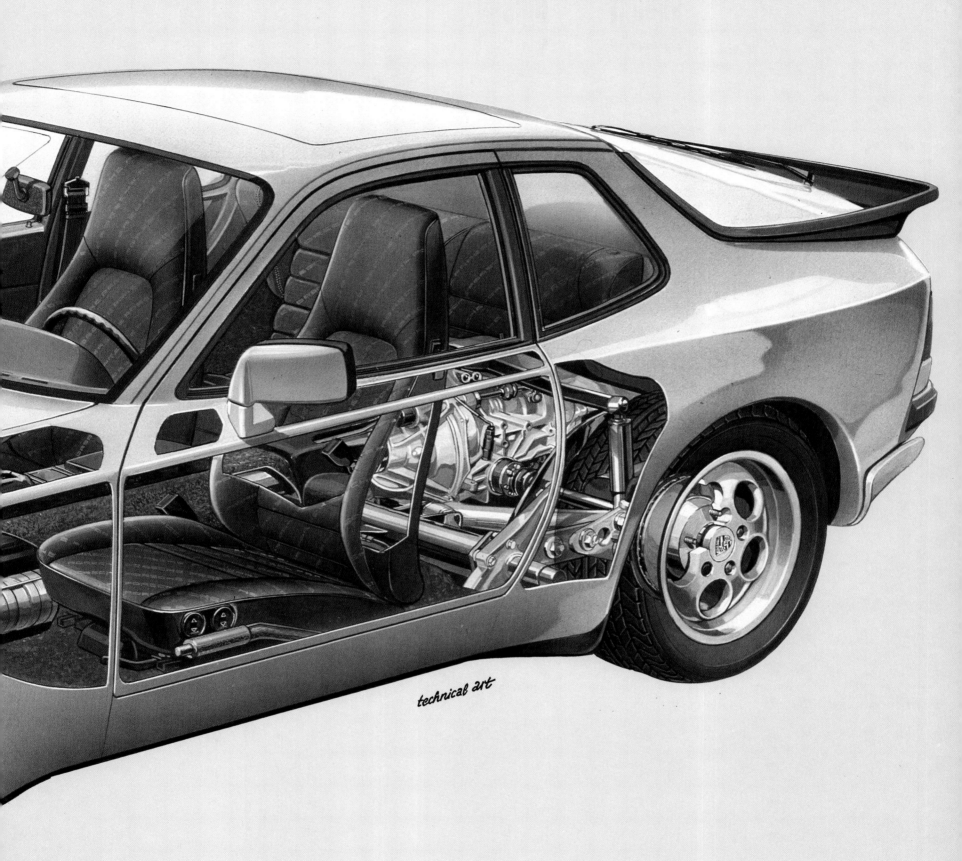

technical art

PORSCHE AND THE 24 HOURS OF LE MANS

To some, Le Mans, the capital of the French department of Sarthe, is known for a very rich sort of pâté produced there. But for most people, Le Mans stands for the famed 24-hour race that jams tens of thousands of fans into a single flight of grandstands lining the course, just like at Indianapolis or Monte Carlo. Located about 125 miles southwest of Paris, with a population of about 150,000 and only moderate significance as a transportation center, Le Mans is a French provincial city like many others. But once a year, in June, the motor sport event that overwhelms the city for a solid week holds the stage. The start is always at 4 p.m. on Saturday . . . exceptions confirm the rule.

Actually, however, the countdown begins much earlier. At the end of each preceding year, the regulations are published, a strict selection committee surveys the list of applicants and issues the invitations. The number of participants is limited to 55. On the Monday preceding the race, the vans which transport the teams arrive in Le Mans. Then, early Tuesday morning, right in the middle of the city, at the Place des Jacobins near the cathedral, the stringent inspection procedure begins.

Training is held on Wednesday and Thursday, up to 11 p.m., in order to give the drivers a chance to acquaint themselves with the night driving conditions. Friday is a day of rest, for the drivers, that is, since the mechanics still have their hands full preparing the cars for the race. It is not all unusual to hear the engines roaring on into the wee hours of the morning, and to catch a glimpse of glaring lights at the nearby airfield – the runway is a popular last-minute test stretch. The race course itself is a mixture of a permanent track – the Bugatti Circuit – and quite ordinary country roads, provided with a few additional guardrails and closed off to everyday traffic.

If you like, climb aboard, for a lap of 8,5 miles in a Porsche 956, with a good 650 hp roaring behind you. Hopefully the road sweeper has cleared away all the nuts, bolts and rocks on the road section – they've often caused blown tires. You're firmly belted in, have pulled on your crash helmet and warmed up the engine with a slow lap. Now, at full acceleration, you leave the Virage Ford and head into the start – finish straight. At the kink to the right at the end of the pits you're in fifth gear, and if the car had a speedometer, it would be reading about 155 mph. The g-loads are tearing you toward the verge, but woe unto you if you let the wheels touch the grass. On top of the rise under the Dunlop bridge the car suddenly goes very light in front, and immediately after diving in you go for the brakes coming up on the narrow, left-right Esses combination. There's no time for a glance at the fairgrounds and the Ferris wheel, because you've suddenly got to make a 90-degree turn to the right, onto national highway 138 heading for Tours.

And there it is – the notorious Mulsanne Straightaway – almost 3½ miles straight ahead, your right foot mashed down on the accelerator. Pick a point midway between the front wheels and focus on the horizon. The landscape screams past you and blurs, the guardrails shrink to dots. Don't think about it now, what would happen if . . . at a speed of 220 mph. The soft bend to the right turns into a full-fledged curve, then the rise and you're tromping on the brakes with all your might. At the village of Mulsanne there's a sharp right turn, at about 55 mph.

And then full acceleration again, and the glowing brakes have a chance to cool down. The S-bend ahead of Arnage, the Virage Porsche, Maison Blanche . . . The rapid alternation of acceleration and brutal braking is making you dizzy . . . the g-loads in the fast curves make your head waggle back and forth. The ground effect sucks the car down onto the road; it's like flying at zero altitude. Finally the grandstands appear, you jag your way through the Virage Ford and the whole thing starts all over again. Still ahead of you are another 23 hours, 57 minutes and 20 seconds to a victory at Le Mans. Or, if you prefer, roughly another 370 laps.

It all began one evening in the year 1922, in Paris. Three friends, all of them car fanatics, were sitting around together talking fuel, on the occasion of the Paris Auto Show. A few bottles of wine were also involved. Suddenly, Monsieur Charles Faroux had a great idea: How about a racing event not for specially built racing cars, but for ordinary touring cars? A true test of performance, one whole day in duration, without a pause. The idea looked better all the time, Monsieur Faroux set about writing up a set of rules, and the 24-hours of Le Mans was born. The punishing race around the clock was designed to match the conditions of the day: Tanking up was allowed only at certain intervals, since the European roads at that time did not boast a gas station every few miles. Repairs could be carried out only with the tools and spare parts carried along during the race in each car.

The response to this challenge was encouraging. On May 26, 1923, 33 cars – all production-line vehicles like those displayed in the sales brochures of their 17 manufacturers – lined up for the first running of this new endurance marathon. Sports journalist and auto expert Charles Faroux probably had little idea of what his stroke of genius had set into motion. Right from the beginning, the auto producers came to Le Mans in droves – there just wasn't a better or more spectacular proof of quality for their products. Nor did that change after the war, when sports cars and prototypes were allowed to compete. The organizers have always managed to find ways to alter their regulations in such a manner as to promote technical developments which might benefit the production-line auto. They have also dared to ignore official sports policy from time to time: The worldwide reputation of their 24-hour event has made them strong and independent.

Ever since the first running in 1923, the 24 Hours has fascinated not only the technicians. An auto race held for the most part on normal roads, day and night, in brilliant sunshine and pouring rain is an ideal stage for the thrill of victory and the drama of defeat. Adherence to regulations is always monitored very strictly; the Le Mans officials are notorious for their merciless scrutiny. Tears of anger and disappointment often flow, but also tears of agony, for Le Mans has always been, and remains, a dangerous race. The fascination of Le Mans is a combination of technical competition, sporting duel, nighttime spectacle and human tragedy.

Ferry Porsche was probably thinking more in terms of performance capacity than competitive potential when his French importer, Auguste Veuillet brought up the subject of Le Mans in the autumn of 1950 – where else but at the Paris Auto Show. Charles Faroux also had a talk with Ferry Porsche, who promised in January 1951 to dispatch three of his 356 Coupés to Le Mans. "Our three Le Mans Porsches were all Coupés with aluminum bodies and spats over the wheels to improve streamlining, but an unhappy fate awaited two of them before the race even started" (J. Bentley and Ferry Porsche in their book "We At Porsche"). The first of the aluminum Coupés, with a 44 hp 1100 cc engine (still built at Gmuend/Kaernten, and still strongly reminiscent of the beetle from which it sprang) went off the course during a test run with Paul von Guilleaume at the wheel. The accident was caused by a careless bicyclist who crossed in front of the car when it was doing 85 mph.

"The car was badly damaged and brought back to Stuttgart for a complete rebuilding. This did not augur well for Porsche's first effort at big-time racing. Of the remaining two cars one was intended for Rudolf Sauerwein, who had built up a good reputation as a race driver, the other for the Frenchmen Auguste Veuillet and Edmond Mouche. But our troubles were not yet over. During the last practise lap at Le Mans Sauerwein went off the road at the White House bend during the night and was taken to the hospital. This left us with only one car, carrying No. 46." (From "We at Porsche").

It had to be entered with French drivers, for the organizers feared that die-hards of the French resistance movement would stone a German car which was also driven by Germans. Auguste Veuillet and co-driver Mouche turned in an outstanding performance: The car bearing number 46, and still carrying its original license plate in the rear, covered a total of 1765.07 miles in 24 hours. That corresponded to an average speed of 73.54 mph, and class victory. A triumph for Porsche and a milestone in the

motor sport reputation of the young company. Since then, Porsche cars have never missed a Le Mans event.

A test report in a 1951 edition of the German motoring magazine "Das Auto" reflects a bit of the fascination generated by the Le Mans victory car. "For anyone at the wheel of a Porsche for the first time, the car provides an entirely new driving flavor. The range of impressions is astounding as, sitting glued to the floor, with your head on a level with the axles of the big trucks, you race over the autobahn at speeds between 75 and 95 mph, almost always in the passing lane. It simply doesn't make sense to drive this car at periods of normal traffic density, weaving in and out between slower vehicles. You feel as if you were sitting in a fast and silent glider, pressed to the road by means of some mysterious and gentle force. The Porsche driver is treated to a sovereign feeling of freedom from all conventional impressions. Calculating driving lanes and braking distances with this quiet 'long wave' vehicle is very different. Its design is the product of genius, which has transported the driving experience into a new dimension, and the vehicle itself into a new era."

Racing drivers were not quite as enthusiastic. In 1953, Porsche racing director Huschke v. Hanstein invited Paul Frère to compete for the factory team for the first time. In his book "The 24 Hours of Le Mans," Frère critically recalls the car he drove: "Our vehicles were rather peculiar constructions, the first Porsche racing cars with the engine mounted in front of the rear axle. Inside it was still the Volkswagen-based 1500 cc pushrod engine, but with a roller bearing crankshaft. There had just been enough time to rotate the rear-mounted drive train – engine, transmission and rear axle – by 180 degrees compared to the production model, but not enough time to redesign the suspension. Thus the swing axles were attached to trailing arms which had been placed behind instead of

155

in front of the axle. As a result, when cornering the rear wheels toed out, and the car tended to oversteer. In general, our cars behaved just like the notorious production-line Porsches of that time. Mounting the engine in the rear thus didn't have much of an influence on the car's traction; the only real advantage resulted from the increased wheelbase, which improved stability in the straightaways to over 125 mph, and permitted a more favorable body form.

The different speeds the competitors were capable of were a problem even back then. Only class victories were possible with the Porsches of that time. The Jaguars, Ferraris, Alfa Romeos and Lancias – programmed for overall wins with their bigger engines – left the Porsches behind, especially on the long Mulsanne Straightaway. Thus, for Paul Frère and his colleagues the rearview mirror was the most important piece of equipment. In the braking zones and coming out of the curves the fast cars passed the Porsche "like arrows." Especially at night, the drivers had great difficulty in "judging the distance and speed of another car coming up on you with all its lights blazing, particularly when you're doing better than 125 mph yourself, and you too have to pass and pay attention to making good time." In that respect, nothing has changed even up to the present day. When you add fog or pouring rain, and the conditioning and concentration of the driver begins to lapse, it gets dangerous.

It was under just such conditions that Porsche achieved one of its greatest triumphs, in 1958. It had been raining cats and dogs all night, and numerous cars hat skidded off the course. The Porsche RSK was running like clockwork, and the team Jean Behra/Hans Herrmann chalked up a sensational third place overall, just ahead of two other Porsches driven by Edgar Barth/Paul Frère and Herbert Linge/ Count de Beaufort. Behra and Herrmann had to drive for hours with defective brakes, and still refused to quit, even when their clutch gave up

the ghost. How much Le Mans meant to Porsche by this time was indicated by the painstaking preparations for this event, an effort that has become typical of Zuffenhausen's approach to all motor sport events. Vacuum chamber measurements were even made just to achieve an optimal aerodynamic cover for the passenger seat of the open sports car, and racing director Huschke v. Hanstein provided his drivers with specially made slippers with rubbercoated back flops for their 24-hour tapdance on the pedals.

But the triumph of 1958 was followed by total disaster the next year. Six Porsches started, and not one of them finished the race – the company's first major defeat ever in international racing. The stakes had been pushed a bit too high, perhaps because of overconfidence after the success at Targa Florio and the sudden role of favorite.

"Put in the sharper cam" Ferry Porsche had decided. All or nothing – after all, the competition had about 150 additional hp under the hood. At first everything went according to plan – halfway through the race four Porsches were among the first seven cars. But after 13 hours and 13 minutes, one Porsche after another pulled out: over-revved engine, dropped transmission, blown clutch. At least the morale didn't suffer: "You have to be able to keep smiling even on the bleakest days," was the comment of v. Hanstein.

There is no record of whether or not Ferdinand Piëch was able to keep smiling in 1968, when once again one factory car after another had to be pushed back to the pits. The plan that year had been to achieve the first Le Mans overall victory for Porsche. When the drivers sprinted across the finish straightaway to their cars at exactly 3 p.m., four factory Porsche 908 s with 3-liter, 8-cylinder engines were right up front. Pre-race tests had exposed this engine's tendency to vibrate, and its destructive effect on other equipment such as the generator. Thus as a precaution, each car had been equipped with a backup generator which, in case of an emergency, the driver could throw into operation by means of a switch in the cockpit. But in vain: The generators broke down one after another, and the backup units were so weak that during the night two of the four headlights had to be switched off. Because the substitution of complete engines was forbidden, two cars were disqualified; others had to be pushed off to the side after total breakdown. Driving an old 907 with a 2.2-liter engine, the team of Steinemann/Spoerry took second place overall behind a Ford GT 40, but in light of the high pre-race expectations that was a meager compensation.

In 1969, Porsche was able to field a new, secret weapon for the first time: the 4.5-liter 917, a 12-cylinder with over 500 hp. Measurements made on the long straightaway resulted in top speeds of nearly 240 mph. Nonetheless, Porsche's real hopes were riding on the four 908s, even though they were capable of a top speed of "only" 205 mph. The 908s cornered better, had been thoroughly tested, and were greatly superior to the competition. And for 20 hours, the race was simply a Porsche show. But suddenly the 917, which was leading by six laps, headed for the pits with clutch problems, followed shortly thereafter by one of the 908s — which had been in second place — with a defective transmission. Suddenly a race that had become a rather uninteresting Porsche display turned into a cliffhanger. After the last refueling stop, only a few seconds separated the leading Ford GT 40 – driven by Jacky Ickx/Jackie Oliver – and the Porsche 908 driven by Hans Herrmann/Gérard Larrousse. Alternately taking advantage of each other's slipstream, Ickx and Herrmann passed each other several times on the long straightaway. It was the most thrilling climax to this race anyone had ever seen. Ickx's clever tactics finally won out. In the final lap he allowed Herrmann to take the lead going into the straight. Then, just before the village of Mulsanne, the Belgian made use of Herrmann's slipstream to pass, and Herrmann was left without any further chance to get by. The Porsche team was dejected: to miss their long-hoped-for overall victory by a margin of two seconds in 24 hours, by only 365 feet over a distance of 3.105 miles!

The next year constituted a total offensive by Porsche. Several Porsche teams were formed, including one under the direction of John Wyer, who had led Ford to two Le Mans victories. Seven 917s were rolled to the starting line. Because at Porsche defects were always a matter of system, the engines were a mixture of 5- and 4.5-liter versions, the cars a mixture of long- and short rear bodies. Ferry Porsche was awarded the privilege of starting the race. For the first time, the drivers started the event already sitting in their cars, and no longer had to sprint across the finish line to get to them. The reason for this change was simply that many of the drivers didn't fasten their seat belts, which couldn't be done properly anyway without the help of a mechanic. The previous year Jackie Ickx had demonstrated his displeasure by pointedly starting the race in last place. The Porsche drivers and technicians were most concerned about the tires and brakes; the suppliers didn't want to issue guarantees when speeds far in excess of 180 mph were to be expected. At Porsche's own test facilities the tires exploded at speeds of 205 mph. In order to prevent accidents in case of sudden showers, intermediate tires were mounted, because two 917s had been wrecked at the VW test track near Wolfsburg when the drivers suddenly ran into rainfall.

At 2 a.m., John Wyer could start packing up to head for home: Accidents and engine breakdowns due to over-revving had finished off his group. But this time Porsche was not to be denied. Hans Herrmann, the luckless loser of the previous year, and his British co-driver Richard Attwood brought Porsche its first overall victory after 20 tries at Le Mans.

In the post-917 era, Porsche didn't have a vehicle capable of producing another overall win. The next Le Mans victories didn't come until 1976 and 1977, with the 2.1-liter turbo Spyder 936. The drama of the 1977 race has never been forgotten, particularly the last hour of competition. The event had been built up by the press as a battle of national prestige, and Renault was determined to beat Porsche. The French put on a flamboyant show for the cheering spectators.

Four and-a-half hours after the start, two of the three factory Porsches had dropped out, and the remaining car, driven by Juergen Barth/Hurley Haywood had fallen far behind following repairs. Porsche bet everything on one card by adding Jacky Ickx to the German-American driving team, and upped the turbocharger pressure from 1.2 to 1.4 bar. Ickx put on a stunning display of driving, chalking up one record lap after another during the night, gradually working the car up in the standings.

Shortly before noon the next day the last factory Renault dropped out, and the Porsche found itself leading by a margin of 19 laps. Without being ordered to do so, Haywood reduced the turbocharger pressure and took it easy. Forty-five minutes before the end, to everyone's horror, he came crawling into the pits with his engine rattling ominously. Engine specialist Valentin Schaeffer quickly diagnosed the problem: a seized piston in one cylinder. In the remaining time, the second-place Renault-Mirage could not overtake the Porsche; but to gain an overall victory, a car has to cross the finish line under its own power.

The Swabians decided to attempt the impossible. The cylinder was simply shut down; that is, the ignition and fuel injection were cut off. Nobody knew whether the engine would even function in that condition, as Juergen Barth took over to complete the final lap. A stopwatch had been attached to the steering wheel because, according to the regulations,

laps slower than 14 minutes and a few seconds are not allowed. Porsche's desperate attempt was greeted with resounding applause from the fair-minded spectators. Smoking, rattling and wheezing, the car disappeared from view of the mechanics. Everyone was glued to the radio set and Barth was repeatedly asked, "Is it still running?" Still running it was, but Barth actually crossed the finish line a few seconds too early and was forced to churn yet another lap before the victor's flag finally ended the suspense and the car's agony.

That's how Le Mans victors were and still are made. Two years later the race produced a similar drama. The factory Porsches had already dropped out or been disqualified (Ickx "coincidentally found" the cogged belt he desperately needed for his injection pump lying at the edge of the course), but the Porsche 935 privately entered by the Kremer brothers of Cologne and driven by the Americans Bill and Don Whittington led the race by a clear margin. Suddenly, Don Whittington rolled to a halt at the side of the track. He didn't understand much about mechanical problems, but by walkie-talkie the Kremer brothers helped him to locate the defect, find the ominous cogged belt, which in this case really was on board, and to make the replacement.

Just a few miles farther, however, the belt flew off again. Running back and forth between the engine and the radio, Whittington managed a minor miracle: He shortened the generator V-belt by winding it with electrician's tape and actually managed to limp in to the rescuing pits. After that it was clear sailing on to the end, and the first overall victory by a privately entered Porsche at Le Mans.

There are so many other stories that could be told, including the one about the total triumph of 1982 with the brand new Porsche 956s, which neatly finished the race in the order of their starting numbers, 1, 2 and 3 — but there was nothing dramatic about Le Mans that year. Or,

1983, when, after the race, Porsche had a poster printed with the headline "Nobody Is Perfect," because among the first ten cars to finish the Le Mans race, one was actually *not* a Porsche.

The Porsche Le Mans story wouldn't be complete, however, without mentioning the village of Téloché. For more than 30 years, the Porsche team set up camp for every race in this village, not far from the course. And every year, Monsieur Prévost pushed aside the little Citroens in his garage and stood there astonished as the sleek, high-powered cars from Zuffenhausen were rolled in. In the village tavern, afternoons and evenings, when the Porsche team members took their places at the long wooden tables decorated with checked table cloths, spirits were high and flowed freely. In Téloché everyone had his own home away from home, quarters he enjoyed year after year. The entire village was caught up in racing fever, celebrating and suffering with its German guests, depending on the outcome.

It was a grand scene when the mechanics chauffered the racing cars through the village's narrow streets to the race course. But that has all been part of history for several years now. Modern racing cars just can't handle even a few miles of country roads; ruts and potholes can ruin their chassis and plastic cowlings all too quickly; today's racing tires are just too sensitive to the smallest pebbles. Ever since sufficient space was created in the driver's camp, Porsche, too, has switched its workshops to canvas walls behind the pits. Now Monsieur Prévost is alone the year round with his little Citroens, and part of the Porsche crew moves into some nondescript hotel. But a few have remained faithful to their hosts in Téloché. "Maybe it brings luck," they say, and you just can't have enough of that at Le Mans.

PETER FALK

33 YEARS
OF RALLY SUCCESSES

We were sitting on the sand at the far end of the Gao airport in West African Mali. We had just learned that our last car still in the rally had fallen out of competition. It was the 14th of January 1985 – 4,700 miles from Paris and 2,800 miles to Dakar. It was the biggest disappointment since the 1959 Le Mans, where not a single one of our cars reached the finish line. Months of preparation, endless commitments and the efforts of the whole team since the start in Paris were all in vain.

Really in vain?

Not in the least, because for an engineer to admit failure would mean revealing the weak points. The weak points must be overcome as quickly as possible as there are only 14 days until the next sport entry and three months for the series entry. This means that difficulties would either never occur or develop much later in a normal test operation. Can you see now why Porsche not only participates in races, but also in rallies, and why these rallies do not necessarily serve as image enhancers for Porsche?

But first let us start from the beginning.

What does rally mean? The word comes from the French verb "rallier" – re-assemble – and, in the original sense, means coming from different directions and getting together at a mutually agreed meeting place. In regard to motor sports, a rally used to be nothing more than a concourse drive. It was later developed into a reliability test course with a common course and given timetables. Nowadays it is usual to combine connecting and special stages. Drivers have to go through the special stages in best time. Common to any kind of rally is the driving of normal cars that are registered for public roads. The rallies also have to take place on ordinary surfaced or unsurfaced or dirt roads.

The first rallies took place when automobiles were just coming of age. Car drivers discovered that this new technology not only served as a means of transportation, but could also be used in sports events. The automobile manufacturers also regarded winning in rallies and races as important for their image. The first automobile race in the world which took place in "Paris–Rouen" on July 22, 1894, can appropriately be called a rally. This is because competition took place among commercially produced vehicles on public roads in order to demonstrate their reliability.

A few more words about history.

June 10, 1909, was the start of the second "Prinz-Heinrich-Fahrt", a rally (in the present sense of the word) covering the course Berlin––Breslau–Budapest–Salzburg–Munich, and full of special challenges. Several Austro-Daimlers were there, one of them driven by Ferdinand

Porsche. The following year, 1910, he won this long distance race.

And sports cars carrying the Porsche name began their winning streak around the world 40 years later.

Which brings us to the subject at hand. I don't think anyone can verify when Porsche first participated in or won a rally. This was because during the 50s, authorities were very tolerant and every motor sports club throughout the country could promote its own reliability test course or rally "around the church steeple." It is certain that the first 356s were among the cars that participated.

"Grass root" rallies were important for the development of rally sports, car popularity and automotive engineering in general.

But we have to limit our focus to the big international competition. It is almost impossible to write about all Porsche entries and successes.

The first international rally successes that are listed in the Porsche files were class victories by Count Constantin Berckheim in the Swedish Rally in June 1950, in July of the same year, by Otto Mathé in the Alps course – both drove a 1,100 cc, 356 Coupé.

The reliability and sturdiness of the 356 in its early years are illustrated by the fact that the following year a light-metal Coupé driven by Paul von Guillaume and Count Heinz von der Muehle won its class and took 3rd place overall in the infamous Liège–Rome–Liège rally. In the same rally a production-model 356 1,1-liter Coupé with Fritz Huschke v. Hanstein and Petermax Mueller at the wheel took 2nd place in its class.

Also in 1951, François Picard came away with class victories in the Morocco Rally and the Tour de France Rally and Count Berckheim repeated as class winner at the Swedish Rally. In 1952, the 356 added class victories at the Sestrières Rally and the Tulip Rally.

Let me describe two events that, although

they took place on public roads, were not really rallies but pure races. These were the Carrera Panamericana in Mexico and the Mille Miglia in Italy. In the former, Prince Alfons Paul von Metternich-Winneburg achieved a class victory and placed 8th overall in 1952 with a 356 Cabrio. The 550 Spyder was successfully entered in many races during the next two years by Porsche and private parties. From 1952 to 1957 every year the Mille Miglia also witnessed two to three class victories with the Porsche 356 (from 1.1–1.6 liter) and the 550 Spyder entered by the factory and its customers in Italy. In 1952, Helmut Polensky and Walter Schlueter gave Porsche its first big international rally victory with the 356 light-metal Coupé (1.5-liter engine), at the rally every driver dreamed of winning: Liège–Rome–Liège; a 86-hour 3,200-mile course that included crossing the Alps twice and driving through numerous unpaved passes.

The following year brought the first double victory. The teams of Polensky/Schlueter and Sauerwein/Castell placed first and second overall in the Alps 1953 (Coupe des Alpes). Polensky became European champion after successive victories in Sestrières and Lisbon.

And once again, a year later, he won the Liège–Rome–Liège Rally, this time with Herbert Linge as co-driver. The choice of Linge had special significance: He was Porsche's chief mechanic and the 356 Alu-Coupé they drove had a test engine, namely the first four-camshaft 1.5 liter engine designed by Dr. Ernst Fuhrmann. This engine was used in all the later Carrera rally cars as well as in the 550 Spyder, the Formula 2 race car and the 904 GTS in different displacement variants.

Herbert Linge boxed up with Claude Storez to win another overall victory at the 1954 Tour de France Rally in a Spyder with the Fuhrmann engine.

Among all the major victories occurred a somewhat less important event: I came into

161

contact with Porsche cars as a young student in 1956. My friend and mentor Alfred Kling took me along in his 356 – 1300 to the International Winter Rally in Garmisch-Partenkirchen. Among these Porsche drivers at the start in Bad Neuenahr was the famous Count Wolfgang v. Trips, driving the same model car. At the end of the three-day rally, which included starting in temperatures of −4 Fahrenheit and a slalom course on frozen Lake Eibsee, we emerged as class winners and had beaten a German sports car champion.

During these years Porsche was occupied with the development and race entries of the 550 Spyders (RS and RSK). There was no time to spare for participation in rallies. But more and more private drivers took part in international Rallies, often with Porsche's support. Names such as Straehle, Storez, Bouchet, Linge and Walter showed up repeatedly on the winners lists. Storez/Bouchet placed second overall in the Coupe des Alpes and the Liège–Rome–Liège Rally in 1956; they won the latter in 1957. The combination Straehle/Bouchet won the 1959 Liège–Rome–Liège Rally and Straehle/Linge drove the 2-liter four-camshaft-engine (356 Carrera 2) to its first victory in the 1960 Corsica Rally. Hans Joachim Walter was 1961 European Rally Champion, winning the German Rally in his Spyder and coming in second in the Liège–Rome–Liège Rally.

I had been in the testing section at Porsche barely a year when I got the opportunity to take part in the Tour d'Europe with Walfried Winkler (who was a Porsche test driver) in a 356 Super 90. This 6,200 mile rally was for amateurs only. There was no service provided along the way and the course had not been checked out in advance. The route was over inferior Balkan roads to Beirut, Lebanon, and back, with numerous special test stretches that had to be driven at very high speed. Winkler and I sacrificed our annual leave in order to drive the car Porsche provided us. During the 14-day tour our provi-

sions consisted of two spare tires, some small spare parts, brake pads, reserve gas cans, tools and a suitcase with our personal effects. We attained a class victory and were fourth in the overall scores at the end of the rally.

Exactly two years later, in 1962, Winkler and I once again participated in the Tour d'Europe with a Super 90. This time the course led through all of Spain to Morocco. The conditions were the same as the Lebanon Rally. The results were also exactly the same. The Tour d'Europe still exists today and as far as I know service is still not provided and the rally is driven without backup service.

1963 and 1964 was an important period for the Porsche production department. Two new cars were developed – the 904 GTS and the 911. Factory driven cars did not participate in rally activities in 1963, but customers took over the field with the models 356 GS/GT or Abarth GT. Two 356 GS/GT models were loaned out to private drivers Bouchet and Klass but were unsuccessful in the 1964 Monte Carlo Rally.

The model 904 was constructed and sold as a road car, but it was designed as a sports car for use on closed racing circuits. Therefore, it was to the surprise of many when a model 904 with drivers Klass/Wuetherich, was entered in the Coupe des Alpes Rally 1964 and three cars were entered with the driving teams of Bouchet/Linge, Klass/Wuetherich and Mueller/Weber in the Tour de France Rally. It should be mentioned that these rallies took place only on asphalt roads. Drivers Bouchet/Linge won a victory and Klass/Wuetherich placed second at the Tour de France.

Porsche entered two 904 models in the 1965 Monte Carlo Rally, which totally confounded the experts. A circuit car in a snow rally? The slightest snowfall would mean getting stuck. Yes and no. While drivers Toivonen/Jaervi did get stuck in deep snow, Boehringer/Wuetherich placed a sensational second overall.

The experts saw another reason to shake

their heads in doubt before the start of this rally. How could Porsche run the risk of entering a brand new, just produced car (911 model) in the hell of the "Monte"? Herbert Linge and I drove this model. We knew the qualities of this new car and we had both participated in the development during the preceding years. We knew every part of the car. This was our "baby" and why shouldn't we christen it?

We drove a test version of the same model twice in trial runs around Christmas 1964. We made up our own personal technical notes for the special phases and sought out favorable service areas. We had at our disposal two service cars for the rally itself but we had to make do with only three types of tires and in addition had to give Boehringer some of our tires for his 904. It was to the astonishment of the experts when we placed fifth overall.

Porsche once again entered the 904 in the Coupe des Alpes Rally in 1965. Drivers Toivonen/Jaervi placed 21st overall while Boehringer/Wuetherich fell out of the competition with a model 904 with a 6-cylinder 911 engine. Another well-known 904 rally victory is the Spain Rally which the Spaniard Fernandez won in his private car.

By the end of 1965 and then in 1966 many private drivers in big international rallies had come to favor the 911. The customer service division prepared three 911s for competition and, with drivers Klass, Bouchet, Walter and Elford, they competed in almost every big rally. In studying the results it's notable that they very seldom dropped out; the 911 lived up to the adage about Porsche dependability from the very beginning.

Guenther Klass drove for Porsche in all the long-distance rallies with the model 911, won the German Rally and became European champion in 1966 with the same model. In 1967 the 911s were homologated with 160 hp. The motor sports department once again built and supported three new cars. Drivers Elford/Stone

placed third at the Monte Carlo Rally, and first in the German, Tulip and Geneva rallies. These wins gave them the European Championship.

It was at this time that the familiar names of Waldegaard and Zasada first appeared on Porsche's listing of results. These names would make history for Porsche during the next ten years. Incidentally, Zasada also won the European Rally Championship for production touring cars with his 912.

I should mention another event which could be considered in-between a rally and a race and which Porsche took part in three times (1967, 1968, 1970) with three cars: Marathon de la Route, which took place on the south and north loops of the Nuerburgring. The old classic long-distance rally Liège–Rome–Liège (or Liège–Sofia–Liège), had been discontinued in 1964. The Royal Motor Union Organization in Liège was looking for an alternative and came up with the idea of holding a long-distance race at the Nuerburgring. This course was to have the exact same duration as the Liège–Rome–Liège i.e., namely 86 hours of driving or four days and three nights non-stop including the route to and from Liège.

The Nuerburgring has always been an ideal test course for our production-line and race sports cars. So it was logical that Porsche would participate in Marathon de la Route with test cars equipped with special novelties. Three 911 models, two of which were equipped with new sportomatic gearboxes, participated in 1967. Drivers Elford/Herrmann/Neerpasch attained an overall victory with a 911 R sportomatic. "R" stands for an extremely light version of the 911 (210 hp) with numerous synthetic parts.

The next entry in 1968 was intended to test the new hydropneumatic, level-regulated spring strut at the front axle of the model 911 as well as the mechanical fuel injection. Drivers Linge/Glemser/Kauhsen came in ahead of Schuller/Blank/Steckkoenig giving Porsche a double victory. And in 1970, three 914/6 models swept the top three places in the Marathon de la Route. Drivers Haldi/Larrousse/Dr. Marko were the winners at the end of the 6,200 mile rally.

But let us return to the year 1968.

It began with one sensation after another: Elford/Stone won the Monte Carlo Rally with a work car, Toivonen/Tiukkanen took second in a private car. These teams drove the 911 T model, which is a lighter version of the 911 equipped with an altered 911 S engine with around 180 hp. After numerous unsuccessful tries, the "Monte" (considered to be the queen of the rallies) was finally won. The list goes on: Waldegaard won the Swedish Rally, Toivonen won the San Remo, Germany, GDR, Spain, the Danube-Castrol and Geneva rallies. He came in third at the Acropolis Rally, which gave him the European championship. Zasada came in second in the German and Acropolis rallies, fourth in the Marathon London–Sydney Rally and first in the Argentina Rally.

The Corsica Rally was once again the site of another test. Drivers Elford, Toivonen and Schuller started in 1968 with 911-R models equipped with the new 6-cylinder, four camshaft engine (916) with 2-liter displacement and 220 hp output. This time luck was not on their side. Schuller had an accident, and due to a defective oil filter, Elford lost all of the oil in his car. The cover of the differential box in Toivonen's car broke. This engine only produced one victory before the development was discontinued. Driver Larrousse won the French Neige et Glace Rally in 1969.

The years 1969 and 1970 were very successful ones for Porsche. Waldegaard won the Monte Carlo Rally twice, which meant that Porsche had won the most famous of all rallies three times in succession. Larrousse came in second twice, which gave Porsche three double victories in a period of three years.

Waldegaard also won the Swedish Rally in 1969 and 1970, which gave him a string of three consecutive victories. Toivonen won the Acropolis Rally in 1969, Waldegaard won the 1970 Austrian Alps Rally and Larrousse won the 1969 Tour de France and Tour de Corse, all with the model 911 R. Zasada took sixth place in the Safari '69 and second in the 1970 Poland Rally. This resulted in Porsche winning the Rally Championship of Makes in 1970 against main competitors Renault Alpine A 110, Ford Escort, Lancia Fulvia HF and Saab V 4.

After this routine listing of successes, let me get back to the technical side. The model 914/6 came on the market in 1970. It had already taken top position at Le Mans and the Marathon at the Nuerburgring and was to make its rally debut in the "Monte" at the beginning of 1971. Despite high expectations, Waldegaard only took third place in the overall scores. The two other cars battled transmission and clutch problems and finally dropped out of the rally because a glued-in ball pin had loosened on the clutch release lever.

The model 914/6 was then used only as a circuit car and hardly as a rally car. This was a shame because the 914 was intended to be a mid-engine car with a long wheel base – an ideal rally car. Its weak points were limited body stiffness and a rear axle suspension that was too light. Waldegaard switched back to the model 911 at the next Swedish Rally in 1971, where he took fourth place. He also came in second at the RAC Rally.

In between was the Safari Rally. Once again the customer sport department provided three factory cars (911 S, 2,2 liter), and took charge of the Kenya rally with drivers Waldegaard, Zasada and Andersson. Only Zasada, who was a specialist in this type of rally, succeeded in reaching the finish. He nearly won, but an electrical defect dropped him back to fifth place. The two other cars had to quit the rally due to an accident and problems with the shock absorber mounting.

In 1972 the 911 engines were uprated to 2.4

liter displacement, 2.5 l for the Monte Carlo and Swedish rallies. Drivers Larrousse and Waldegaard took respective second-place finishes. Zasada received a factory car for the Safari (which was safari driveable) due to his excellent performance in Kenya the previous year. He showed his appreciation by coming in second. The Safari Rally would eventually become a trauma for Porsche.

The Corsica Rally was the only one on the test schedule for 1972. This was the first time Porsche entered two Carrera RS models with rebored 2.8 liter displacement. This model was supposed to play a major role in the coming years in rallies and, as the RSR, in racing. But the debut of this model was unsuccessful. Waldegaard dropped out of the competition due to an accident and Larrousse developed a defective axle shaft in his car.

Time drew near for the 1973 Safari. Two Carrera RSs were made ready for Waldegaard and Zasada and taken charge of by the customer service branch. But once again the drivers were unlucky: defective shock absorbers and gears forced both cars to withdraw from the rally. After the cars and defective parts were shipped back to the factory, we analyzed the damage intensively. While it was possible to correct the transmission defect fairly quickly, the development of a safer shock absorber took time. We built a test car in the original Safari version. The shock absorbers held up for merely 32 miles of the rally course in the Weissach test area. Numerous major and minor changes were made on the shock absorbers and mounting points. Through systematic testing of every single step on the test track a distance of 620 miles was finally covered without any problems.

This meant a twentyfold improvement. More than 3,200 miles were driven and the test lasted all through the summer and fall of 1973. We often conducted test drives into the night, and of course on weekends.

The next Safari Rally in 1974 almost made it

worth our while. The shock absorbers were not the focus anymore. This time the rear axle suspension of Waldegaard's lead car broke. Once again, he only came in second. The second car with Schuller/Herrmann had a broken ball pin on the front axle and the third car withdrew because of a defective oil cooler.

Porsche's rally section was comparatively inactive for the next two years. The development capacity was concentrated mainly on the models 924 and 928, as well as the various turbo engines for production and racing cars. But a decision was made at the end of 1977 to make an all-out push to win the Safari Rally 1978. Waldegaard had won the Rally in 1977 with a Ford Escort. Zasada had his private Carrera made ready by Porsche within two days for the 1977 London-Sydney Marathon. He withdrew his car in Australia because of defective steering while still leading the rally. This was important for the next preparation. A stronger steering box had to be built. A car not previously tested was taken by Waldegaard to Kenya before Christmas 1977.

Two cars were entered for the 1978 rally (the second car was driven by the Kenyan Preston Jr.) and a test car was also constructed. In the middle of preparations Nicolas stunned everyone by winning the Monte Carlo Rally in his privately-owned Carrera. A good omen?

The best test mechanics flew to Kenya. Preston Sr. placed garages, vehicles and a service crew at our disposal. We were provided with CB radios and two airplanes as our relay stations. In short, no other professional team was better prepared and equipped. And again it was not meant to be: The rear axle trailing arm of Waldegaard's car and Preston's front absorber strut broke. The result was only fourth place and again second place. Winner of this rally was the Monte Carlo winner Nicolas, with a factory-owned Peugeot.

Again Porsche withdrew from rally sports for two years. The 924 Turbo, 924 GT and GTS

165

were developed during this time. A course of action was being looked into for the GTS and by coincidence Walter Roehrl was unemployed at the time. For one season Roehrl drove a factory-owned GTS in events for the German Rally Championship in 1981, winning four times. Porsche's Juergen Barth and Roland Kussmaul had previously taken the initiative for rally entries with the models 924 and 924 Turbo on a private basis. They achieved the first rally class victory for the 924 in Australia 1978, drove in the 1979 Kenya Safari and several times in the Monte Carlo Rally.

In contrast to its big brother, the 911, the 924 GTS has never won a big international rally. Its motor efficiency was inferior to the special rally cars of the period (Audi, Opel, Toyota, Lancia). This is also the case with the model 911 today. Even the driving genius Henri Toivonen (son of the successful 60s winner, Pauli Toivonen), only placed second in the European Rally Championship in 1984. He drove an exceptionally well equipped 911 SC RS, an improved 3-liter 911.

The rally scene then underwent a basic change. The drivers could previously only rely on their own improvisations and limited spare parts. There were no available instructions, only road maps, and the drivers could not test the rally course. Today the professional rally drivers can count on the help of dozens of service vehicles and mechanics. For each special phase all the tires are replaced according to the road and weather conditions and the length of the rally course. Transmission, wheel suspension or engine parts can be replaced at every service station.

The drivers are in touch with their racing manager by radio. Racing manager, mechanics and spare parts are in a helicopter hovering overhead and the drivers are able to practice extensively on all the special legs of the rally course beforehand. This enormous escalation in cost is one of the reasons why Porsche shied away from participation in the International Rally Championship for Makes.

The engineering of the rally car has also changed. All-wheel drive, high-performance turbo engine, race chassis and synthetic body shell have now become standard. Porsche had been developing an all-wheel drive 959 based on the 911 model for some time. And Porsche wouldn't be Porsche if this new technology had not been tested in a competition at the next opportunity.

This opportunity was the Paris–Dakar Rally in 1984. The rally had already taken place five times and has become one of the toughest rallies in the world. Prototypes (not homologated cars) are allowed to take part. This rally has very special characteristics: Service cars as well as helicopters and radios are forbidden. Spare parts and tools must be transported either in the cars or in escort cars, which also have to be rally cars. Only previously approved airplanes can fly spare parts to not more than five designated areas along the 7,500-mile course.

We built a test car for training purposes: 911 body, 911 SC engine, 911 rear axle, a new front axle and all-wheel drive. A 320-mile desert test was conducted in Algeria to the accompaniment of a cross-country car and an all-wheel drive truck loaded with spare parts, fuel and tools. The crew was on the road for three weeks. Weak points were noted, the best tire combination was chosen and fuel consumption was determined. They decided on the appropriate transmission gear ratios and measured engine and transmission temperatures.

Back at the factory, three entry cars were built, taking into account the training results, two all-wheel drive trucks were prepared and loaded with spare parts, tires, fuel- and water tanks and crews were picked. Finally the start in Paris on January 1, 1984: In the cars were Jacky Ickx (initiator and head of the expedition and winner the previous year) with co-driver Claude Brasseur; driver René Metge (former overall winner) with co-driver Lemoine; Roland Kussmaul (Porsche rally engineer) with co-driver Erich Lerner. There were two French drivers and two mechanics in each of the trucks.

The organization supplied two airplanes with which team mechanics could be on hand and flown ahead to the end of the daily leg. Three mechanics and myself were in one of the planes. It was an advantage to have the mechanics check the rally cars on their arrival before the trucks reached them. Besides, small repairs could be done with tools the cars had on board. Sleep if any, was possible in sleeping bags on a cot beside the cars. Meals were brought to us by a food wagon provided by the organizers.

We developed problems during the rally. The cable harness in Ickx's car was charred and he slipped into 139th place after repairs. While trying to gain ground, his car fell into a deep ditch, causing damage to the front axle. Metge had a collision with a cow. His windshield and fender had to be replaced. There was damage to tires and torn rubber bellows on axle shafts. But still we were in luck; all the cars including the two trucks finished and Metge was the winner, Ickx came in sixth and Kussmaul was in 22nd place.

In my opinion the Paris–Dakar victory, along with the Targa Florio win (1956), was one of the most impressive Porsche successes in motor sports. For every other big international challenge Porsche needed several attempts before a victory.

This is also true of the Liège–Rome–Liège Rally, Formula 1-Era 1962, Monte Carlo Rally, Le Mans, TAG Formula 1-engine 1983–84. A Safari Rally has never been won by Porsche. The Paris–Dakar Rally, which is considered the hardest, was won on the first try with the first all-wheel-drive Porsches. In addition, all cars finished.

Luck naturally plays a part in a rally victory. The luck we had in 1984 could only be wished for in 1985 when all three cars entered dropped out of the rally competition. Two cars had accidents and the third had to withdraw because a small oil line on the production SC engine broke, causing loss of oil. The cars themselves mainly consisted of parts of the 959. The body, transmission, transaxle, front- and rear axles passed the acid test for production release. Only the new turbo engine was not quite ready.

And here we sit on the sand at the edge of the Gao airport. The 1985 Paris–Dakar Rally is at an end for us. But we are quite sure there will be a Paris–Dakar 1986 for us. And the Safari is waiting for us sometime in the future...

167

REINHARD SEIFFERT

THE PORSCHE MYSTIQUE

We live in the century that brought mankind the automobile. With a bit of optimism we can count this among the positive phenomena of our century – even if, as we near the year 2000, the auto has become the subject of controversy, and is subjected to an increasing number of restraints. However, the desire to command perfect technology is by no means a product of our century; it is of mythical origin and that desire has always played a major role in automotive engineering. The Porsche legend and Porsche philosophy – which began with the Volkswagen project for "everyman" and with the indestructibility of VW engines on the fronts of the World War II – are also rooted in this ancient aspiration.

The Porsche mystique first became a psychological factor when small numbers of a certain vehicle began appearing on the roads in the early 1950s like the harbinger of a new age. The first Porsche was designated the 356; its successors all bore type designation numbers beginning with a "9." The cipher symbolism is lovingly cultivated, but it has only a decorative function. The true phenomenon is to be found in the uniqueness of these automobiles.

The history reads like a fairy tale: A design office, lost in a remote Alpine valley, brings to life the dream car of the small company's boss in the dreary post-war world. The car is a hit with friends and acquaintances; more of them are built. Fifty hand-made models just aren't enough, so a small production site is established in Stuttgart, with an initial goal of 500 vehicles. The rest of the story is well-known.

The secret of the fascination is by no means a factor of engine performance, which started out at a rather modest 35 hp. It is more a matter of the acceleration and speed which were wrung from this unassuming engine rating thanks to the lightweight construction and low drag of the body. There was a certain irrational response to the body styling, but also to the technical concept of a rear-mounted, air-cooled, horizontally-opposed engine and to the special system of suspension and springing. For this concept demanded very specific skills of the driver. A Porsche driver was someone who could manage to handle a Porsche. And if that didn't work out, the driver's capabilities simply had to be adjusted to those of the car – and not vice-versa.

Not a hint of the usual production and consumption mentality: The Porsche is not built to be bought, and is not bought to be used. The Porsche driver is not concerned with unadulterated comfort – there's something of the old instinct of the rider involved, for whom the most interesting horse is the one who throws him most often as they're getting to know each

168

other. The young aristocrats and the sons of wealthy parents who in the early 1950s battled for laurels in that oversteering Porsche were inspired and motivated by the idea of demonstrating their ability with this particular car.

Of course, a lot has changed in the meantime: The handling of the rear-engine Porsche has become more neutral, there are transaxle chassis and water-cooled front-mounted engines. But even these cars are still genuine Porsches, for it is part of the Porsche philosophy to exploit any and every technical means to reach the desired goal. And the fascination has not diminished, even with 300 horsepower instead of 30, with acceleration and top speed doubled. One also has to be able to handle a 944 Turbo or a 928 S, cars which have pushed the physical limits of driving into areas inaccessible with normal vehicles. Even if they are not utilized, they manifest themselves like the six legs of the mythological stallion.

It is a myth of the present time, for names like Daimler or Ford are much more closely related to the industrial history of the automobile. Ferdinand Porsche was not one of the great auto pioneers, but a renewer... as a designer, a rejuvenator of technology that had often lapsed into lethargy. That is his historic contribution, and the basis of the Porsche legend, the Porsche mystique.

Did Ferdinand Porsche, who once started out from Maffersdorf in Bohemia to Vienna to change the world of technology, did this famous designer ever build a Porsche? No, he had worked for Lohner, for Austro-Daimler, for Daimler-Benz, for Steyr, for Auto Union and many others. He never worked for Porsche – he died in the same year in which Porsche first became an auto manufacturer. The man who chauffered Emperor Franz Joseph and impressed Kaiser Wilhelm II, the engineer to whom Hitler listened always stood more in the background than at the focus of events.

Is it a coincidence that his life's work coincides exactly with the first half of our century? In the world of technology and transportation the name Ferdinand Porsche was first mentioned when the Lohner-Porsche – a coach with electric wheel-hub motors – appeared at the 1900 Paris World Fair. Porsche was a student of electrical engineering – for him it only made sense to equip a vehicle with small, lightweight electric motors which were safer, easier to operate and quieter than the combustion engines of the day, or the steam engines, which were also used to power vehicles.

World fairs were of immense importance in the relationship between man and technology, which was advancing at a furious pace. Such fairs shaped the consciousness of the technological age – Porsche had come on the scene at just the right moment. The Lohner electric cars played a role in city transportation right up to the start of the World War I. But by that time Porsche had long been working for the Austrian Daimler company which, like its British counterpart, had achieved increasing independence from the parent company in Stuttgart. Porsche became technical director of the company in Wiener Neustadt. Conventional automotive history accounts usually assert that at this point, after tinkering with peculiar electrical contraptions, Porsche finally embraced the internal combustion engine. And in fact, he did at that time design outstanding gasoline engines, remarkable for their simple construction and favorable power-to-weight ratio. But he also continued to build electric vehicles.

Never in his life did Porsche commit himself to any specific technical principle. He was always interested in the immediate task, for whose solution he was willing to exploit any technical means or measure. As far as powering vehicles were concerned, in the year 1900 the electric motor, even including its accumulator in the power-to-weight ratio, was a worthy competitor of the piston engine of the day.

In 1910 it proved to be the internal combustion engine which – thanks to improved ignition and carburetion systems and higher rpms – was the better power plant for a vehicle independent of rails. Porsche's decision to devote himself to the combustion engine was based on – as it might be put in this sober age – systems analysis.

Porsche didn't build just automobiles, however – he became just as well known, if not better, for his aircraft engines, railway locomotives, streetcars and all-wheel-drive trucks. The same basic concept of distributing the drive among many axles was also applied to his locomotives, which served mainly to transport heavy military equipment, providing better traction than conventional railway engines or tractors. And his cars? They were remarkable not just for their speed and reliability, but also for their attractive, almost fashionable styling: He had instinctively recognized that, in contrast to rail vehicles and trucks, the passenger vehicle would be strongly subject to aesthetic and emotional factors. That was reflected in the cute little car that he presented his son Ferdinand Anton Ernst ("Ferry") on Christmas Day in 1920, and in his small "Sascha" car of the same period.

In the pre-war years, Porsche's designs were never particularly inexpensive. But around the year 1920, during a period of financial hardship, he immediately found ways to build good cars simply. As the director of a renowned company for whose continued well-being he was also responsible, he would never have considered the path to low prices taken in America: churning out enormous numbers of vehicles. He was not Henry Ford, the mass producer, he was Ferdinand Porsche the design engineer. So he designed cars that could be built at favorable prices even in small quantities.

He wasn't confronted with the idea of larger production series until the 1930s, when he moved to Daimler in Stuttgart following an interlude with Steyr. He remained true to his

principles and, even though the entire economy was in dire straits, set out to do business independently. After two attempts with Zuendapp and NSU, which broke down because of financing problems, he finally found state support for the Volkswagen idea – the peoples' car. At the same time, he was also busy designing one of the most powerful and successful racing cars of all time, as always, according to his own idiosyncratic ideas.

When the war did away with the construction of the Volkswagen plant and his new plans for racing and world records, Porsche remained Hitler's technical advisor. For he understood just as much about heavy armored vehicles as he did about lightweight automobiles. The war-time projects also contributed to the Porsche legend, even though most of them remained secret and were more a matter of rumor – admired and sometimes ridiculed, like the gigantic tank "Maus." But many a trooper during the war learned the advantages of an air-cooled rear-mounted engine: The lightweight, Jeep-like VW "Kuebelwagen" eased many a soldier's life and saved many others when retreat was finally sounded on all fronts. Porsche had not discovered these technical solutions, but his Volkswagen made them popular.

The resurrection of the Volkswagen under the direction of Britain's occupation forces, and its career as Germany's number one export article is the final chapter in the legend of that great design engineer, Ferdinand Porsche. It began shortly before his death in 1951; the old and ailing professor just managed to witness the opening chapters of this peacetime success story. And it confirmed that, despite his eclecticism, he had usually chosen to develop the right ideas. With his death, the age of the grand and solitary design engineers came to an end.

The same year marks the beginning of the sports car maker Porsche's history – modern times, so to speak. For the first time in Stuttgart a larger number of those unmistakable little

Coupés were built, where on the low flat hoods the name Porsche could be found in stretched letters. The history of the engineering design company Dr. h. c. F. Porsche goes much farther back, however, to the year 1930, when Ferdinand Porsche opened his own office in Stuttgart's Kronenstrasse, which was entered in the commercial register the following year.

That designing firm still exists today, an ongoing link between the first half of the century and the present. Hard at work in the Stuttgart office back in 1931 were Ferdinand Porsche's son Ferry, and engineers such as Karl Rabe and Erwin Komenda, who served as the mentors of the Porsche engineers still active today. The orientation – which had been set by Ferry Porsche since the new beginning in 1945 in Kaernten-Gmuend – was based on the thinking and working procedures of that design office. A Porsche philosophy that continued uninterrupted.

What is the philosophy and what are the concepts on which it is founded? One of the anecdotes that Ferry Porsche tells in this regard goes like this: Two identical Porsche Spyders during the first years of racing differed in one way – one handled well on the road, the other poorly. The springs of the second were replaced, the shock absorbers, the suspension... but nothing made any difference. Ferry asked, "Did you check the measurements?" Of course, all the dimensions had been inspected: wheelbase, track, camber, toeing and a number of other factors. "Then give me a piece of string," said Ferry. With this string the head of the entire company personally checked the car body, which had already been inspected and passed: He measured the distance from the left front to the right rear wheel, and from the right front to the left rear wheel. The measurements differed by nearly an inch – the car was crooked.

Is that a philosophy, using a piece of string instead of a piece of measuring equipment? No, of course not – some deviations simply can't be detected without precision optical instruments. The philosophy is not a matter of the means selected, but of approaching each and every problem with the simplest solution. If that doesn't suffice, then the second simplest solution is attempted. Under certain circumstances that can lead to quite complicated solutions. But the approach remains simple, for that is the only way to avoid the danger of not being able to see the forest for the trees.

Whether in string measurements or in electronically stored matrixes for the regulation of ignition, injection and air pressure, there is no solution at Porsche for which a simpler one hasn't been attempted. Helmuth Bott, the director of the Weissach development center with more than 2,000 engineers and technical specialists under him, began his career as a young engineer in the 1950s. In those days the simplest solution was greeted enthusiastically because of the lack of expensive measuring equipment and of the time needed for comprehensive calculations. Today Weissach features the most advanced computers, which in seconds can produce results that formerly required months of work. But cad-cam and finite elements cannot replace simple thinking. On the contrary, they make it possible, even when faced with complex problems, to maintain a manner of thinking that is simple and success-orientated.

Success orientation is a product of the uniqueness of the independent Porsche design office. Right from the beginning it had to accomplish tasks successfully, and almost invariably on a limited budget. Creativity instead of money – even today that is part of everyday life in Weissach. For there is always a border between red and black ink, and its importance rises proportionately with the number of digits ahead of the decimal point. The development engineer earns his salary on the path between the acceptance and the fulfillment of a contract. When the budget is fixed, whether money is earned or lost depends on the shortness of that path.

Is that philosophy? Does it have anything to do with Kant or Hegel? The term has to be stretched a bit in order to include an approach in technical thinking under the term "philosophy." But on the other hand, each and every sentence – no matter how complicated – in "The Critique of Pure Reason" constitutes the simplest way of expressing a particular relationship. The tasks confronting modern technology cannot be solved by means of pseudo-science – they require a fundamental approach. And that approach can be spelled out: It can be applied to problems in vehicle handling or in environmental protection, to comfort or safety, to acoustics or ergonomics. The approach that determines whether something is done correctly or incorrectly has to be established right at the beginning of any development: This is a basic part of the Porsche philosophy.

Even without the first car hand-crafted in Gmuend, the first Porsche design to carry the name "Porsche," the legend of Ferdinand Porsche and the philosophy of the Porsche design office would have survived. But it was that car which first exposed the effectiveness of the Porsche philosophy in its entirety, and which turned the philosophy into mystique.

The car named Porsche soon developed its own dynamics. Increasing orders and the quick growth of a good reputation led to the evolution of a true auto factory. Ferry Porsche, who had actually wanted only to build the car that appealed to him personally, found himself in the role of manufacturer.

An engineer built cars because there was a demand for them. For him the fundamental idea was not to make money by manufacturing cars. Once the sports car manufacturer path had been trod, funds had to be accumulated for production equipment, employees had to be hired, space rented. Ferry Porsche scrupulously applied himself to these necessities, but at heart

he remained the engineer, and saw automobile manufacturing as a branch that, once it had appeared, had to be approached with the same conscientiousness as a design contract.

Even today the numbers produced at the Zuffenhausen plant are inconsiderable when compared to the auto industry as a whole. Porsche has remained true to the principle of not building more than there is a demand for. And the engineer Ferry Porsche, who built "his" car, remained the prototype of the Porsche driver. The psychological profile of the Porsche driver could thus be a psychological profile of Ferry Porsche. But it is not necessary to dissect the character of the individual personality – the typical elements are reflected in the entirety of Porsche drivers.

That by no means constitutes uniformity. Quite the contrary: A Porsche driver is conceivable only as an individualist. After reading through survey results, the very perceptive swiss market observer Henry Keller once commented: "I realized that everyone who drove a Porsche had at least one thing in common – the Porsche."

They really don't have much in common, not even sex: The proportion of women Porsche drivers is much higher than in the case of other sedans comparable in price. Also a wide variety of professions are represented, with an increasing percentage of employees in the traditional professional categories.

There are a number of contradictions involved in that. The employee can no longer be associated automatically with workaday dependence. In terms of choice and opportunity, the employee often enjoys more freedom than the free-lancer or self-employed professional, who must struggle to make a living. For all of these groups, the Porsche represents freedom, for men and women. The women are no longer relegated to the passenger seat. A Porsche is no less attractive to car-loving women than men. But since women do not

172

uniformly disdain the passenger seat, the Porsche also serves to promote male attractiveness.

The web of psychological reactions and influences could be spun out even further. But its importance can also be over-estimated, for despite all of the comparisons with expensive watches or jewelry, the Porsche is quite simply a very different kind of object: a sports car. The effect of its external appearance on other people is indisputable, but the drivers themselves react to very specific factors, like the handling or the qualities and characteristics of a vehicle. Its specific characteristics in the critical range of lateral acceleration and its excellent traction are part of this classic concept.

And it is part of the psychological profile of the (rear-engine) Porsche driver that he or she identifies with all of that. Like the young aristocrats or the sons of wealthy parents in the early 1950s, who, using this car in rallies and on race tracks, proved that both the car and their own driving ability were not to be underrated. There is still something to the adage that, at the wheel of a Porsche, the driver must prove himself, and be willing to learn. At normal traffic speeds such a vehicle is as gentle as a lamb and presents no problems whatsoever.

But the challenge to explore the car's outer limits is always present. The driver who accepts this challenge with the proper caution and seriousness – for instance in driving courses – gains not just in driving ability, but also in self-respect and spirit: It might not alter the personality, but it will surely develop it.

That is certainly one of the reasons that Porsche is not so much a symbol of an economic status – which can be demonstrated with other expensive makes – but that of a personal one. Despite its high price, the car does not erect social barriers. It generates enthusiasm – among school children in Italy, city-dwellers in Poland or Hungarian farmers. People still tend to spend more for a Porsche than they can actually afford, and not just for the sake of prestige. But catchwords like "status" and "esprit" are simply inadequate to explain why an idea born in a remote Alpine valley proved to be so successful. There seems to be a bit of mystique involved after all.

HENRY KELLER

PSYCHOGRAPH OF THE PORSCHE DRIVER

Am I the Porsche type? I wanted to know more. All right, a pilgrimage to Weissach to look for the answer.

What was my wish? I answered timidly that I wanted to know more about the Porsche types.

Certainly, answered the man. Which one then? He pointed to a cabinet containing many files. 356? A, B, or C? 911, 912, 914, 916? 924, 944, 928? Or maybe 904, 906, 908, 917?

No, I stammered. You misunderstood me. I would like to know about the type who drives these types of cars. And if I personally am a Porsche type?

Now he understood what I wanted. Market research? Then you will have to go to Tamm. By that, he meant the Porsche sales distribution center in the Ludwigsburg suburb of Tamm. So I drove through the villages to Tamm.

There, I met with full understanding. The heavy safe was opened and I was inundated with data.

When I surfaced, it was with the understanding that people who drive Porsches have one thing in common: the Porsche.

I also understood that the keeper of the safe was particularly interested in this one common factor. A Porsche driver who changes to BMW, I determined, is considered pretty wishy-washy. A BMW driver who buys a Porsche – that makes them sit up and take notice in Tamm.

But first I wanted to know more about myself. I found out that here I wouldn't be rated as a Porsche driver or a Porsche owner, but as a primary user. I am only interesting to them as a user.

This is easy to explain: Whoever bought my Porsche, whoever writes it off his taxes is not important. It is important who uses the Porsche, that is – the primary user. Certainly, this is normally the owner. Although this ratio decreases as the price increases: Out of a hundred 924's, 86 are driven by the owner; out of one hundred 928's only 73.

The trend is to fewer owner-users. One reason is that leasing is becoming more common; another is that often someone other than the primary user makes the purchase.

With the 924, this is, in particular, "other private persons." I was told that under this heading are mainly husbands whose wives are the primary users of the 924. On the other hand, wives who buy and husbands who drive are rare. The wife buys and the wife drives is more common and there are reasons for this. I will come back to this later.

The company buys and the man drives – this is often the case, particularly with the 928. However only about one-fourth of these valuable objects are owned in this manner. It should be said that these get intensive use.

174

The income – I shamefully kept to myself that I earn less than the average primary user in my class. I will try to find the reasons for this and take the necessary steps to remedy it.

In Ludwigsburg they are happy to have more of the top earners as customers than BMW or Mercedes. I would like to see more people with smaller incomes with Porsches – somehow this will be possible.

The number of automobiles in the household: Use of a Porsche often makes it possible to leave another vehicle in the garage. One out of ten 928s is a third car. Another trend: I learned that the third car is a necessity for large families. Now I know what I can expect. The 928 driver is especially strong in the family question. The average household is 2.7. I was told that this is because of the available seating. The 928 Porsche is used more often by people who travel with four in the car. The 928 can be compared with a Sedan in this respect.

Even for the other Porsche-type owners, having children is not unusual. Even the 911 can meet the requirement as a family car. It is necessary to discuss the question of marriage: This old tradition is popular with Porsche owners. Although the average user age of 40 is attractive to the playboy existence, 67 percent of 911 drivers always have the same lady next to them in the passenger seat. And the 928-person, not much older, is usually married.

The fact that the number of Porsche-driving women is increasing is not – I determined from the subtle psycho-profile – because of the feminization of the Porsche. No, a woman achieves a touch of masculinity by conquering the sports car. And a touch of masculinity is a necessary part of the comprehensive personality of a woman – just as a touch of femininity is essential to the inner make-up of a man. So women are not only at home in the passenger seat of the male automobile.

Also, the Porsche-driving mother is not a rarity. The Porsche is not only for the one-man-

family: Of the 2.5 persons in the average Porsche household, 0.3 are children under thirteen who cannot be considered users. So it is accurate to figure one person per vehicle.

Because of this, the Porsche seldom stays in the garage... While the average West German automobile is used only on an average of 7,500 miles a year, the Porsche user doubles that average with 15,300 miles.

The 928 overshadows even the well-known sedans that have established themselves in the company and service car sector. The 928 averages 19,204 miles a year. These miles are not driven around the church steeple – obviously these automobiles are often used as total alternatives to airplanes and intercity trains. The objections of the tax people are nullified, because such milage point to a real business use of an automobile that is considered a pure luxury by a lot of people.

A private airplane with four wheels say some; traffic-jam bomber say others. In the end, the speed of forward progress is completely dependent on when one is driving. And 928 drivers seem to be nonconformists, driving at off-peak periods. They can afford to be; 77 percent are self-employed or work as free-lancers. These groups prevail over the 911 – I can see that, as a married free-lancer, I am in the right group of Porsche users.

Porsche people are avid periodical readers and their choice of magazines tends to those that are car-oriented, for example, "Auto, Motor & Sport". The leading German news magazines "Stern" and "Spiegel" enjoy approximately equal readership. Drivers of the 911 and 928 are more interested in "Capital" and "Frankfurter Allgemeine Zeitung" than the corresponding group of 924 and 944 drivers and the 928 S group. A diversity of interests is evident in the above-average readership rates for both "Die Welt" and "Playboy."

In my spare time activities I am an atypical Porsche driver as a non-tennis player and typical as a skier. Inasmuch as I have taken part in safety training at Hockenheim, I am even a model driver. More than half of Porsche drivers would like to study systematically the skills of proper cornering and braking habits, but only a few have actually taken part in such training.

Porsche drivers are, after all, only people and it sometimes happens that they look around for another make of car. It is seldom a yearning that drives them to this thought, but more often the good life with four doors and a large comfortable interior.

It can be argued hypothetically that Porsche drivers will sooner or later turn away from the pure sports car doctrine. In reality the exact opposite is true. Porsche can count on customer loyalty rates of which other firms can only dream. At the top is the 928 with 94 percent of the drivers buying the same model again. This is true even of drivers of cars without the "S" and the tail spoiler. Well above the average are also the 911 drivers, with 80 percent. The only other company to reach this average is the previously mentioned well-known sedan manufacturer.

The loyalty of the 911 driver is without question when it comes to buying a new car. 93 percent want to buy another Porsche and the trend shown by the drivers of the other models is similar, 80 to 88 percent.

This flourishing loyalty, a term used in mar-keting research, is particularly important for the peaceful sleep of those who make the policy concerning sales and new models for the future. Of course, Porsche will only be able to sell Porsche users certain automobiles in the future. In this point they are particular and they will only change little in their program. The easiest of the Porsche users to seduce are the drivers of the 924 and 944, of whom 15 percent dream of the 911. Out of hundred 911 drivers only 7 would consider switching to another type of Porsche. And the drivers of the 928 S show about the same reluctance to change to another model, or even another make of car.

Back from Tamm and filled to the brim with information, I fell into a deep sleep and dreamed I was unexpectedly standing before a high court. The judge asked me if I would ever think of buying a four-door sedan instead of my Porsche. No, I answered firmly.Or a comfortable coupé from (here, two cities in Southern Germany were mentioned)? No, then what about an exo-tic from Italy? N-no, I stammered, quickly reviewing the new prices, after-sales service and resale values.

The jury withdrew to decide the verdict. Finally the judgement came: You are the Porsche type, recognized as one of many pos-sible Porsche-types.

Smiling contendedly, I woke up.

71

72

73

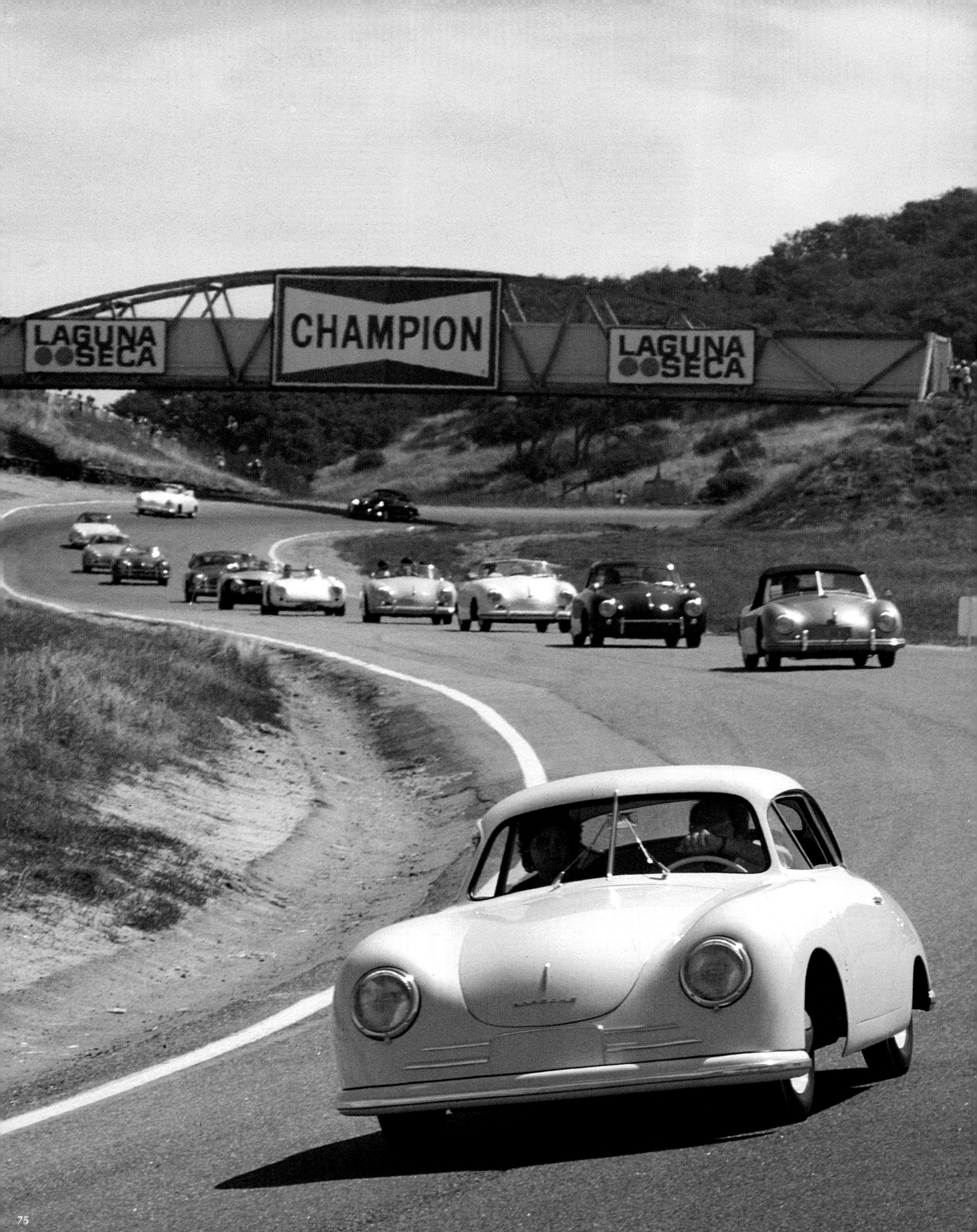
LAGUNA
SECA
CHAMPION
LAGUNA
SECA

RUDI NOPPEN

FIRST AND FOREMOST – QUALITY

Porsche – affectionately referred to as "the biggest little auto factory in the world" – receives a lot of visitors every day who want to take personal delivery of their vehicles at the Stuttgart plant. This practice has a tradition going back several decades, and we're pleased to note that more and more customers are taking advantage of it. Before "driving in its finest form," it's an experience to be present when your very own car receives the finishing touches prior to delivery, and to have a look at all the procedures and processes through which it has passed in the preceding days, during a tour of the factory.

The personal pick-up program is just as popular with us as it is with our customers. The buyer's visit underlines his or her interest in the product and a feeling of loyalty to the company, especially when the customer has demonstrated faithfulness to the Porsche make for years or even decades – as is often the case. Customer visits also provide first-hand opportunity for debating the pros and cons of our vehicles and our after-sales service. Is there any more valid information on our performance than the personal reports of our loyal buyers?

Another matter of interest is of course the buyer's motivation: Why does it have to be a Porsche? Design, technical standards, handling, reliability – these are all factors which are repeatedly quoted, with variations only in the order of priority. And naturally, the exclusivity of Porsche, a factor of its high quality and its highly individualized equipment and finishing.

That is, in fact, the prime factor in production at Porsche. Individualistic vehicles with top quality, luxury equipment. The guideline for our work is not only to maintain the level that has been reached, but to improve it continually, on a day-to-day basis, and in longer-term planning.

Just a quick glance at our production program indicates how successful continuous development has been. Gone are the days of the "single-model 356-age." We now offer 4- and 8-cylinder engine models with the transaxle concept, some with two- and some with four-valve-technology; naturally aspirated and turbocharged engines, with five-speed standard transmissions or automatics. There is also a variety of 6-cylinder air-cooled engine series: coupés, targas, convertibles and turbos.

But that is really just the basis of even greater variety. Depending on the particular type, we offer our customers between 70 and 100 optional extras, which allow highly individualized, personal Porsche styling. What's more, day after day we fulfill a wide range of special equipment and finishing wishes – of course, only when they don't conflict with the

201

safety requirements and handling characteristics of our vehicles. Although we offer 15 different colors of paint in our standard program, roughly one out of every twenty 911s or 928s is given a special paint job.

Another example: Including all the technical, material and color-scheme variations, we offer several hundred different seats as standard equipment. Nonetheless, each and every day five to ten individualized seating wishes are requested and produced.

All these and other factors are responsible for a remarkable situation at Porsche: If all the vehicles produced in Zuffenhausen over a period of three months were lined up side by side and inspected down to the last details, it would be a rarity to find two that are identical. Of course, producing individualized vehicles necessitates the maintenance of an extraordinary variety of manufacturing, quality control and logistical processes. However, we don't regard that as a disadvantage. Quite the contrary: I think the special fascination of our production work lies in reliably mastering this range of techniques and procedures.

The key factor is the commitment and flexibility of our highly qualified employees, who see themselves as "co-workers" in the most literal sense of the term. Their experience and craftsmanship are our most important tool when it comes to manufacturing and expanding an already wide range of top-quality products, despite having to work at capacity levels. All this depends on a good working climate. That we have, and we're just as proud of it as of the fact that each of our employees has been with us for an average of more than nine years. Progressive technology alone is not enough; the hearts and minds of our employees are essential to the sensible application of such technology.

That is especially true of our parts distribution center which, in our factory, serves as the focal point of material supplies for all the various plant operations. Measured against today's technical standards, this center and its integrated quality assurance constitute one of the most modern and highly automated facilities of its kind. In order to properly appreciate the importance of this system for Porsche, it is essential to understand one very significant aspect of our production strategy: In its own workshops, Porsche places maximum priority on high-technology and quality-assuring manufacturing processes for engines and vehicles.

The fact that we purchase more than 70 % of the parts we require from well-qualified suppliers – most of whom are located in the vicinity of Stuttgart – is simply the reverse side of this strategy. In fact, many of these suppliers could actually be regarded as extensions of our own production, because most of the parts we purchase are Porsche designs. This intense interrelationship with suppliers, and of course the above-mentioned product diversity, underline the significance which the distribution center – our logistical clockwork – has for our company.

The system itself handles more than 10,000 different types of parts. On arrival at the plant, the parts are subjected to statistical quality inspection. A computer provides the required data and stores all the inspection results over a relatively long period of time. Thus, we are always aware of the quality of our parts and can therefore react very quickly, when necessary, to critical situations.

But reacting is not what we're really after. The motto is: preclude errors in the first place. For instance, all suppliers are checked out before they receive their first order from Porsche. A team of specialists takes a close look at the quality "capability" of each supplier's manufacturing and inspection facilities. Binding acceptance standards are worked out together with potential suppliers – with the goal of establishing consistent-quality processes and of systematically eliminating failure sources right from the beginning. Quality must be solidly built in – checking for its existence after the fact is not enough. We'll run into this philosophy again later when we go on a tour of Porsche's own production facilities. But first let's return once more to the distribution center.

After inspection, parts are automatically transported to their holding areas in the high-bay storage depot. Over terminals located in the assembly areas, the parts are requisitioned on the basis of production requirements, and transported – once again automatically by an unmanned underground transfer system and elevators – to the proper sites. To ensure a punctual flow of material without long holding periods, the system can be pre-programmed 23 hours in advance. The computer automatically sorts the "orders" and ensures that they are reliably filled. The computer also handles express deliveries separately. If need be, the period between the requisitioning of a part and its arrival at the assembly site can be reduced to less than ten minutes.

This flexibility and speed often proved their value when "the rush is on." The computer also directs those parts which do not pass through the storage depot. For example, seats used to take up huge storage space and necessitated complicated handling procedures. Today, thanks to the stupid but reliable direction of the computer, they are delivered at short intervals direct from the suppliers to the proper assembly sites, in accordance with exactly specified delivery and transport schedules.

Highly automated techniques in the distribution center: What is Porsche's fundamental approach to automation? Well, we are not prejudiced against such developments. We consider automation primarily when it can help us to achieve higher quality and greater flexibility, improved economy and better working conditions. Above all, automation must not be allowed to interfere with the requirements involved in manufacturing exclusive products: We simply cannot afford automation at the cost

of quality, for example – even if it appears so much more economical on paper!

Now that we've had a look at logistics, and seen how the material flow is controlled and regulated, let's follow the evolution of a Porsche, from the initial order on paper on up to the finished vehicle, just as if we were taking a tour of the factory.

All engines – even the 4-cylinder power plants later built into the vehicles in Neckarsulm – are produced and inspected in Stuttgart-Zuffenhausen. This process begins with the precision-machining of main components, for example, grinding of the close-tolerance cam profiles, precision-drilling of the tappet guides, diamond milling of the cylinder head and gauged honing of the drill holes in the sinter-forged connecting rods. Finish machining of the cylinder barrels is carried out with a special etching technique that removes layers of material so thin that they can hardly be measured, let alone perceived by the naked eye. This procedure, which we pioneered worldwide in series production, produces highest-precision surface characteristics with a wide range of advantages: longer life, lower fuel consumption, high efficiency and the best engine break-in qualities, to name just a few.

With the help of special measuring instruments, our employees monitor the precision of each operation, before the finished parts – combined with purchased components from the distribution center – are transported to the engine assembly area. Outsiders may find it hard to believe, but, counting our basic engine types and the many modifications required to meet specific national regulations, for example in regard to exhaust emissions, we now produce almost 100 different engine variations, in a completely variable sequence, but always synchronized with the fabrication of the respective vehicle bodies and allocated to the individual customer's order.

Almost every employee in the engine

department is capable of assembling and inspecting each of these variations single-handedly. Each and every step in the procedure is stored on videotape cassettes – the employee can voluntarily view "his" specific tasks and movements as often as he likes, until he has absolutely mastered them. He himself assumes the responsibility for the quality of his work by entering each step into the register that is maintained for each engine, including all assembly data and the results of test runnings. By the way, test runs: "The heart and lungs" of each engine are checked under load conditions for about 15 minutes by running the engine through all rpm ranges. Together with the precision component processing mentioned above, this ingenious test program eliminates the need for subsequent breaking-in of the engine in the classical sense.

In synch with engine assembly, the body shop prepares the sheet metal elements which are subsequently pressed to form the configuration that is immediately recognized the world over as "the Porsche." Most people assume that it's simply a matter of putting together two doors, a roof, the fenders and a floor assembly and there you have it. That's far from the truth, however. Altogether, including the smaller components, a total of some 600 sheet metal parts go into a Porsche body. And that is just for the sheet metal shell; it does not include interior fittings and related parts.

Arranged on fixtures which in some cases almost reach room size, the sheet metal parts are brought together in the correct positions and then spot-welded, for the most part. Did you know that each vehicle gets as many as 5,000 spot welds and, depending on the particular type involved, up to 33 feet of seam welding? The fitting and jointing process in the body shop is carried out with the utmost precision, since any deviations which occur there are almost impossible to eradicate later.

A couple of notes on the materials used: For its vehicle bodies, Porsche utilizes non-corrosive aluminum or sheet steel that has been insulated against corrosion by means of a coating of zinc. Among other advantages, this coated steel tends to "repair" itself during later use when minor damage occurs. Scratches and small dents caused by stone chips have a tendency to "heal": Due to the influence of the surrounding atmosphere, the zinc spreads out over the scratched steel, sealing off the surface from rust. We have impressive examples of the resilience of this system; for example, an unpainted auto body that was left outside, exposed to the elements. Even after years, it showed no signs of rusting.

Of course, specialized processes are necessary to handle such materials, particularly when it comes to welding. We developed and perfected such processes for production-line application long before we became the first company, many years ago, to offer our customers a seven-year warranty against corrosion of the sheet metal parts.

Before the body shell moves on to the paint shop, its exterior "skin" is specially finished. The goal of the process, which alternates machining and inspection operations, is to achieve a surface as smooth as possible. Manual labor is the key here; for instance, the operators wear special sensory gloves which, in the event of even the tiniest blemishes or irregularities, make the auto body surface feel like a cobblestone path.

All of these steps are necessary to achieve the subsequent paint job that has come to be synonymous with Porsche. Did you know that each vehicle receives three to four coats of paint, which together are less than eight-thousandths of an inch thick? Or that between the individual coats the body shell is repeatedly heated and cooled to ensure that the paint always has the proper consistency? Or that between coats the body surface is repeatedly polished? The smoother the surface, the more homogeneous the coats of paint, and the more brilliant and glossy the final appearance of the car.

The exterior paint. Once the vehicle type itself has been selected, the paint job seems to be the most important factor in the buyer's mind. We offer 15 different colors in our standard line, but during the course of a year we make use of more than 200 different colors in order to fulfill the wishes of customers – including mixtures that are prepared specially by the paint shop foreman himself. It is not just myth that we are occasionally given lipsticks, scarves, wash cloths and other objects as pattern and color schemes for the vehicle paint. Spurious, however, is the assertion that such requests come only from women customers! Nor is it true that only American buyers supplement their orders with customizing wishes of this kind.

Special orders, of course, have their price, and tend to extend the delivery period, but in principle we are quite flexible in this respect, as long as vehicle safety and operation are not impaired. For example, we have been asked to paint a Porsche in the typical red used by the fire department, perhaps because the customers figured this might have an especially "liberating" effect on the open highway. But because of existing regulations, we had to turn down such requests.

From the paint shop, the car body is transferred to the assembly shop, where it meets up with "its" engine – see above – and with several thousand other parts. In light of such diversity, the much-acclaimed reliability of our parts distribution center is not a luxury for our assemblers, but an absolutely essential foundation of their work.

After all, the assemblers don't just have to master the many different vehicle types, but also about 28 different characteristics per type depending on the country of destination, and another 70 to 100 optional extras per type.

Assembly work at Porsche is not organized along strict production lines, where the workers repeatedly perform the same tasks at intervals of one minute or less. Aside from the fact that this would impair the all-important relationship of our employees to their jobs and to the product, our highly diversified production program simply couldn't be carried out optimally in this way. Instead, at Porsche, groups of three to four, sometimes even more workers, man successive assembly stations, carrying out operations that typically require about a half hour per station.

One assembly area that has steadily grown in importance can literally be scented out: the saddlery and upholstery workshop. Experienced specialists have plenty of opportunity to apply their creative talents to the task of turning the various materials and designs into well over a hundred different interiors. The convertible tops are also fabricated here. There were periods when the demand for convertibles far outstripped our capacity to deliver them. The problem was not a lack of facilities or suitable top material or frames. No, the problem was simply that we couldn't find enough auto saddlers with the supreme craftsmanship that has always been and remains the standard at Porsche. It goes without saying that, just as in the case of the painters, our master saddlers could tell quite a few tales about the completion of special orders, and the reactions of satisfied customers.

The final assembly area is a combination of inspection, filling, adjustment and tuning jobs. Tanking up with fuel, oil, water and air; checking the overall vehicle tightness, shaking in the springs, an electrical test, adjustment of the chassis and suspension, a roller test and exhaust emission test are just some of the operations carried out here on every Porsche.

Did you know that we also subject each vehicle to an extensive test drive before it leaves the factory on its way to the customer or dealer? In fact, a test drive in everyday traffic used to be standard procedure even for Porsche racing cars. That, of course, is no longer possible. But we maintain that tradition for all our production-line vehicles – for which we're envied by a number of other manufacturers. A test drive is simply the only way that some 40 different characteristics can be properly checked: rattles, interior fittings that squeak, etc., things that can be adjusted and corrected within minutes by an expert, so that the customer's first impression is valid.

Thus, each and every Porsche is literally a used car, with quite a few miles already on the odometer. That has never been seen as a blemish, however. Quite the contrary: Like so many other factors, this characteristic is regarded as a fundamental aspect of Porsche quality. And quality has the highest priority: That was true in the days of the 356, is still valid today and will continue to be in the future.

I think that, with this approach, the production department makes its best contribution to the satisfaction of our customers and thus to the future of Porsche as well.

PORSCHE STYLING

In talking about the art of bodywork construction, the first thing we have to do is define three terms whose meanings are manifold and the subject of a lot of arguments: the designer, the stylist and the body shaper. In German-speaking countries, the designer is seen as someone who "specializes in designing and giving Gestalt (shape) to objects of everyday use." In American usage, he is quite simply an engineer or constructor and finally a body shaper. A stylist is someone defined by a renowned German dictionary as "one who gives Gestalt to industrial forms, especially in the automobile industry." In the Oxford Guide to the English Language, the term "stylist" attains even greater honor: "A person who has or aims at a good style – or a person who styles things."

In his book "The Designers," the author, L. J. K. Setright, quite simply uses the term "body shapers" when talking of famous designers of automobile bodies. And if you really want to flatter the designers, stylists and body shapers, you might define them the way a German auto historian defined Ettore Bugatti; for the Alsatian genius, the designing and building of motor cars meant – paraphrasing Spanish philosopher Ortega y Gasset – "to conceive in beauty" and to consider technology as a pleasant sensation. But that's wishful thinking. Reality looks different. In his controversial book "Kritik am

Auto" ("Car Criticism"), Otl Aicher compares the Fiat Uno and the Porsche Carrera and attempts the following definitions: "One who is concerned with the car for its own sake is a designer. One who is concerned with its associations is a stylist. You can build a car in order to make it a proper car, and you can build it in order to make it signify something... Unlike the designer, the stylist has a model. There is something he can imagine: a certain form, a certain style. He will give his car an artificially added expressive touch. He will give it an elongated hood and soft curves tapering away at the back... He who prefers precise, matter-of-fact appearances to expression of this sort is dealing with design, not with styling."

Putting it simply: The Fiat Uno is "designed," giving marvelous credence to the theory that design is art making itself useful. In that case, Otl Aicher would consider the Carrera a "styled" automobile that is something rather more special by virtue of the shape it has been given. Quoting Aicher again: "The Porsche Carrera is a streamlined creature that wants to show how fast it is. It moves even when it's standing still." Is there any greater compliment one could pay the stylist of a sports car? This is what Ferdinand Alexander "Butzi" Porsche, creator of the 911 body, has to say about it:

207

"I am one of those who believe the 911 to be an incredibly harmonious sight even today. As a sports car, it is compromised by its size. But as a sports car it is also a two-seater with enough luggage space for its passengers. And its engine is powerful enough." In automobile literature, the 911, including all its variations, is honored as a singular feat of styling outlasting all the vagaries of fashion. Says "Butzi" Porsche:

"Form isn't based on fashion. It's really the other way around. I think a fine form can become fashion if it's good enough. Take the Volkswagen, the beetle, as an example. It was accepted because it was good. And because it dominated the market for long enough, it became fashionable.

"The same could be said of our 911. It always got by without any gimmicks, whereas the Americans, with their rapidly changing models on an old chassis, had to rely on 'cosmetics' and on new colors to point out something new. This is something that Porsche has never had to do, as it simply isn't possible for us to work with that sort of diversity in models. In my mind, the 911 is based on a very matter-of-fact, classic, serene concept."

The design of the 911, incidentally, is by no means the result of one single stroke of genius, but the fruit of many years of evolution in styling. It all began with "Butzi" Porsche being commissioned to develop the 356 C into a four-seater coupé – by way of experiment. In his book, "Porsche – Excellence Was Expected," one of the most important on the subject, Karl Ludvigsen remarks that "the completely newly formed four-seater body developed as part of the 695 program represented a milestone in the evolution of the contours of the Porsche 901" (Later rechristened the 911. Editor's note). The nose section of the completed 695 prototype was used for the 911 two years later.

These days, no automobile designer or stylist can just come along and do what he likes with an automobile body or decorate his four-

wheeled objects with all sorts of trendy gimmicks. British auto historian D. B. Tubbs, in his book "Art and the Automobile," sheds a tear for the passing of the cars of the Jazz Age, when design engineers like Marc Birkigt (Hispano-Suiza) and Gabriel Voisin, ex-airplane builders, applied their World War I fighter-bomber experience to the enormous luxury limos they built in the twenties, and when it was considered a faux-pas to arrive in Biarritz or Deauville year after year in the same Hispano-Suiza or, even worse, to wear the wrong car model with that year's new mink coat. The cars of the Jazz Age were grotesquely impractical, l'art pour l'art on four wheels. Small wonder that the word functionalism hardly ever crops up in books about the automobiles of the Roaring Twenties.

The criteria for today's automobile bodywork are much more sober and reasonable. In a 1978 Porsche commercial, for instance, we are told that "the form of a new Porsche body must satisfy many demands. First of all, it must be 'unmistakably Porsche' and at the same time quite distinct from the others – the others from the same company and above all the others of rival make.

"It has to be technology-oriented in two respects: regarding the car itself, for which it has to be the ideal suit of clothes, and regarding the possibilities of industrial mass production. It must be of thoroughbred sports car quality and fulfill the strictest requirements in regard to torsional rigidity, handling, comfortable seating and vision. It has to have exemplary aerodynamic qualities and precisely defined passive safety properties. Down to its smallest details, it must match up to hundreds of laws, guidelines, regulations and specifications of all the various countries that will buy it. And most of all, it should have long-term properties that will make it desirable to discriminating buyers of all possible tastes for a period of ten or fifteen years, without the model having to undergo major retouching."

208

Obviously, there is little room here for the overly creative. And even with all of these restrictions, the Porsche look must be preserved. Anatole C. Lapine, director Style-Porsche, describes this unmistakable look as follows:

"Traditionally, Porsches have bumpers sprayed the same color as the car; a nose section without any notable openings for cooling oil or water, even in water-cooled models with the engine in the front; they always have very low hoods, thus avoiding all obstructions to the driver's field of view; and for years, the body of the car has been aerodynamically sound.

Porsches were able to get along with very little chrome trim at a time when rival makes still had to rely on it to identify their products. Today, there are hardly any automakers that haven't followed our example of using dark ornamental moldings, not to mention dark windshield wipers."

Designers or stylists are always being suspected of having to diminish their creativity in order to satisfy the engineers and of having to let their imaginations be shackled by technical requirements. Taking the 928 and its subsequent developments as an example, one can see that, ideally, engineers and body shapers can function like two adjoining tubes.

Says Anatole C. Lapine: "We at Porsche thought it was logical and right to now build automobiles that entireley measured up to the strict safety requirements. We who had to form the cars were given the task of dressing technology in a new suit of clothes and moving body design in the direction of safety. One point of much controversy was the absence of bumpers on the 928. We're very proud of our radical solution: We skipped the 'integrated' bumper stage and turned the body itself into bumpers.

When the Porsche share-holders first saw the plasticine model of the 928, they said: 'What a great car that will be once it has bumpers!' Here we found a highly functional solution that's also aesthetically pleasing. In this case, our engineers respected the wishes of the styling department. We asked them if it was possible to build the body in a way that would enable it to function as a bumper itself in the 'classic' bumper area, without suffering any harm. And it was possible.

"This rolling the ball to one another has for instance been continued in the 944 Turbo. Its nose section was technically and visually redesigned to provide optimal air inlets for charge-air cooling, engine water cooling, engine oil cooling and ram-air cooling of the front wheel brakes. Additional high-beam headlights, fog lamps and parking lights are installed in the shock-absorbing plastic nose section.

"There's a further example for the creative interchange between engineering and styling. We'd always appreciated the fact that in our air-cooled rear-engine cars we could design a nose section that managed without huge air inlet openings. Then, when watercooling came along in our front-engine cars, we had to ask our engineers for two things.

"First, we wanted to have the hood so low that the view ahead would be as unimpeded as in a rear-engine car. The engineers fulfilled this wish by putting in a V-8 engine that didn't spoil the view. Second, we didn't want any apertures in the front, at least no large ones. As a result, even those for the water cooling were kept exceedingly small, which at the same time helped the aerodynamics and was aesthetically pleasing."

Porsche aesthetics have taken on a mythical aura. The advertising department in Stuttgart talks about "love at second sight." There is no Porsche, they say, that immediately pleases the eye. That which appeals at first sight usually doesn't last for more than 15 years. Every time a new Porsche appears in the showrooms, Porsche fans sentimentally bemoan the passing of the previous model. Even within the company, sides are taken. Only since a 911 body has been put up in the Museum of Modern Art in New York as an exemplary masterpiece of industrial design, have 356 fans started to cool down a little.

"Introducing the 928 was one hell of a job," remembers Hans Klauser, former Porsche general service manager. This particular 8-cylinder car had a rear section that put an end to a lot of Porsche clichés. The 911, "still a fascinating beast" (Hans Klauser), emits a sort of ascetic virility and signaled good standing as far as sex was concerned. Many machos among 911 drivers associated the 928's wide hips with "femininity," "softness" and "motherliness."

Well, just as in politics, you can sit back and wait for success in new-car design. By now, the 928's more muscular brother, the 944, has become Porsche's absolutely most successful car; the 928 S consolidated its position as the world's fastest sports touring car long ago. The fact that it didn't encumber itself with provocative bumpers served to irritate all those who like to burden their cars with symbolism. Massive bumpers were regarded as a sign of strength, as a sort of symbolical minefield. My car is my castle. Along comes Porsche to put an end to these antiquated defense systems, cheekily turning the body itself into the bumper! That way, preconceived notions are bound to take a beating.

Stylist Anatole C. Lapine has a convincing explanation for the 928 S's by now proverbial wide hips. They're the result of performance specification. "We had a gearbox that partly stuck up into the passenger compartment. Then we had a passenger on either side of the gearbox. Then we had 7-inch wheels on the left and on the right that had to move toward the middle of the car quite a bit when they deflected. And these wheels had to be covered in a way that still enabled you to put on snow chains. So you had one specification necessitating another. I'll admit the 928 seems wide; to a large extent that's due to the fact that it's relatively low cut.

It's proportions would have been even better if we could have made the car longer. But that would have meant exceeding the length of the 911 many times... They only let us have 7¾ inches more. And if we hadn't chopped off it's rear corners, the 928 would have seemed even wider."

The nagging question whether the 924 was still a "real" Porsche was something the 928 had to put up with a lot more. In his book, Karl Ludvigsen also quotes Ferry Porsche's eldest son, Ferdinand Alexander Porsche. When asked if a new Porsche had to be built exactly like the old ones, Porsche said: "Obviously, it has to become a new Porsche that is just as good as or better than the old one, in the same style but not necessarily in the same form."

"Butzi" Porsche is talking here about the transition from the 356 to the 911, but he could just as well be thinking of the introduction of the water-cooled front-engine models. This is Karl Ludvigsen's comment: "Easier said than done, especially when you try to create the successor model of a car that is already considered a classic." In this way, the sensitive stylist has to negotiate between the Scylla and Charybdis of the automobile business. As the Frankfurter Rundschau of February 16, 1985, remarked, "Buying a car is obviously not entirely a matter of cool reasoning. Far from it. With private buyers, imponderables like the desire to make an impression, individual taste, the compensating for apparent personality deficits, and subconscious desires that would fascinate psychoanalysts sometimes play an important part. To the chagrin of statistically-minded marketing executives, the automobile buyer remains a creature that is hard to fathom."

Can these imponderables be countered with aggressive styling? Anatole C. Lapine is sceptical. "You can be sure that we are not going to strain our customers' imaginations and expectations excessively. That would be reckless.

There are about 7,000 people employed at Porsche. That's a great responsibility for us. It would be easy to just change something. It's a lot harder improving on something that's already good. We would for instance go beyond our customers' expectations if we loaded their imaginations with changes on the existing models amounting to more than 15–20%.

"Too many innovations and improvements can lead to dissatisfaction. On the other hand, we had to take this giant step into new territory when we introduced the front-engined models. People were very disappointed; the interested public's initial reactions were negative. The protests boiled down to: 'How can Porsche suddenly build water-cooled engines?' It's not as if we didn't give a damn about our customers' opinions; quite the opposite is true. But we can't always lie with our ears pressed to the rails in order to detect the slightest warning noises.

"Let's face it, the market and the customers just aren't creative. Let me give you this example to show what I mean: You don't usually go into a good restaurant and tell the cook what he has to put on his menu and above all how he has to prepare it. He'll probably try to recommend that which he considers good... And I take his advice, especially because I've been familiar with his culinary prowess for a long time.

"In other words, we are not mavericks. We identify ourselves with the wishes of our clientele. We are prototypes of our customers regarding aesthetics. You see, we have quite a bit of training and experience. The Porsche driver's identifying himself with his car is more pronounced than in the case of any other make. So he trusts us, saying, 'They'll do the right thing, I guess.' We're really in an enviable position just by being able to make sure very quickly whether what we see before us is Porsche-like or not; because if Professor Porsche thinks it's Porsche-like, that'll make it easier for the customer to decide. Getting back to the 928 S: Professor Porsche saw it often enough while it was being developed. And then one day he gave us the decisive 'go-ahead.' Because we had spent a lot of effort for him to be able to reach that decision."

LOTHAR BOSCHEN

SUPER-PORSCHES: FROM 917 TO 962

For over 35 years, sports car manufacturer Porsche has been extremely successful in international motor sports with upgraded production-line cars and thoroughbred powerhouses. The people who were directly involved believe the period from 1967 to 1973 to have been Porsche's finest years in this respect.

It all began with the 910/47 (2-liter, 6-cylinder) and 907 (2.2-liter, 8-cylinder) racing cars that created a sensation in the World Endurance Championship Race of 1967 thanks to their dependability. At the end of the year, Porsche needed only one more point to wrest the World Championship from a competition that was superior in displacement and power.

Then the rules that (as of January 1, 1968) permitted prototypes with a displacement of up to 3 liters and homologated sports cars (a minimum of 25 cars built) with a maximum displacement of 5 liters opened the door to full-scale racing for Porsche.

There *was* a hitch. Since generally only the "3-liter Formula" was expected with the new rules, Porsche also concentrated on development in this direction. Thus, the 3-liter, 8-cylinder 908 made its debut at the 24 Hours of Le Mans preliminary training, but due to the two-part rules it was, in fact, already obsolete, being inferior in high-speed performance. If, like the other companies, Porsche had known in

time that there would be two classes, they would certainly have avoided their detour via the small prototype, instead entering the big class directly.

While all the world was still debating the absurdity of the rules, Porsche got busy. In March 1969, taking even experts by surprise, the people from Stuttgart were already able to present the 4.5-liter, 12-cylinder, 580-hp 917 type in racing trim. Hardly a month later, Porsche even presented the required minimum of 25 of these "sports cars" to a board of examiners. Twenty of these Super Porsches were to be bought by private teams at 140,000 deutschmarks apiece.

As early as May, at the 1,000 Kilometers in Spa, Belgium, a Porsche 917 was for the first time entered in a race. But this racing vehicle, built in record time, had more flaws than a dog has fleas. Even experienced company drivers shied away from getting behind the wheel of this "monster", thinking up a myriad of excuses for being unable to drive it.

As far as the 917 was concerned, Porsche had no choice but to be content with 1969 as a year for testing and experimenting. In the meantime, the racing Coupé let it be known what of the sort of potential it had. To gather experience, those in charge therefore entered a 917 in the 1,000-kilometer race on the Nuerburgring's north loop. However, none of the company drivers wanted to ride this particular bucking bronco, claiming it didn't have a winning chance anyway. Thus, BMW drivers Hubert Hahne and Dieter Quester drove the white Coupé in training, but not in the race. That was left up to the Anglo-Australian team of David Piper and Frank Gardner, specially flown in from London. Despite all the dire predictions, they drove the unloved stepchild to eigth place in the overall scoring and placed second in the Group 4 scoring.

Le Mans in June saw the 917 entering its third race, one of the two works cars that had been entered dominating for almost twenty hours until the clutch quit and prevented a probable victory. In the 1,000-kilometer race at the Oesterreichring in September 1969, drivers Jo Siffert and Kurt Ahrens finally got the first victory.

When the 917 had finally gotten over its growing pains after serious attention to details, it not only took a leading position at races but also decisively consolidated Porsche's technological image. Sometimes used by private teams, the 917's multifarious versions held the upper hand over the Ferrari 512s, Mirage-Cosworths, Matras, McLarens, Lolas and others.

Incidentally, the Porsche 917's engine performance data very precisely mirror the fact that the above-mentioned competitors were always close on Porsche's tail. Whereas a 4.5-liter, 580 hp, 917 with an air-cooled, 12-cylinder, horizontally opposed engine still managed to take a leading position over three quarters of the 1969 Le Mans race, in the following years a 600 hp 4.9-liter, a 630 hp 5-liter and a 660 hp 5.4-liter were necessary to do this.

In the races during the 1969 season however, Porsche was faced with another problem: Developing, preparing and entering the 908 and 917 racing cars proved to be too much for the engineering staff at Weissach to handle alone. The people at Stuttgart began to look for a part-

ner who would be able to lead the 917 factory armada victoriously into battle. Briton John Wyer, who had previously been successful with the Ford GT 40, became a partner. Wyer entered racing in 1970 with the backing of Gulf Oil. He was joined by the semi-official factory team of Porsche-Salzburg (Austria). Incidentally, the Martini Racing Team took over this "factory stable" a year later.

In their first race, the Daytona 24 Hours, Wyer's team with drivers Rodriguez/Kinnunen and Siffert/Redman gained a double victory, and at the end of an association lasting two years, Wyer had more than done his bit, winning a total of eleven races in the World Championship of Makes. The factory's only official success in 1969 was in Austria. In 1970, the Salzburg team won a race, and a year later, the Martini Team came in first in two World Championship of Makes races.

Porsche's effort with the 917 cost the company approximately 15 million deutschmarks; taking the 43 models (short-tail and long-tail), that figures out to about 350,000 deutschmarks per racing car. Whereas the first 917 cost no more than 140,000, private customers already had to shell out 280,000 for a 917 short-tail in 1971, at least 325,000 for a new 917-10 (Spyder), and at least 450,000 for the same two-seater with a turbocharged 12-cylinder engine.

Without a doubt, the greatest success in the Porsche 917's singular career was winning the Le Mans endurance race in 1970. Twenty years before, the people from Stuttgart had accepted their first invitation to this popular race and had sent two cars of the 356-Alu type to France, one of which gained a class victory that caused quite a stir. The Swabians celebrated their first overall victory after twenty years on the scene in a big way: The short-tail 917 in the Porsche-Salzburg colors rolled in triumph from the Zuffenhausen plant right through Stuttgart to the city hall. There was something else to celebrate: One of the victorious drivers, next to

213

Great Britain's Dick Attwood, was local boy Hans Herrmann.

A long-tail version developed by the Sera company in conjunction with Porsche measured 24 inches more than the short-tail and reached a theoretical maximum speed of 248 mph with a drag coefficient of 0.36. The long-tail 917 (dubbed "hippie" because of its colorful paint job) did take second place with Larrousse and Kauhsen piloting, the Austrian Porsche coming in first.

The Sera engineering office also came up with another special 917 version nicknamed "Big Bertha." A body shorter than usual in a 917 K was mounted on chassis No. 917-20, it did however have an enormous width of 87⅜ inches. Although it won the four-hours plus "training" race at Le Mans in 1971, this car did not match up to expectations and only made one other appearance, at the Le Mans 24 hours in the same year.

Having won the World Championship of Makes from 1969 to 1971 (twice with the 917), the Porsche factory withdrew from this particular competition. The reason for this was a change in the existing rules as of January 1, 1972. After this only vehicles with a maximum of 3 liters displacement were allowed, and a minimum weight of 1,432 pounds was required." However, in the period of active 917 entries, a new field of racing activity had been "tested". The Can-Am (Canadian-American racing series) overseas seemed like a perfect place for the 917, albeit not as a Coupé but as the much lighter Spyder. In the summer of 1969, works driver Jo Siffert received a hastily constructed Spyder of this type named the 917 PA, which was technically still constructed like the first Coupé. PA, by the way, here stands for Porsche-Audi, the entrant at the overseas races. Although Siffert only participated in seven out of eleven races, he was fourth in overall scoring at the end of the 1969 season, which proved that a suitably prepared 917 had a chance to win here

as well. This chance, however, didn't come until 1971, as there just wasn't enough time to prepare for the 1970 race.

Once again it was Jo Siffert who caused a stir among the U.S. teams with his Can-Am success from the middle of 1971 on. After only six races, he and his new 5-liter, 630 hp 917 Spyder were already in third place overall behind two factory McLarens. But when the great racing driver, who also drove in Formula 1 races, was killed at the Brands Hatch Grand Prix, Porsche withdrew "his" car.

Nevertheless, in 1972, Porsche continued the indirect factory participation it had already begun and gave the American Roger Penske team and its driver Mark Donohue the chance to be in the forefront with the 917-10, a car developed especially for the Can-Am. For a power plant, the Can-Am Spyder had a turbocharged 12-cylinder engine that drew just under 1,000 hp from a 5-liter capacity! The first tests with this engine booster, which was largely unknown in racing at that time, were carried out with the 4.5-liter engine; right from the start, two turbochargers, one for each cylinder bank, were used. With a performance of about 850 hp, this version scored numerous successes in the European Can-Am Inter series. Porsche knew how powerful the McLaren Chevrolets were, so this "derated" version wasn't entered in the overseas series at all.

After a spectacular crash, Mark Donohue was out of business for several months, and American George Follmer, totally unaccustomed to cars as potent as these, got into the bucket seat. Nevertheless, after a very short period of acclimatization, he drove the Porsche 917-10 to a superb overall victory.

For the following season, Donohue was again available. The 917-30 built for him was the most powerful race car that has ever run a race. Follmer had usually been able to beat the McLarens, but often by only the barest of margins. In order not to take any risks in the 1973 season, Donohue's 917-30 Spyder was equipped with a power plant consisting of a 5.4-liter 12-cylinder engine boosted with only one super-charger. It had an engine brake power performance of over 1,500 hp, and 1,100 hp or so in the car. Not surprisingly, fuel consumption was high; the 400 liters of high-test gasoline on board were barely enough for a sprint race. In addition, the 917-30's wheelbase was longer than that of its predecessor; it had a wider front track and a narrower rear track. And the body was not only longer, but also narrower.

With this powerhouse, Donohue succeeded in winning the 1973 Can-Am series. Because of the superiority of these Porsches (in the meantime, several 917-10's were also being driven by private teams), the organizers changed the rules for 1974 in such a way that turbo vehicles were left with hardly a chance. Porsche officially withdrew and left the field to private drivers.

But without the participation of the spectacular turbo Porsches with internationally renowned drivers, Can-Am with its anti-Porsche rules survived for only one year and the Inter series suffered a similar fate a little later. The last of the marvelous 917s disappeared into the museums.

Not all of them, however. One of the two 917-30's, the entrant car, remained in the U.S.A., where "the most perfect racing car in the world," as its driver Mark Donohue called it, won its final glory. The 245 mph maximum speed attained during test runs on the Paul Ricard testing grounds in France at the end of 1972 seemed a perfect prerequisite to Donohue for setting a very special kind of record: the best performance in one lap on a circuit race track. Up to then the record was held by A.J. Foyt (Coyote), with 217.8 mph. During training on the Talladega, United States, testing grounds, however, two engines broke down. Porsche came to the rescue and sent one of the 1,100 hp engines with an improved cooling system. On August 9, 1975, things went right for the first

time, Mark Donohue setting a new world record in his Porsche 917-30 with 221.11 mph.

But at this point in time, a new product of the Weissach think-tank already had its first race behind it. In 1973, the Porsche Carrera RS (2.8 liters, 305 hp, 6 cylinders) had had a successful entry at Daytona Beach. In the next season, the Carrera pilots worked their way into the phalanx of genuine prototypes thanks to a supercharged 2.1-liter, 490-hp, 6-cylinder engine. Although these silver-painted race-car "hermaphrodites" were never able to win an overall victory, they always placed near the top. By way of the 934 (3 liters, 485 hp) for private customers with an eye on their dollar, development went directly ahead to the 2.85-liter, 590 hp 935.

With their sights on a new set of rules, Porsche did some no-nonsense developing. After all, a Group 5 world championship under the general heading of "production racing cars" was to start in 1975. But the people who made the rules suddenly decided to postpone everything for one year, thereby once again forcing Porsche to take a break. But at the start of the 1976 season, the Swabians were back in racing as promised. The switch from the abstract racing cars like the 917 to the production cars went with almost a hitch thanks to the 935 and its World Championship victory.

The 1977 season didn't go quite as smoothly. Out of the eight World Championship of Makes runs, the factory only won four. Entering just one factory car (2,85 liters, 630 hp) in the face of continually weak competition had backfired more than once. Luckily, Porsche's reputation was only slightly tarnished; none of the important World Championship points were lost. That year, quite a few Porsche teams again appeared and made a splendid impression with their privately built and entered 935s.

Parallel to the 935 entries in the World Championship of Makes, which were only half-heartedly raced in the first place, the engineers

215

had already been looking around for new fields of endeavor. Because the people in Stuttgart were also afraid that the Group 5 series would be canceled due to a lack of manufacturers' participation, they hastily built a two-seater Spyder in 1976 for the Sports Car World Championship (Group 6). The think-tank at Weissach hoped to compete against the powerful factory-entered Renault Alpines in at least a few races for this championship. However, the 2.1-liter, 520 hp Spyder (named the 936) was so successful right away that it usually clearly dominated the races in which it participated.

One of the highlights in any racing season for Porsche is without a doubt the Le Mans 24 hours. Every new racing car has had to prove itself here, including the 936 Spyder. Although one of the two Porsche 936s entered had to quit after 14 hours, the second car, with Belgian Jacky Ickx and Dutchman Gijs van Lennep driving, won by a clear margin.

A year later, Le Mans witnessed a dramatic racing struggle that fans still remember. Right at the start, the 936 (Nr. 4) had had to cope with a number of problems, and after one quarter of the distance had been covered, it was seemingly hopelessly mired in 41st place! But after a breathtaking chase lasting more than 18 hours, Jacky Ickx, Hurley Haywood and Juergen Barth brought the Porsche back to first place.

At the end of the 1977 season, Porsche put its factory 935s into mothballs, built a low-volume series (935-77) of this successful Group 5 car for private customers and, from 1978 on, left this racing car class to their clients worldwide. The factory 935 did make one or two further appearances, but only to try out some new technological feature like the four-valve, supercharged 6-cylinder engine or a long-tail body dubbed "Moby Dick."

In 1978 and 1979, Porsche also kept a low profile in racing, for which it was promptly punished, losing the Le Mans races due to breakdowns and accidents. Actually, this was only the case with the factory cars, since Porsche's clients took all the prizes there were at Le Mans and elsewhere in their 935s and 936s. In 1979 alone, they won over 20 national and international championships, including the World Championship.

Once again, the bureaucrats of motor racing, i.e. the people who make the rules, saved Porsche from having to make a decision regarding its racing future. The 935, still based on the 911 but technically taken pretty much to its limits (3.2 liters, 750 hp), no longer complied with the new rules, which permitted fewer alterations than before and were specifically aimed at limiting performance escalation by regulating fuel consumption.

The first results of reflecting on how to remain in compliance with the new rules were made public at Porsche as early as the end of 1979: based on the 924 road turbo, the homologation model 924 Carrera GT (210 hp, 150 mph), and, as its derivation, three 924 Carrera GT/Le Mans cars (320 hp, 181 mph) turned out for the obligatory endurance race festival in France. It was practically the same initial situation as in 1973, when the Carrera RS had been developed from the normal 911, in its turn evolving into the 935.

Although the three factory 924s stood the 24-hour test magnificently and came in 6th, 12th and 13th, Porsche's clients failed to react as had been hoped. Uncertainty regarding the still unfamiliar new rules caused the private teams to go on entering 935s, which were being continually modified.

Like everyone else, Porsche was uncertain about the future of motor sports, so they went on experimenting with the 924 GTR (the external designation of the Carrera GT/Le Mans), and with a 924 GTP. The latter differed from the GTR in having a 2.5-liter, 4-cylinder engine which, with 4-valve cylinder heads and a turbocharger, mustered 410 hp and reached a maximum speed of about 187 mph at Le Mans. Inci-

216

dentally, this GTP was the technological predecessor of the 944 road model that was to come.

To be able to win again at Le Mans in 1981, Porsche engineers reactivated two museum 936s. These Spyders were fitted with the 6-cylinder horizontally opposed engine of 2.65 liters displacement (albeit with 4-valve cylinder heads, air/water-cooling and two turbochargers), since it had initially, with even greater power, been intended for entry in the Indianapolis 500. This engineering package ensured a solid 620 hp and a maximum speed of over 225 mph.

With the victory of one of the two 936 Spyders, an impressive era lasting from 1976 to 1981 drew to a close. It entailed winning the World Championship of Makes four times, as well as countless other titles for the Porsche make. At that time, the development of the 935 and 936 race-car types was considered to be completed. A new vehicle for the rules valid as of 1982 (with a new group division) was already in the works.

Porsche decided on the Group C and accordingly built a totally new racing machine, the 956. Apart from the stipulated measurements for length, width and height, consumption limitation is a challenge for automotive engineers. A maximum of 100 liters of fuel was allowed on board, which, in conjunction with the refuelling stops permitted (for instance five times in a 1,000-kilometer race), made for a consumption of 50 to 60 liters.

For a Coupé weighting only 1,762 pounds, with a unitized-body construction instead of a tubular frame, Porsche's home computer calculated a power-to-weight ratio of 2,976 lb/hp and a maximum speed of over 220 mph. In this case, the tried and tested 6-cylinder horizontally opposed engine delivered 600 or so hp out of 2.65 liters displacement.

The Porsche 956 had its premiere in May 1982, in the 6-hour race at Silverstone, Great Britain. R & D director Helmuth Bott personally directed the proceedings and got Porsche's first completed Group C racing car into second place in the overall scoring. But the entry at Le Mans a few weeks later saw a result not even the greatest optimists had dared to predict. After a heart-stopping race, three Porsche 956s (the one which had come in second at Silverstone and two new ones) came in first, second and third. One must bear in mind that the development crowned by this success had only begun ten months previously.

True to its tradition of making fully developed race cars available to clients, Porsche in the winter of 1982/83 built a mini-series of ten 956s with the technical specifications of the Le Mans factory cars. Some of these so immediately successful race cars went to the United States, but these were only permitted to enter in the Can-Am series. The IMSA series, however, also known in Europe and comparable to an international U.S. championship, was closed to the Porsche 956 due to another changing of the rules. In the interests of overseas clients, Porsche took appropriate measures, and engines modified to meet IMSA specifications were cleared for installation in Lola, March and other chassis.

As far as the Group C was concerned, 1983 may be considered the year of the private drivers. In almost every race of the World and European Championships, the clients' cars racked up successes. The factory cars remained objects for continual further development. Next to chassis improvement and aerodynamic refinements, the introduction of electronic engine management systems had priority. This new technology permitted an increase in compression and thus in efficiency. The engines' performance increased without a rise in fuel consumption. In spite of all the powers of persuasion of Porsche and others concerned, the IMSA organizers stuck to their indirect barring of the 956. For this reason, Porsche decided at the end

217

of 1983 to supply American clients with a racing car made to comply with IMSA regulations.

The 962 was 1984's model. And although the European 956 and the American 962 are optically very similar, their technological differences are considerable. For instance, one of the IMSA conditions is that the driver's feet must not pass the middle of the front axle. Since this isn't the case in the 956, the wheelbase had to be lengthened by 4 ¾ inches for the 962, which now measures 109.05 inches. This required reworking of the monocoque construction necessary. But in order to retain the vehicle's overall length, the front overhang was correspondingly shortened, which led to changes in overface and underbody aerodynamics.

As far as the engine was concerned, a long debate led to the decision to use the 2.86-liter, 2-valve engine with only one turbocharger (650 hp). This version had the advantage of giving the vehicle a minimum weight of only 1,872 pounds; the 2.1-liter engine with two turbochargers would have meant a 1,982-pound minimum. The engine is basically taken from the 935 and has air-cooled cylinder heads, as opposed to the 4-valve 962 engine's water-cooled cylinder heads.

On October 17, 1983, layout work on the new monocoque was begun, and chassis construction commenced in the middle of November. One day before Christmas Eve, the monocoque was completed, and on Monday, January 24th, 1984, at 6:00 in the evening, the 962.001 was finally assembled. Without the customary tests, the car was transported directly to the Paul Ricard race track in the South of France. An engine fault at the start of the first day of testing only temporarily upset the schedule. At the end of a short tryout, it was certain that the 962 could be run as fast as the 956 short-tail.

At the Daytona 24 hours in February 5th, 1984, this 962 with 21-year old Mike Andretti, son of the famous Mario, at the wheel, occupied the best starting position after the time trials. However, the race soon had to be abandoned due to a gearbox fault and later on, after repairs, due to an engine problem.

In 1985, the Porsche company and the private teams share the low-volume series of new racing cars with the standard designation 962, differing only in the engine they are fitted with, for their entries in the U.S. series IMSA (= 962) and the Makes World Championship (= 962 C). For the same racing distance, fuel consumption has been reduced from 100 liters to 85 liters per 100 miles. This presented a great challenge to the engine electronics engineers who have come to master their subject with more and more perfection during the course of the season.

The name Porsche has been associated with motor sports for over three-quarters of a century – after all, Professor Porsche as a young man took every opportunity to drive a car himself when a sports tryout was called for. Later on, he and his team developed racing cars for a great variety of clients. The transition to the product "Porsche" went just as smoothly as the commitment to racing and rally activity. Enthusiasm for meeting technological challenges head on is as old as the company, and it is only in this connection that the company is going to grow old and at the same time stay young.

JUERGEN BARTH

CUSTOMER-SPORT SERVICE WORLDWIDE

Porsche customer-sport is almost as old as Porsche vehicles themselves. Even in the 1950s, the production-line 356 models proved to be ideal for sports events. In the year 1950, Walter Gloeckler won the German Championship for the first time with a sports car built from Porsche parts. Then, in 1954, the decision was taken at Porsche to build a small series of racing cars for factory use, and, of course, for customers as well: That was the 550 model.

In the years following, a small series of about 100 vehicles was produced each year, exclusively for racing fan customers. There can be no doubt that the victories captured all over the world by these customers played a key role in determining the direction of the Porsche image. Since in the past the racing cars were almost identical – especially the engines, transmissions and in most cases the chassis and brakes as well – it was possible to handle spare parts distribution by means of the normal Porsche in-house and dealer channels. Not until 1964, with the production of the 904, was a special spare parts warehouse built in Stuttgart, from which customers were supplied directly.

At that time, all Porsche sports activities were coordinated by Baron Fritz Huschke v. Hanstein, who was well aware of the lack of young talents on the German racing scene. So, in cooperation with the Volkswagen corporation at Wolfsburg, the first VW Super V racing car series was broken down into parts, flown from the United States to West Germany and then built into 12 chic, inexpensive racing cars by the customer-sport mechanics for the first race in Germany. The high-caliber drivers hired on by Huschke v. Hanstein put on a great show, and in the following years, German racing was able to count on a successful batch of up-and-coming drivers.

But because it was becoming necessary to produce one new racing car after another – mainly as the result of pressure from racing competitors – factory sports were given priority over supplies of new racing cars to customers. For example, in the case of the 908 or 907, private drivers were allowed to purchase only one used vehicle each, which had already appeared in one or two races for the factory team. As a result, spare parts supplies became somewhat complicated. Another difficulty was, that different versions of each model were built, in order to remain competitive with the Ferraris and Chevrolets. In the case of the "long-tailed" 908, there were two versions: The "long narrow" and the "long wide." There was also a variety of engines. Thus, from time to time, customers had to make do with parts already used once by the factory.

The telephone rang. It was 2 a. m. Friday

219

morning and the voice was Spanish. A spare parts order for a Porsche 908, that had had an accident during practice. The race was due to begin in less than 30 hours. A flood of pleas poured from the telephone, in the hope of getting the car back into the race and helping it to victory. Seven a. m. Friday morning in the racing department: The search for new and used parts for a 908 Spyder was underway, because there was no specific spare parts depot for this racing car. By noon we had managed to gather together all the parts required. On the basis of the customer phone call in the wee hours of the morning, we had decided to board an early afternoon flight to Barcelona, Spain, with the required parts in our hand luggage.

The customer was overjoyed. He spent the entire night Friday and all Saturday installing the spare parts in his car and – believe it or not – won the race on Sunday with ease in his Spyder. That took place in 1968, when Porsche's customer-sport service was still in its infancy.

In the meantime, that service has been developed to such an extent, that situations like that don't arise anymore. It should also be mentioned that, during the same period, the customer-sport department directed several rally entries in which the customers did the driving, but with the direct support of the factory. That was how the 911 rally car came into being in 1968, for example, for the endurance race from London to Sydney. The car was equipped with a number of special features for the 6,220-mile run. The most unusual extra was the roll-bar, that extended over the entire vehicle and even included a special screen device over the windshield, designed to catch monkeys, which might be run into along the way. By air and by car, three mechanics accompanied the racing vehicles all the way to Australia. Unfortunately, of the three entries, one dropped out, one finished third and the other fifteenth, but the exercise had provided a lot of valuable experience for future events.

Then in 1969, the overall Rally World Championship and the European Rally Championship were handled by the customer-sport department, responsibility for which was shared equally by the repairs department and the public relations department, under Huschke v. Hanstein. Our small team – with a maximum of five mechanics and two or three attendants – joined in the battle with two or three 911 T rally vehicles. The schedule included the rallies in Monte Carlo, Sweden, the Acropolis event in Athens, the Alps, Yugoslavia and others. Besides the factory drivers Waldegaard and Andersson from Sweden and Sobieslav Zasada of Poland, privately-entered Porsches also had to be serviced and supplied. So it was not all that unusual at the various service areas, to find not just the three semi-factory vehicles in for a change of tires, but up to ten privately-entered cars as well.

How well the assignment was handled, was demonstrated by overall victories in the 1969 World and European championships, and later, in the one-time-only Rally Argentina, which was won by Zasada. In 1969, Gérard Larrousse had captured the Tour de France Rally for himself and Porsche. But in order to do as well against the Matra prototypes entered in 1970, Larrousse needed a special vehicle. He wanted the lightest 911 ever built, and as an incentive, offered a bottle of champagne for each and every kilo (2.2 pounds) under a total weight of 1,762 pounds. Unfortunately, Larrousse hat to content himself with second place in the rally, but the customer-sport department shared eleven bottles of champagne – the car weighed in at 1,738 pounds. In 1970, the first independent customer-sport department, headed by Herbert Staudenmaier with five employees, was established in Korntal, not far from the main factory in Zuffenhausen. Operating out of a rented apartment and warehouse, this department was finally able to offer customers direct-order service on the parts they needed.

In the years following, the service was extended to include the race tracks themselves. Using a small truck loaded with about 1,000 parts and various replacement engines, it was possible to provide customers a sort of on-course emergency service during a racing weekend. That applied especially to engines. A customer could exchange his 908 or 917 engine on-the-spot for a new one, and later received a bill for the cost of overhauling his original engine. The customer service department couldn't complain about lack of work. No fewer than 24 Porsche 911s und 914/6s took part in the 1970 running of Le Mans. In 1971, a total of 33 Porsche starters had to be serviced there.

The same year also marked the advent of the Porsche Cup for private drivers. Private Porsche drivers throughout the world were eligible to compete in this series of events based on a point system, and offering 250,000 deutschmarks in prize money. The first winner, who rang up a total of 50,000 deutschmarks in prizes, was Erwin Kremer. Then, starting in 1973 with the construction of the 911 RSR, an almost ideal customer racing car, private drivers turned the Porsche Cup into an even tougher and more exciting competition. Herbert Staudenmaier was succeeded by Elmar Willrett as the head of customer service, and, simultaneously, as the chief of construction of future customer racing cars. The years 1975 to 1979 produced outstanding developments, in particular the construction of the 935 models. One problem with this racing car did arise, however, and that was the matter of further development. Since, in the years preceding, excellent Porsche customer racing teams had evolved – for instance, the Kremer brothers in Cologne, or the Reinhold Joest team – in World Championship of Makes events, it occasionally happened that a customer car suddenly wound up leading a factory car. The result mainly of tougher competition in the German Racing Championship, this situation might be characterized as a period of total technical inflation. In almost every race new technical masterpieces appeared, which did not always comply with the Porsche principle of reliability and endurance.

The situation was similar in the United States, so the decision was made to include more than just the "Big Two" events – Daytona and Sebring – in the customer service package. In 1977, with assistance from Volkswagen of America, Gerd Schmid initiated a similar customer service operation with spare parts supply and racing service at almost all American events in which Porsche customers participated. That helped ensure that parts authorized by Porsche were utilized, and the chances for success by customers once again increased. In 1977, the total prize money in the Porsche Cup was also hiked to 300,000 deutschmarks – quite an incentive for successful customers.

In the same year, Sobieslav Zasada had once again entered a 911 in the London-to-Sydney-Rally. This time, however, he wanted to handle the servicing himself, which functioned fairly well, but before the arrival of the teams in Australia he was only in second place, behind a factory Mercedes. So once again the Porsche customer-sport department was called on to pull off an overnight miracle. In a matter of three days, a mechanic and myself were dispatched to Australia. Don't ask how we managed to make all the travel arrangements and get visas so quickly, but it worked. We were able to meet Sobieslav Zasada as he arrived at the Port of Perth (the cars came by ship from Singapore). What followed was a very tough week for the drivers and team crews. A total of 9,320 miles criss-crossing through the Australian bush country still had to be covered. Our Australian importer provided us with the crews and a small airplane with pilot, so that we were almost always able to fly right above Zasada and to be on the spot whenever problems arose. And arise they did: After about half the distance to be run in Australia, Zasada plowed into a washed-out riverbed at such high speed that he ripped the entire steering system out of its supports. As unbelievable as it sounds, he managed to provisionally repair the steering housing with wire and limp into the designated service area – somewhat behind schedule – at "Rabbit Flat," a municipality consisting of a single building. Nothing but desert prairie and a landing strip for 310 miles in any direction. Fortunately, the family that lived there, owned an old tractor, out of which we sawed two angle-irons which we used to re-attach the defective steering system to the supports.

Zasada was able to continue the rally, but had fallen back in the standings because the repairs had cost several hours. Because it had already grown dark, we weren't able to take off again, and spent the night in our sleeping bags under the plane, out in the middle of the desert. At the end of the week Zasada finished the rally in fifth place, and we had covered a total of 10,000 miles in the air. We insisted on dismantling the steering assembly, that had been repaired out in the bush and took it back to the factory with us as a sort of souvenir. Our innovative emergency solution was even subjected to a stress test and – believe it or not – turned out to be more durable than the comparable production-line model.

Today we try to offer Porsche racing customers a service based not just on the central spare parts depot in Weissach-Flacht, but also on the Porsche customer service truck, loaded with about 3,000 different parts, which is present at all major international races in which the racing types 956/962 or 935 and others participate. And this service is not limited to parts supplies at the track. It also includes the expert advice of experienced Porsche technicians and mechanics. Since 1982 the customer-sport department has been integrated into the Weissach racing department, so the customers also benefit directly from improved communication with the factory racing teams.

It should also be mentioned that, since the introduction of the new sports regulations in 1982, a total of twenty-five 956/962 racing cars have been built just for customers. In addition, in 1983, a small series of 20 specially built 911 SC/RS vehicles were outfitted primarily as rally cars. Among others, Henri Toivonen of the newly-established Rothmans private team competed in the European Rally Championship and just missed taking the title because of a back ailment.

In 1984, Saed Al Hajri won the FIA title for Porsche in the Middle East Championship. The customer-sport department was especially pleased with that victory, because it had taken complete responsibility for the overhauling of the engines and transmissions, and for the construction and sale of the cars.

Rothmans wasn't the only successful rally team. In Belgium, too, the championship went to Porsche. And after the Porsche factory team had made the decision not to compete in the 1984 Le Mans-24-hours (there were problems with the stability of the regulations laid down by FISA for Group C), the Porsche customer teams were eager to do well in the race against the works teams entered by Lancia, Jaguar and Peugeot. By supplying additional material along the course, the Porsche customer service operation tried to help out wherever possible.

The Wednesday practice session had hardly begun when the first damage occurred. A Bruns team 956 was pretty badly mangled in an accident; even the cockpit was ruptured, although the driver escaped without injury. After a lengthy discussion, we made the decision to repair the vehicle. Walter Brun chartered a plane so that we could fly in the necessary spare parts, especially the sheet metal for the cockpit. Working day and night, the car was rebuilt in the garage of the Rondeau team and with the help of its mechanics.

On Saturday morning, just in time for the warm-up, Walter Brun was finally able to run

222

the first laps in the repaired car. The race itself went very well for this team, which finished in an outstanding fifth place overall. The stamina of the mechanics was especially remarkable – they had to slave away without interruption from Wednesday night until Sunday morning. And although six hours before the end of the race, the prospects of yet another Porsche triumph looked anything but good, the proverbial reliability of Porsche once again produced a class victory for Porsche customers at Le Mans. Certainly a factor in that win was the contribution of the members of the customer-sport department – in particular, Gerd Schmid, Rainer Gohl and Bernd Mueller – and of the Porsche mechanics.

Up to now, only one spare parts truck has been operated on the U. S. market, which is of enormous importance to Porsche. In order to offer service comparable to that in Europe, in the future an independent company (Porsche Motorsport North America) – headed by Al Hol-bert, himself a successful private Porsche driver with great experience, and backed up by a small team of advisers, including Peter Schmitz from West Germany – will completely take over the American racing customer service, which until now has been handled by Volkswagen of America. That will give American customers the chance to direct-order the spare parts they need for various racing cars in the United States, and will greatly reduce delivery times. In addition, a version of the Porsche Cup will be established for the numerous races in the United States. All that is just a small sample of what the U. S. Porsche organization has in store for customers there.

And in the future, European customer service will no longer be limited to contemporary vehicles. A small team is going to begin servicing "old-timer" races, which are becoming increasingly popular. The many thousands of Porsche sport drivers can thus look ahead to a bright future: The customer is king.

HANS KLAUSER / HERMANN BRIEM

HOW IT ALL BEGAN

Hans Klauser has been in Porsche's employ for more than 40 years. In 1933 he started out as an apprentice designer in the firm of Doctor of Engineering h. c. Ferdinand Porsche, located at 24 Kronenstraße in Stuttgart. When Klauser was born on July 8, 1913, his future boss was already famous throughout the automobile industry. The Porsche Electromobile was a sensation at the Paris World Fair of 1900. Ferdinand Porsche became the technical director of the Austro-Daimler factories in Wiener Neustadt in 1906. He designed his first real aircraft engine in 1909. Porsche won the "Prinz-Heinrich-Fahrt" one year later in a "big Daimler" that he had designed, reaching a maximum speed of 91 mph. The era of the famous Porsche aircraft engines began in 1911. For instance, among these was the colossal 9-cylinder, double V engine arranged in three banks of three cylinders each. This aircraft engine had a total displacement of 10.9 liters and a performance rating of more than 300 hp at 3,000 rpm.

Director Ferdinand Porsche received the highest honor in 1912 from Austrian Emperor Franz Josef I. The emperor declared Porsche "the devoted follower and technical director of the Austrian Daimler Engines Corporation in Wiener Neustadt and knight of the Franz Josef Order." Hans Klauser indeed made the right choice of employers when he decided to turn his passion for automobiles into a career. He learned a lot from the legendary chief engineer, Karl Rabe, and the young Ferry Porsche, who was at that time a design engineer and assistant to his father. From 1936 on, he was involved in the development of the Volkswagen – as a test driver.

After World War II, he was in charge of servicing the brand-new Volkswagens for the French occupation forces in Baden-Baden. Thirty mechanics were kept busy maintaining the "Beetles," which were delivered from Wolfsburg after production had been resumed under British supervision. It was an advantage during these hard times to hold such a lucrative job, because the German mechanics were able to bring food, schnapps and cognac to their families when they went home every two weeks. The year 1949 meant a big change for Hans Klauser. Ferry Porsche informed him: "We're going to start building cars in Stuttgart again. Do you feel like joining us?"

Hans Klauser relates:

The beginning in Zuffenhausen was relatively primitive. We had to improvise a lot. Everything took place in a small shop of about 5,400 square feet. It formerly belonged to the Reutter body shop. We took our first chassis from Austria (Gmuend) as a model and started building new cars, or rather "old ones" with modifications.

We rapidly abandoned aluminum bodies. The reasons for this were: First, aluminum was hard to get and second, only a few specialists could weld aluminum after an accident, for instance. This meant we had to switch to steel. We signed a contract with the Reutter firm, which became responsible for engineering and styling of the 356 body under Porsche's direction. Our lofty aim: We wanted to build about 500 units of the 356!

This is the way I gradually worked into a multi-purpose position. I was the factory manager, test director, production and service manager and salesman all in one. The day before Good Friday (1950), I drove with my wife to Wiesbaden to present a coupé to Rudolf Sauerwein, a well-known long-distance rally driver. While returning to Stuttgart we took the longer route to the Gerstenmaier Firm in Baden-Baden. They specialized in luxury cars (the Horch, for example) before the war. Selling the first 356s was definitely complicated and involved. The most important VW wholesalers like Gloeckler (Frankfurt), van Raffay (Hamburg), Hahn (Stuttgart), Krauss (Nuernberg), Haberl (Munich), Fleischauer (Cologne) – just to name a few – were invited. They were asked how many cars they would order and pay for in advance. We made it clear that without their previous orders, the 356 would not go into production. Gradually the wholesalers put their orders in. Fritz Hahn ordered four, Gloeckler wanted five, Gottfried Schultz from Essen requested eight and the firm Fleischauer even asked for ten ... and so it continued.

Amid all this enthusiasm, we were concerned with the problem of whether we could fulfill these requests. But our joy was more overwhelming and we toasted our good fortune with champagne. I was often asked how we motivated potential customers. One way was the Porsche name, another was the styling of the

car, but also there was the "chutzpah" which we presented. Probably the most important feature of the 356 was its speed. With a top speed of 84 mph, the 356 had no competition among the new German cars at the time. And it was also a steady car. Driving on the autobahn at full speed was no problem for the 356, a fact which could not be argued by other manufacturers of sports cars. The basic engine of the 356 was the same as the VW engine. The latter was produced a by the thousands during World War II. We only added more horsepower and decorated it up a little: the engine had proved itself in untold numbers of Kuebelwagen and amphibious vehicles. One can say in retrospect that the VW Kuebelwagen was the jeep of the German Wehrmacht. Needless to say, the 356 engine was not exclusive. It was to the astonishment of the public that we eventually changed the original 23-horsepower engine to 40 hp.

This process was child's play for technicians like us. Handbooks and owner's manuals were put together after we realized the attention our car attracted on the market. We also noticed that the specialists in the numerous VW workshops had to be trained to work on the model 356. I recruited mechanics with teaching ability from the production department and trained them to become service advisers. The guidelines were strict. I instructed them on several grooming points: "Wear a tie, get a decent haircut, always keep your fingernails clean and short ... and act accordingly, because you represent the name of Porsche."

As the one responsible for our after-sales service worldwide, including warranty work, I had some wild adventures. We succeeded in gaining a hold on the giant U. S. market, from New York to San Francisco, in a manner that is unimaginable today ... The legendary importer, Max Hoffmann, took care of the advance preparation; our two after-sales service specialists, Herbert Linge and Hermann Briem, trekked back and forth like pioneers from coast to coast as Porsche's emissaries from faraway Stuttgart. (But my former colleague Hermann Briem will tell you all about that.)

The most exotic market was the Middle East. Although the department responsible for international sales was located in Zuffenhausen, once a year a trip was made to Beirut, which then was still glamorous and known as the Paris of the Middle East. Masses of food and drinks were consumed and talk was plentiful but we seldom got any concrete results out of it. Jordan's Hussein was without a doubt our best customer. He bought several Spyders for hill climbs. If any technical problems developed in the few Porsches in the Middle East, a mechanic was sent by plane. The most important foreign market was the U.S.A.; but soon there were also many Porsche owners in Italy, France and Great Britain.

Our firm took part in the 24 Hours of Le Mans for the first time in 1951. Naturally I was a part of this new activity, as well as the next 14 Le Mans entries. We entered three cars in the 1951 competition. Ferry Porsche assigned Paul von Guilleaume as chief of the Porsche team, while Wilhelm Hild and myself were put in charge of the technical responsibilities. Due to unfortunate circumstances, two of our cars had to be withdrawn before the race.

Guilleaume was testing the Sarthe course himself when the unfortunate incident occurred. A bicyclist crossed the course and was struck. The first car had to be withdrawn. Guilleaume was only slightly injured, but the car was unusable for the race. The cyclist did not survive this tragic accident. The second car also had to be withdrawn because of an accident. Rudolf Sauerwein, who was already an accomplished race driver before World War II, ran his car off the course at the Maison-Blanche curve and was taken to the hospital with injuries. His car sustained heavy damage and could not be repaired in time for the race.

We concentrated all our hopes on the only car left in the race. The Coupé with the number 46 was driven by the French importer Auguste Veuillet and by Edmond Mouche. They won the 1,100-cc-class and placed 20th in the overall scores. The winners were Whitehead and Walker in a Jaguar.

The 24 Hours of Le Mans in the 50s wasn't as thoroughly organized as today. Life was not easy for the drivers, but circumstances were often idyllic and simple. For economic reasons, I shared a double room with Ferry Porsche in 1951. After the race we went back to our room to relax from the hectic activity, and woke up at 11 p.m. to the revelry of the Aston-Martin-team, who were celebrating their class victory and fifth place finish overall.

Porsche's headquarters was a small service station situated in a little village called Téloché. Lodging was cheap and we were afforded the peace and quiet needed to work. I later had to take up lodgings in a small guest room in the owner's home because the hotel room I was in (near the Le Mans railway station), was too loud. We also had to economize at the pits; there was no extravagance involved compared to the present. That time Mrs. Dorothea Porsche and Ursula v. Hanstein made the sandwiches for the drivers and mechanics, and journalists who were sports fans, such as Paul Frère and Rainer Guenzler (who has since passed away), helped keep time.

Ferry Porsche always took the route where the gourmet restaurants were when we drove to Le Mans together ... It can be said today that the French whistled when we won a class victory ... Another thing can be said: Ferry Porsche and myself had smuggled money into France by sewing the cash inside our ties ...

Le Mans turned into a merciless test which brought satisfaction to us. The 356 with the number 46 endured 24 hours non-stop at full speed while the Cunninghams, modified V-8 Chryslers, soon lost power and could only be driven in first gear. The Porsche team spirit got an enormous boost from our class victory in 1951. Porsches were also overall winners in the Liège–Rome–Liège Rally, the "rally of rallies," in 1952, 1954 and 1957. And in the Targa-Florio our cars scored repeated victories: in 1956, 1959, 1960 and an unbroken victory skein from 1963 to 1970.

These Targa-Florio triumphs for Porsche are reminiscent of the celebrated success of the Mercedes developed by Paul Daimler and perfected by Ferdinand Porsche in 1924: The overall winner with Christian Werner driving. Upon his return to Stuttgart hundreds of thousands cheered him in the streets and all the church bells were ringing.

It is noted in the Porsche's annals: „The Wuerttemberg Technical University in Stuttgart awarded Ferdinand Porsche, Dr. of Engineering h. c. (director and executive board member of the Daimler Corporation), the honorary degree of Doctor of Engineering. He was honored for his excellent achievement in automotive engineering in general and especially as the design engineer of the car that won the Targa-Florio in 1924."

I attended every important German racing event up to the 60s, especially at the Nuerburgring. I later concentrated my attention only on the Le Mans races. Ferry Porsche had questioned the necessity of his presence at Le Mans. The reason for this was the beginning of a big change in Zuffenhausen: The 911 was under development. It meant a turning point for all of us. As Porsche's general service manager, I was of course asked what criteria this car would have to meet. "Naturally, easy to repair," was my reply, to which the mechanics retorted, "You won't have to repair this car." My reaction to this was "That would be nice..." (My basic expectation from my friends in Weissach has always been that our cars should receive the same service in North Dakota as in Tierra del Fuego. And if that cannot be achieved, you can forget about it!)

According to the opinion of many auto fans, a real engine has at least six cylinders. The Porsche fans were content when we produced the model 911 with a 6-cylinder, again with an air-cooled rear engine. This car reflected the wishes and demands customers had expressed for years...

The 911 had more power, more room and a narrower shape than the 356 (despite its successes), which resembled a "Bavarian laundry woman" from the rear. The changeover to the 911 was difficult, despite its advantages. We had to put a lot of effort into training the mechanics in the service centers to work on the new engine. Only in this way could we keep our customers satisfied. To answer a question often asked: The 911 concept was not based on scientific marketing research. Our only considerations were the wishes and dreams of the customers.

The 911 was not only a technical challenge for us, but for the drivers as well: The first models of the 911 series dictated to the driver how they should be handled, not vice versa. These cars soon developed the reputation of behaving like headstrong horses that could only be tamed with force. Stories were told of these Porsche drivers: Tough lads and men who needed to prove themselves; older Porsche drivers worked hard to impress their very young girl friends. Psychologists soon referred to this car as the "sexy 911," with which men could satisfy their most secret libidinal fantasies driving in the speed lane...

It was also hard to pit the 928 against the 911 because 911 drivers considered themselves a kind of knightly order. And yet, it was not intended for the 928 to replace the 911, but instead to offer a new variety of Porsche feeling. But when a 911 fan switches over to the 928 S and drives from Stuttgart to Hamburg – with the stereo blaring – he gets out of the car at the "Jungfernstieg" completely relaxed... and prejudices are put aside. The 928 S is an exception-

227

ally fine car and the 911 is still a fascinating beast.

In my years as general service manager, I have often been asked why people buy a Porsche. And why it has to be a Turbo, for instance, which costs more than 100,000 deutschmarks. People who buy these cars are far from being conventional drivers. In order to drive from point A to point B, it is not necessary to drive a Porsche, Jaguar, Ferrari, Mercedes 500 SE, Aston-Martin. A reliable, inexpensive and quiet car with four wheels will suffice. Nevertheless, there are more than 50,000 people a year who buy Porsches with 4-, 6- or 8-cylinder engines.

When asked why people buy Porsches, I have always given the following example: The price of a Timex watch is between 200 and 300 deutschmarks, a Rolex costs between 4,000 and 5,000 deutschmarks and a Cartier set in diamonds, about 15,000 deutschmarks. They all tell the same time. But still...

Or take people who only wear custom tailored suits which cost 2,000 to 3,000 deutschmarks. Exclusive ready-made clothes cost 600–700 deutschmarks, and still...

Or: Why do people buy race horses? Or bicycles made of titanium, which cost 10,000 deutschmarks? Is it because they only weigh a few pounds less? And why do gray-haired men over 50 believe that a Porsche will make it easier for them to get younger women – which wouldn't do any good anyway.

I believe that driving a Porsche is deeply psychological, which is why there are very few convincing answers to the meaning of the Porsche philosophy.

When Porsche made the decision to get into the American market in a big way a few of the most experienced and capable after-sales specialists from Zuffenhausen led the westward march. Hermann Briem was one of them. Here is his story:

Hermann Briem, experienced master automotive mechanic, was for many years race mechanic, service specialist, troubleshooter and chief of the repair section in Zuffenhausen. He was on the road for many years serving Porsche in Europe and the United States and is one of the pioneers of Porsche.

The year 1921, in which he was born, was full of breakthroughs: Dr. Ferdinand Porsche introduced to the public his Austro-Daimler "Sascha," a sensation for the times; Fritz Rumpler astounded the car experts with his streamlined "teardrop" car; Friedrich Bergius succeeded in making synthetic gasoline from coal, and Albert Einstein won the Nobel Prize in physics.

For as long as he can remember, Hermann Briem has been a car buff. He started in 1935 as an apprentice auto mechanic with a company that handled cars and motorcycles made by Auto-Union, NSU-Fiat, NSU and DKW. The great passion of all young Germans at that time was motor sports. Most of all, there was a lot to marvel at in the Stuttgart area: Numerous races on the Solitude circuit and test drives of the Mercedes-Benz Silver Arrows on the autobahn. Excursions to the legendary Nuerburgring were out of reach of an apprentice who took home 2.50 reichsmarks a week. Hermann Briem could only experience the races at the "Green Hell," as the Nuerburgring was called, on his radio.

In 1938, Hermann Briem put off his journeyman examination and got his driver's license. When the war broke out he was lying in the hospital: While test driving a motorcycle he had been involved in a bad accident. After months in the hospital and numerous operations he was finally released. Two years later he was drafted and came through the war without any serious ill effects. He was taken prisoner of war near the Remagen Bridge in April 1945.

Soon after his release from a POW camp he is able to resume his job at the company where he started his apprenticeship. His ambition is to become a master mechanic, so he looks for a job that will give him time to study for the master mechanic's test on the side. He becomes a chauffeur at the Finance Ministry in Stuttgart, gets his master mechanic's license, and has his hopes set on a job with Daimler-Benz because the staff car he drives is a Mercedes 170V.

But something sensational happens one day on one of his job-related drives: His Mercedes is passed by a low-slung silver-gray sports coupé on the autobahn from Karlsruhe to Stuttgart. The car shoots by the 170V like a phantom. Briem has never seen this type of car at full speed before, but he recognizes it from press photos, it must be the new Porsche. This encounter with one of the first 356 models will change the life of Hermann Briem decisively.

He applies for a job with Porsche. Hans Klauser interviews him for the job. Briem proudly produces his master mechanic's certificate and expresses his wish to work for Porsche. Hans Klauser replies matter-of-factly: "We don't need master mechanics and we don't need certificates, we only need people who can work." Aside from that, the 1.50 deutschmark per hour wage the young mechanic is asking for is too high. They don't reach an agreement – but a few months later, Briem receives a card which informs him that he can start work for Porsche on October 1, 1950. His pay: 1.50 deutschmarks per hour.

Hermann Briem relates:

Naturally, I was proud. The name Porsche meant something special to me, most of all because of the Auto-Union race cars before World War II. My first job was taking charge of the aluminum bodies that were brought in from Gmuend. Porsche registered for the Le Mans Race in 1951, and we had to begin preparing for the demanding race well in advance. Soon I was named the first race mechanic. How successful the Porsche cars were in Le Mans, is related in another part of this book.

I was a race mechanic until 1954, preparing cars for competition and servicing them. Actually, I was a "jack-of-all-trades" for tests and race entries. This time period also became a difficult test for me. This is probably the reason why I was transferred to the after-sales service department in 1954. Together with my colleague, Gustav Woelfle, I conducted training courses in after-sales service. Because we did a good job, we were promoted to field service specialists.

Woelfle and I covered all of Western Europe, which would be unthinkable today. Woelfle was in charge of Northern Europe, which included Scandinavia, whereas my presence was always required in the European regions south of the Main River, i.e. Switzerland, Austria, Italy, France ... But it did not compare with my colleague Herbert Linge's region: the U. S. A. from the East to the West Coast! It was no wonder that he desperately asked for reinforcements from Zuffenhausen.

I was consequently assigned to the U.S.A. for an initial three-month probationary period. I quickly learned a smattering of English, and left for New York in January 1956, accompanied by Herbert Linge. Incidentally, my job change went according to the usual Porsche pattern: "We intend to send you to the U. S. A. Discuss it with your wife und let us know by tomorrow. It will be for a trial period of three months." No beating about the bush, you were just thrown in the water to sink or swim.

Three Porsche specialists had already been hired by American Porsche dealers as regional "missionaries": Sigmund Mayerlen in Sebring, Harry Weber in San Francisco, Erich Bucklers and Rolf Wuetherich in L.A. (who was a passenger in James Dean's Porsche Spyder, in which the actor was killed September 30th, 1955, on Highway 466).

The American Porsche owners needed troubleshooters who could assist them in any area, and who also possessed technological

229

know-how in dealing with Porsche cars. We mapped out our strategy in Max Hoffmann's New York office. Soon after my arrival, Herbert Linge returned to Stuttgart; the second man who followed was my colleague, Herbert Tramm. We split the U. S. A. region between us: He took over the eastern region, and I was responsible for the whole region west of the Mississippi, with headquarters in Los Angeles with the West Coast importer Johnny von Neumann.

Before that I had started some kind of after-sales service school with Herbert Linge in New York. We used a room to improvise with sets of machines and invited mechanics from as far away as Chicago and Miami. At that time there were about 3,000 Porsches in the U. S. A., about half of them in California and some 300 in the greater New York area. Although the transfiguration of Porsche's image was a bit romanticized, I was immediately impressed by the legendary reputation Porsche had already acquired in the U. S. A. For instance, the prevailing story was that Porsche cars were produced in small workshops, by a few hardy mechanics somewhere in the Black Forest, "Autos all made by hand!"

The American Porsche customers differed a lot from German Porsche customers: In the 50s, Porsche buyers in Germany consisted mainly of members of the nobility and high society. Whereas, in the U. S. A., the buyers were not the so-called well-to-do but technicians, engineers, pilots, doctors ... and most of them with German ancestors.

On the one hand they were, as individualists, fascinated by the car's high technology; on the other hand, they took their Porsche as a perfect example of the "made in Germany" hallmark. The Porsche was considered a jewel of the Old World. Anybody who was interested in engineering and at the same time valued reliability, dreamed of owning a Porsche. But the amateur auto sports enthusiasts too, were crazy about Porsche. Racing with a Porsche as a

hobby was not very expensive because there were very few repairs involved. Fuel consumption was low, and there was a comprehensive six-month warranty. Incidentally, I was responsible for handling warranty claims.

Porsche troubleshooters in the U. S. A. in the 50s, like Herbert Linge and myself, certainly belonged to the last and most envied adventurers of the auto industry. We were instructed to be extremely frugal, turn each dollar twice, and still be quick and highly effective – all that in spite of the gigantic distances of the New World!

I loaded my Chevy Bel-Air station wagon to the brim with all sorts of spare parts when I headed from New York to California. I made detours through a number of states and combed the Porsche garages. I spent four weeks alone in Houston, Texas, overhauling a Spyder engine, gearbox and chassis. In some cases, I was on the road for three days just for one single repair: One day to get to my destination, one day for repairs (training of the mechanics included), and one day to get back. Porsche owners were always highly impressed when a Zuffenhausen specialist showed up. A helping hand was appreciated, and especially tips that were passed on to the American mechanics.

After three months of work in the U. S. A., I realized that we needed more extensive time to get a grasp on the service for the American market. It was for this reason I extented my stay, and in December 1956, my wife and two children followed me to the U. S. A. We bought a house in North Hollywood. I did this by driving around the neighborhood looking for a place to rent. I saw one that I liked very much, and the owner noticed my interest in his house. The conversation didn't last long. I didn't rent his house, I bought it! It takes a lifetime to make such a decision back home. But the clocks tick differently in America, especially in California.

Or can anyone in Germany imagine a Porsche-driving film star who comes in the shop to demonstrate how fast he can draw a pistol? I experienced it with Steve McQueen, who unfortunately passed away too soon. Steve was not only a Porsche fan (he drove a black speedster with central wheel locking system), he was also crazy about pistols. He got a kick out of challenging us with his Colt 34. He practiced with his Colt in front of a mirror three hours daily: a fast draw, spin the pistol around his forefinger like John Wayne, etc. He often practiced the following exercise with us: "Hold your hands waist-high, about three feet apart! Someone give the word, and before you can clap your hands, I'll have my Colt between them! That's how fast I am!" But Steve soon was unable to take part even in small races anymore – the film company he worked for had forbidden him to race.

The key word was: racing. It was clear that besides our regular service job, we had to be present at some important race every weekend. We were there to service the top drivers. For example, Jack McAffee (1956 American sports car champion), or Eddi Crawford from Illinois, or Ken Miles. With the increasing Porsche successes, drivers started turning up in our garages, who later became famous on the international Grand Prix circuit (even though many drove other makes): Phil Hill (1961 World Champion), Richie Ginther, Dan Gurney (who won the 1962 Rouen Grand Prix in a Porsche) – to name only a few.

Porsche garages attracted the connoisseurs like bees drawn to honey. They could get their Zuffenhausen cars optimally tuned and have a small touch-up job done. The engines were taken apart, intake ports were rubbed to a polish shine for better flow. This method enabled the Porsche engine to be jacked up to an extra 5 hp, which at 50 hp meant an increase of 10 %.

On the various race circuits of the U. S. A. Porsches behaved like foxes in a chicken coop: They evoked consternation among the bulky British, Italian and American makes with con-siderably greater engine displacement. If, for example, Briggs Swift Cunningham showed up with his fleet of Jaguars and spotted Linge and me with our Stetsons, he smelled trouble ahead for his flashy, big-engined racers. This annoyed Cunningham and caused him to make sarcastic remarks such as: "If you throw a Beetle or a Porsche on a scrap heap and pick it up the next day, it's still running." In order to participate in the more important races, an American Porsche race car driver, who was not a millionaire, had to overcome many obstacles. Californians would load their Porsches on trucks, and cross the country to get to Sebring, which took many days to drive. From there, they would then drive to the Elkhart Lake Circuit, which was situated north of Chicago.

Porsche cars stirred excitement in the so-called Handicap Races – Group F races – modified group up to 1.5-liter engines. The first three finishers from the modified group were allowed to race in the large class and here also our small Spyders entered in the top group along with the bigger cars occasionally won. In the 1958/59 seasons, the small cars were excluded, at least in California, because the sponsors of big cars didn't like the fact that the "little" Porsches were showing up their big bombers.

An interesting sidelight: During the Group F races, English makes like the Triumph, MG and Lotus principally participated beside Porsche. The big classes were also dominated by cars from the Old World: Jaguar, Ferrari, Maserati, Aston Martin, 300 SL "gull wing," etc. Participants in these semi-amateur races did not win much. Price money was first given out at the end of 1958 and beginning of 1959.

Nevertheless, no matter how fascinating working for Porsche was in the U. S. A. – it took its toll. My health, most of all my nervous system, was not in the best shape after three years. Since the children also had to be enrolled in school, we decided to return to Germany. Just how hard this exciting job of after-sales service representative in the U. S. A. was can be noted in the 150,000 miles I covered. We returned on April 1, 1959, shortly after my friend Kenneth Miles (one of the most successful American Porsche race car drivers), achieved the biggest success up to that time with a Spyder – the overall victory in the Pomona Sports Car Races.

After my return to Zuffenhausen, I was soon named senior foreman, responsible for chassis and engine repair shops as well as for customer sports service activities. I later advanced to manager of the Porsche repair shops and in the fall of 1984, having reached the age limit, I retired from the firm.

81

82

77 The 1955 Berlin Grand Prix for Gran Turismo cars. Four Porsche 356's in the AVUS north bend. This famous (and notorious) steep bend was 66 feet high, with a width of roadway of 39 feet and at an angle of 43 degrees, permitting speeds of up to 112 mph.

78 Richard von Frankenberg, one of Germany's most successful sports car pilots in the fifties and sixties, and for many years editor of "Christophorus," in a Porsche 550 Spyder 1500 RS (1955).

79 1959 German Grand Prix at AVUS. Four Porsche drivers in Spyder 1500 RSK's jostling for elbow room. No. 23 is Wolfgang Count Berghe v. Trips (later to win), No. 21 is Jean Behra, No. 28 is Heini Walter and No. 22 is Joakim Bonnier.

80 A Porsche 356 B – 1600 GS/GT being filled up at the Reims 12-hour race in 1961. On the right, is Richard von Frankenberg, wearing the crash helmet, behind the car, wearing the cap, is Fritz Huschke v. Hanstein.

81 Porsche Nr. 500 leaving the Zuffenhausen plant on March 21st, 1951. Hans Klauser is behind the wheel.

82 In 1951, Porsche for the first time participated in the Le Mans 24-hour race. A 356 Alu (No. 46) with French pilots Auguste Veuillet and Edmond Mouche came in first in the 1100 cc class and twentieth in the overall rating.

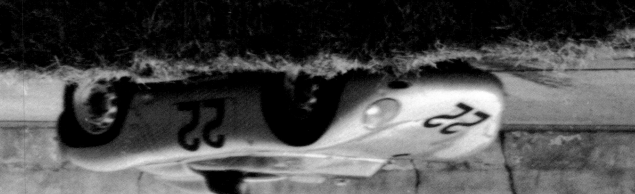

84

83 Max Nathan in a private Porsche 356 A at the 1955 Mille Miglia.

84 1000-kilometre race at the Nuerburgring in 1958. Hans-Joachim Walter and Paul Ernst Straehle took turns at the wheel of a 356 B 1600 GS/GT speedster and were first in their class.

85 Le Mans, 1955. Richard von Frankenberg and Helmut Polensky win in their class in a 550/1500 RS Spyder and come in fourth in the overall rating, with an average of 99,25 mph, quite apart from topping the index rating.

86 Jean Behra in a Porsche 718/1500 RSK on the Schauinsland race circuit in the south of the Black Forest, 1958.

87 In 1958, the Zeltweg airfield races were made popular by German pilot Wolfgang Count Berghe v. Trips, who won in a Porsche Spyder 1500 RSK, followed by Jean Behra and Edgar Barth, also driving Porsches.

85

86

88 The Gaisberg race circuit near Salzburg is one of the fastest circuits for hill climbs. Here is Yugoslav pilot Milivoc Boczik in a Spyder 550 A/1500 RS at Gaisberg (1958).

89 Two Porsche 718/RS 61 being rolled off a transporter to practise for the 1961 Targa Florio. From right to left, Porsche mechanics Herbert Linge, Erich Lerner and Ludwig Schmidt.

90 Young Italian motorcar-freaks are flocking around the Porsche of German rally driver Paul Ernst Straehle (Sicily 1961).

91 The Solitude race circuit consisted of closed-off public roads in the woods surrounding Castle Solitude southwest of Stuttgart. Here we see Joakim Bonnier in the Porsche Formula 2 with which he came in fifth at the 1960 Solitude Grand Prix.

92 The Nuerburgring 1000-kilometre race in 1960, the Dutch driver Carel Count de Beaufort behind the wheel of a Porsche 718 RS/1600 cc. Together with Belgian pilot Paul Frère he was first in his class and fifth in the overall rating.

93 The Nuerburgring 1000-kilometre race in 1961, celebrities crowding around a Porsche RS 61. Graham Hill on the right, Dan Gurney at the cockpit, and Huschke v. Hanstein talking with Joakim Bonnier at the nose section of the car. The Bonnier/Gurney team had to quit in the last lap due to distributor trouble.

94 The 1961 Targa Florio. A 2-litre Porsche RS 60 with more famous faces. To the left, in front of the car, German pilot Hans Herrmann. On the right, Graham Hill with Stirling Moss to his left. Car No. 136 had to give up three miles before the finish because of a rear axle defect.

95 Jean Behra in a centre-steering Porsche 718 at 1957 Reims Grand Prix.

96 Richard von Frankenbergs spectacular crash at the Berlin AVUS race circuit on September 16th, 1956. Tens of thousands of spectators saw his 645 Porsche, "Mickey Mouse," suddenly swerving to the right, zooming out over the highest point of the embankment like a rocket and fireballing into the paddock. Because he was tossed out of the cockpit, von Frankenberg remained uninjured.

97 Wolfgang Count Berghe v. Trips (No. 14) and Jean Behra (No. 12) practising for the 1959 German Grand Prix at AVUS. Behra's Porsche is a self-built Formula 2 based on a 718.

98 Hans Herrmann behind the wheel of a Porsche Formula 2 car at the 1961 German Grand Prix at the Nuerburgring. Herrmann's best result during practising was 9.12,7 minutes. During the race, he had to give up due to transmission trouble.

99 Joakim Bonnier's and Dan Gurney's Porsche 718 RS Coupé out of the race in the twentieth hour of the 1961 Le Mans 24-hour race due to a broken crankshaft.
100 Jean Behra at the 1958 Gaisberg hill climb in a 718/1500 RSK.

101 Before they were run for the last time in 1957, the "Thousand Miles" (Mille Miglia) were the most exciting and most dangerous road race in the world. It took the pilots from Brescia in Northern Italy to Rome and back, exclusively on public roads. After World War II, Porsche cars scored many victories in their respective classes in this race. In 1955, Wolfgang Seidel (left) and Helm Gloeckler (right) made first place in their class in a 550/1500 RS.

102 Michael May, of Switzerland, installed an "air brake" in his Porsche 550/1500 RS, seen here being tested at the Nuerburgring. With this device, May aimed for additional road holding stability and higher speed in bends, without significantly increasing the car's total weight. At the 1956 1000-kilometre race, however, he had to drive without this aid.

103 Two Porsche Spyder 910's before the start of the 1966 European Hill Climb Championship in Trento-Bordone. Next to No. 108, Peter Falk (today Porsche's director racing development) and Porsche associate Theo Huber are talking cars. No. 112 on the right was piloted to victory by Gerhard Mitter.
104 Count Berghe v. Trips in a 718/1500 RSK at the 1958 Schauinsland hill climb.

AFTERWORD

To be honest, by myself I would never have come up with the idea of doing a Porsche book. I had been primarily interested in vintage cars for much too long to have fitted into the cliché of a Porsche fanatic. However, when I showed the first photograph proofs of my book on oldtimers to Porsche public relations director Manfred Jantke during an excellent Swabian dinner in the Porsche canteen high above the roofs of Zuffenhausen about four years ago, he matter-of-factly asked me when I intended to do a similar book on Porsche.

Imagine my surprise! After all, I knew how many Porsche books (of which a large number are mentioned in the appendix) already existed, most of them carefully researched studies, informative reference works written with much attention to historical accuracy. After meticulously reading a large number of them and silently acknowledging my respect to their authors, I was still no closer to putting my finger on the legendary Porsche mystique.

It isn't that easy, after all. To begin with, one must realize that "normal" motorists and Porsche drivers are worlds apart! Porsche cars are a philosophy on wheels; they are vehicles that can only be described with a vocabulary taken from psychoanalysis; they are cars that Sigmund Freud, were he still alive, would have embraced as perfect objects for psychological

study. On the one hand, they are regarded as four-wheeled phallic symbols; on the other, as superb examples of German automotive technology. Both descriptions are correct and yet insufficient for a complete analysis of the Porsche phenomenon. Even the slogan, "Porsche – Driving in its finest form" can only partially do justice to the charisma this make exudes. But I must admit that, after having interviewed Professor Ferry Porsche and Peter W. Schutz, to both of whom I again offer my heartfelt thanks, I now know much about the Porsche mystique that I hadn't realized before.

When I had finished hunting down rare Bugattis, Hispano-Suizas, Duesenbergs, Bentleys etc. for my book on vintage automobiles, I made up my mind. One day, I would do a Porsche book. But one with a difference!

Another experience that brought me to this decision was the 1983 annual meeting of the Porsche Club of America (PCA) in Missouri, where I met a Porsche fanatic who had collected astronomically priced objects and mobiles by Alexander Calder before swapping them for Porsches that now adorn his house like sculptures. Imagine: sports cars from Zuffenhausen elevated to works of modern art! I was also fascinated by those American Porsche lovers who cleaned the treads of their 904s with the same Q-tips with which they removed the lint from their infants' belly-buttons. Was I dealing with madmen?

This almost fanatical relationship between the make and its drivers is an important aspect of the Porsche mystique. Another one is the fact that Porsche has been competing in races ever since they started building cars. In doing this, they aren't primarily concerned with gathering first-prize laurels, but with keeping up their image and international reputation. For Porsche, developing competition vehicles is also a means of testing advanced technology for the benefit of their stock cars. Porsche drivers can take a lot and they're highly sensitive at the same time. Take the 911 with its rear engine as an example. Its drivers, be they male or female, need a lot of forearm muscle. Technologically, the 911 is the product of a bygone era, but it is no less in demand than before; it would be a sacrilege, an act of barbarity to cease its production.

PORSCHE – PORTRAIT OF A LEGEND only mirrors my own personal interpretation of this subject, with the aid of impressive photographs and contributions by authors with inside information. It is neither a book for air-headed zealots nor an esoteric tome intended exclusively for sports-car aficionados or technology buffs. I wanted to demonstrate that Porsche is above all a synonym for "pure driving," a name that makes even successful executives and trend-setters of both sexes (i. e. otherwise down-to-earth and sensible people) totally flip out. Candidly and proudly, they confess to their passion for Porsches. And they admit that the Zuffenhausen power package has made many of their automobile dreams come true. As I believe I can (still) see this irrational devotion to one single make in an objective way, I thought myself capable of producing this book. My task was made that much easier by the Porsche people, who permitted me to give both the 911 Carrera and the 944 try-out spins in Northern Italy.

I am proud of the prominent and highly qualified authors and photographers featured in this book, and especially of the fact that (with the exception of fig. 82) all of the black-and-white shots were done by Julius Weitmann, mentor of a whole generation of sports lensmen. For the sake of accuracy I should mention that I contributed two articles and about one fourth of the photographs myself.

But I must also emphasize that my work on this book was substantially aided by associates of the Porsche company. I am especially indebted to Klaus Reichert of the Porsche press department, who let me get on his nerves for two years and always reacted in a creative and helpful way. His colleague Klaus Parr made himself very useful by double-checking during the final phase of the book, and without Juergen Barth's assistance, the photograph captions wouldn't have been possible.

Regine Stuetzner of Hoffmann & Campe publishers, energetically put copy, proofs and deadlines in order and sensitively directed the team of translators for the English-language version of the book, which was simultaneously produced in the Hamburg publishing house. (This will also be of interest to the German readers; the English version is of particular importance since approximately sixty percent of Porsche's total yearly production is exported to English-speaking countries.) Lothar Boschen was an expert and patient adviser, contributing many valuable suggestions. I am grateful to Porsche owners on both sides of the Atlantic for their encouragement and readiness to help. For the English-language version, Gerhard Koestner's and Norman Zeigler's assistance was invaluable; the former was responsible for the technical accuracy, the latter for the overall correctness of the English text.

Finally, a few hints on how to use the book: It was not my intention to come up with yet another Porsche reference work and compete with similar books by Karl Ludvigsen or Lothar

Boschen and Juergen Barth. All the same, the reader will find a wealth of useful and interesting information, not only in the main part but also in the appendix. The photo captions consciously exclude detailed technical data in order not to detract from the visual impact of the photographs. For these, I refer the reader to the end papers, which list the most important sports and racing-car types with their specifications.

We racked our brains over a solution to the following problem: How should we translate into English the weight and performance data given in kilograms, kilometers per hour and horsepower. You will find the solution we came up with in the aforementioned comments inside the end papers of the book and in the table of contents.

In closing, a final observation about the timing of this book: The original publication deadline was the end of June 1985. Therefore, the careful reader will discover, on the one hand, certain facts and details which are no longer current and, on the other hand, missing figures and results that would have been worth including but that came in after the deadline.

APPENDIX

LIST OF TYPES AND QUANTITIES

Type	Production Period	Displacement	HP (DIN)	Body (Type)	Quantity	Remarks
Porsche 356—356 C						
356 - 1100	1950—1954	1100 cc	40	Coupé, Cabriolet	4,670	—
1300	1951—1957	1300 cc	44	Coupé, Cabriolet	7,085	from 1955: 356 A
1500	1951—1952	1500 cc	60	Coupé, Cabriolet	632	—
1500	1952—1955	1500 cc	55	Coupé, Cabriolet, Speedster	3,869	—
1300 S	1953—1957	1300 cc	60	Coupé, Cabriolet, Speedster	2,669	from 1955: 356 A
1500 S	1952—1955	1500 cc	70	Coupé, Cabriolet, Speedster	116	—
356 A - 1600	1955—1959	1600 cc	60	Coupé, Cabriolet, Speedster	8,367	—
1600 S	1955—1959	1600 cc	75	Coupé, Cabriolet, Speedster, Convertible*	5,981	*) until 1958/59
356 B - 1600	1959—1963	1600 cc	60	Coupé, Cabriolet, Roadster*	18,609	*) until 1962
1600 S	1959—1963	1600 cc	75	Coupé, Cabriolet, Roadster*	6,637	*) until 1962
S 90	1960—1963	1600 cc	90	Coupé, Cabriolet, Roadster*	5,694	*) until 1962
356 C - 1600 C	1963—1965	1600 cc	75	Coupé, Cabriolet	13,509	—
1600 SC	1963—1965	1600 cc	95	Coupé, Cabriolet	3,165	—
					Total 81,003	
Porsche 356 A—356 C Carrera						
356 A - 1500 GS	1955—1956	1500 cc	100	Coupé, Cabriolet, Speedster	appr. 700	incl. "1600 GS"
1600 GS	1958—1959	1600 cc	105	Coupé, Cabriolet (Hardtop)		
356 B - 1600 GS	1960—1961	1600 cc	115	Coupé	40	—
1600 GTL	1960	1600 cc	115	Coupé	18	incl. Abarth
Abarth	1960	1600 cc	128	Coupé		up to 135 HP
2000 GS	1961—1963	2000 cc	130	Coupé	310	—
356 C - 2000 GS	1963—1964	2000 cc	130	Coupé	126	—
					Total 1,194	
Porsche 904 GTS						
904 GTS	1964	2000 cc	155	Coupé	Total 110	—
(VW)-Porsche 914-4/6, 916						
914-4	1969—1975	1700 cc	80	Roadster	118,900	—
		1800 cc	85	Roadster		—
		2000 cc	100	Roadster		—
914-6	1969—1972	2000 cc	110	Roadster	3,350	—
916	1972	2400 cc	190	Hardtop	11	—
		2600 cc	210	Hardtop		—
					Total 122,261	
Porsche 912/912 E						
912	1965—1968	1600 cc	90	Coupé, Targa	30,300	Targa from 1967
912 E	1975	2000 cc	90	Coupé	2,100	USA only
					Total 32,400	
Porsche 928/928 S						
928	1977—1979	4500 cc	240	Coupé (regular gasoline)	9,268	1 car: 3,9 l
928	1979—1982	4500 cc	240	Coupé (premium gasoline)	8,442	USA: 230 HP
928 S	1979—1983	4700 cc	300	Coupé	10,205	USA: 252 HP, from 1982
928 S	1983—1985*	4700 cc	310	Coupé	6,572	USA: 272 HP/292 HP
					Total 34,487	
Porsche 944/944 Turbo						
944	1981—1984	2500 cc	163	Coupé (old interior)	63,132	USA: 150 HP
944	1985*	2500 cc	163	Coupé (new interior)	9,633	USA: 150 HP
944 Turbo	1985*	2500 cc	220	Coupé	54	KAT: 220 HP
*) until April 1985					Total 72,819	

List of Types and Quantities 1950—1985*

LIST OF TYPES AND QUANTITIES

List of Types and Quantities produced 1950—1985*						
Type	Production Period	Displace-ment	HP (DIN)	Body (Type)	Quantity	Remarks
Porsche 924/924 Turbo/924 Carrera GT/GTS/GTR						
924	1976—1985*	2000 cc	125	Coupé	121,672	USA: 100/115 HP
924 Turbo	1978—1980	2000 cc	170	Coupé	8,153	USA: 150 HP
924 Turbo	1980—1982 (in Italy up to 10/83)	2000 cc	177	Coupé	5,275	USA: 154 HP
924 Carrera GT	1980	2000 cc	210	Coupé	400	—
924 GTS/GTR	1981	2000 cc	245	Coupé	50	Sport: 270 HP; Rally: 280 HP; Race: 375 HP
				Total	135,550	
Porsche 911/911 Turbo (930)						
911	1964—1967	2000 cc	130	Coupé, Targa	10,723	Targa from 1967
911 T	1967—1969	2000 cc	110	Coupé, Targa	6,318	—
911 L	1967—1968	2000 cc	130	Coupé, Targa	11,610	—
911 S	1966—1968	2000 cc	160	Coupé, Targa	2,950	—
911 E	1968—1969	2000 cc	140	Coupé, Targa	2,826	—
911 S (E)	1968—1969	2000 cc	170	Coupé, Targa	2,106	—
911 T 2.2	1969—1971	2200 cc	125	Coupé, Targa	15,082	—
911 E 2.2	1969—1971	2200 cc	155	Coupé, Targa	4,972	—
911 S 2.2	1969—1971	2200 cc	180	Coupé, Targa	4,691	—
911 T 2.4	1971—1973	2400 cc	130	Coupé, Targa	13,687	USA: 140 HP
911 E 2.4	1971—1973	2400 cc	165	Coupé, Targa	4,406	—
911 S 2.4	1971—1973	2400 cc	190	Coupé, Targa	5,094	—
911 SC	1972—1973	2700 cc	210	Coupé	1,590	"Carrera RS 2.7"
911 2.7	1973—1975	2700 cc	150	Coupé, Targa	9,360	—
911 S 2.7	1973—1975	2700 cc	175	Coupé, Targa	7,904	USA: 165 HP
911 SC	1973—1975	2700 cc	210	Coupé, Targa	2,184	"Carrera 2.7"
911 2.7	1975—1977	2700 cc	165	Coupé, Targa	18,177	—
911 SC	1975—1977	3000 cc	200	Coupé, Targa	3,646	"Carrera 3.0"
911 Turbo (930)	1974—1977	3000 cc	260	Coupé	2,873	USA: Carrera Turbo with 245 HP
911 SC	1977—1979	3000 cc	180	Coupé, Targa	19,012	—
911 Turbo (930)	1977—1985*	3300 cc	300	Coupé	8,195	USA: 265 HP, until 1979
911 SC	1973—1974	3000 cc	230	Coupé	109	"Carrera RS 3.0" Street: 58 Expl. RSR: 51 Expl. (320 HP)
911 SC	1979—1980	3000 cc	188	Coupé, Targa	9,083	USA: 180 HP
911 SC	1980—1983	3000 cc	204	Coupé, Targa	25,861	USA: 180 HP
911 SC	1980—1983	3000 cc	204	Cabriolet	4,097	USA: 180 HP
911 Carrera	1983—1985*	3200 cc	231	Coupé, Targa, Cabriolet	15,605	USA: 207 HP
911 SC RS	1984	3000 cc	250	Coupé	20	Rally: 280 HP
*) until April 1985				Total	212,181	

Quantity breakdown by types					
Porsche 356 - 356 C	81,003		Porsche 944 Turbo	54	72,819
Porsche 356 Carrera	1,194 (incl. Abarth)	82,197	Porsche 924	121,672	
Porsche 904 GTS	110	110	Porsche 924 Turbo	13,428	
VW-Porsche 914-4		118,900	Porsche 924 Carrera GT/GTS/GTR	450	135,550
Porsche 914-6	3,350		Porsche 911 2.0	36,533	
Porsche 916	11	3,361	Porsche 911 2.2	24,745	
Porsche 912	30,300		Porsche 911 2.4	23,187	
Porsche 912 E	2,100	32,400	Porsche 911 2.7	39,215	
Porsche 928	17,710		Porsche 911 3.0	61,828	
Porsche 928 S	16,777	34,487	Porsche 911 3.2	15,605	201,113
Porsche 944	72,765		Porsche 911 Turbo (930)	11,068	11,068
*) excluding VW-Porsche 914-4			Total	573,105*)	692,005

279

MAJOR LANDMARKS OF AUTOMOBILE HISTORY

Pre-petrol pioneers

Ca 3500 BC First recorded use of the wheel on Sumerian chariots.

Ca 500 BC 'Sicilian' surface oil (petroleum) used for lighting by Romans.

308 BC Demetrios (Greece) builds an enclosed 'war wagon' occupied by two men, one steering, the other treadling a wheel driving the rear wheels.

1420 Giovanni Fontana (Italy) builds one-seater four-wheeled 'sedan,' propelled by occupant pulling on endless rope working a drum and gears (Pictured above).

1649–63 Hans Hautsch (Germany) builds 'wonder' horseless carriages, operated by men concealed within, working cranks.

1673 Christiaan Huygens of Holland demonstrates possibilities of internal combustion by exploding gunpowder in a cylinder, thereby raising a piston and causing a vacuum, atmospheric pressure then forcing piston down and lifting a weight.

1689 Legless cripple Stefan Farffler of Altdorf, Germany, builds hand-operated three-wheeler 'for going to church'.

1694 Elie Richard (France) proposes a carriage treadled by a footman behind passenger's seat.

1771 Nicolas Cugnot (Lorraine) builds working three-wheeled high-pressure steam powered gun tractor.

1784 James Watt (Britain) patents specification for steam road carriage with three-speed variable transmission.

1784 William Murdoch (Britain) builds working model steam vehicle.

1787 Oliver Evans (USA) patents a high-pressure steam wagon.

1788 Pistons on articulated connecting rods first prescribed in an engine by Robert Fourness in a steam engine design.

1791 Nathan Read (USA) projects a twin-engined, rack-driven steam car.

1801 Richard Trevithick (Britain) builds fullscale working high-pressure steam road vehicle.

1803 Charles Dallery (France) patents four-wheeled steam car with change-speed gears.

1807 Isaac de Rivaz (Switzerland) makes a working vehicle propelled by gas electrically fired in a cylinder.

1815 Josef Bozek (Bohemia) builds Watt low-pressure steam-powered four-wheeler.

1823 Samuel Brown (Britain) successfully climbs Shooter's Hill, London, with two-cylinder 'gas-vacuum'-powered four-wheeler.

1825—ca 1840 First steam carriage era brings working vehicles by Gurney, Burstall & Hill, Hancock, Nasmyth, Napier, James, Fraser, Ogle & Summers, Heaton, Macerone, Scott Russell and others of Britain; Dietz (France); Bordino (Italy); Fisher (USA) and others.

1828 Onésiphore Pecqueur (France) patents four-wheeled steam wagon with differential drive.

1858 Thomas Rickett (Britain) builds first of several light passenger-carrying steam carriages, one being used to tour the Scottish Highlands by Earl of Caithness.

1863 J-J Etienne Lenoir (Luxembourg) builds and runs a three-wheeled 'break' on coal gas.

1873 Amédée Bollée Snr (France) completes 'L'Obéissante,' first of several practical, working steam carriages, driving it 135 miles to Paris without mechanical mishap two years later.

1858–1885 Second steam carriage era: vehicles built by Yarrow, Cooke, Tangye, Thompson, Carrett & Marshall, Inshaw, Prew, Mackenzie, Todd, Blackburn, Grenville and others of Britian; Dudgeon, Roper, Reed, War, Carhart, Copeland and others of USA; Ravel, Bollée, De Dion-Bouton and Trépardoux of France; Nussberger of Sweden.

1875 Ferdinand Porsche was born in Maffersdorf, Bohemia, on September 3. After attending elementary school in Maffersdorf and the State Industrial School at Reichenberg, Bohemia, he began his professional career.

1876 Nicolaus Otto (Germany) patents four-stroke cycle, only to lose rights ten years later on grounds that principle was propounded in 1862 by Alphonse Beau de Rochas (France).

1881 Jeantaud (France) builds and runs electric car powered by 21 Fulmen batteries.

1885–1904
The veteran era

1885 Carl Benz builds first practical petrol-powered tricar; single-cylinder, single speed; belt drive.

1886 Gottlieb Daimler builds first 4-wheeled petrol car with fast-turning single-cylinder engine, two speeds, and belt-cum-gear drive.

1888 Frau Berta Benz and two sons complete first extended motor drive (125 miles).

1889 Daimler introduces twin-cylinder engine and sliding-pinion four-speed transmission.

Panhard and Levassor acquire licence to manufacture Daimler engines.

1890 First Peugeot and Panhard-Levassor cars, both Daimler-engined.

1891 Peugeot car covers 1280 miles, following the Paris—Brest—Paris cycle race.

1892 Panhard-Levassor build the first front-engined petrol car.

Wilhelm Maybach of Daimler introduces constant-level float type jet carburettor.

1893 First four-wheeled Benz car, the Viktoria, is introduced.

Ferdinand Porsche joined Vereinigte Elektrizitätswerke AG in Vienna. After his apprenticeship, he worked as a mechanic and ultimately became head of testing operations.

1894 Panhard-Levassor and Peugeot share first prize in Paris—Rouen 'Concours', the world's first motoring contest.

Panhard introduce countershaft sliding gear system.

Frank and Charles Duryea found first American motor manufacturing company at Peoria, Illinois.

1895 Emile Levassor in a Panhard-Levassor with 1.2-litre Daimler 'Phénix' in-line twin-cylinder engine and enclosed gearbox wins world's first motor race, the 732-mile Paris—Bordeaux–Paris.

First pneumatic tires used on a car by Michelin brothers.

Rudolf Egg of Switzerland develops lever controlled gearless variable transmission.

1896 De Dion-Bouton market proprietary aircooled, single-cylinder 1500rpm engines from 1hp upwards for use in light two-, three- and four-wheeled vehicles.

Léon-Bollée produce 650cc tandem-seated three-wheeled voiturette.

First four-cylinder engine built by Daimler for Panhard-Levassor.

British Daimler Motor Company founded at Coventry. Henry Ford builds first experimental car.

1897 First petrol-engined car with two-speed epicyclic gearbox and shaft final drive to live axle made by F. W. Lanchester.

Mors of Paris produce 45 deg. V4 aircum-watercooled car with low tension coil and dynamo ignition.

First front-wheel-drive car built by Graef und Stift in Vienna, using De Dion engine.

Low tension magneto introduced by Bosch in collaboration with F. R. Simms.

Benz introduce 5hp 'Kontra' horizontally-opposed twin-cylinder engine.

With the design of an electro-motor housed in the wheel-hub of a vehicle, Ferdinand Porsche laid the cornerstone for numerous inventions.

1898 Louis Renault builds prototype small car with front-mounted De Dion engine, direct drive top gear and universally-jointed shaft final drive.

Decauville 'Voiturelle' has independent front suspension by transverse leaf spring.

Daimler-designed four-cylinder engine used in touring Panhard-Levassor.

Porsche joined Lohner & Co. and built his wheel-hub-engine into a vehicle which, two years later, caused a sensation at the Paris World Exhibition. During the following years, he was able to score remarkable competitions successes with this car.

1899 Four-cylinder German Daimler 'Phoenix' has honeycomb-type radiator, pressed steel frame and gate-type gearchange.

First monobloc four-cylinder engine made by Amédée Bollée Jnr.

Automatic advance and retard ignition control used by Hiram Maxim and Packard in USA.

1900 Acetylene (carbide) lighting supplements oil and kerosene.

1901 Daimler's first Mercedes car has throttle-controlled engine, improved honeycomb radiator, twin side camshafts operating inlet and exhaust valves, and gate gearchange.

Oldsmobile 'Curved Dash' is America's first car to go into high quantity production.

1902 Bosch introduce high-tension magneto.

Spyker of Holland build six-cylinder four-wheel-drive car.

First straight-eight engined car (two 4-cylinder units coupled together) with single-speed gearbox built by CGV of Paris.

Truffault of Paris introduce friction-type shock absorber.

Disc brake patented by F. W. Lanchester of Britain.

Single overhead camshaft engine with pressurized lubrication marketed by Maudslay in Britain.

1903 Ader of Paris build V8-engined car.

1904 Napier of Britain market first successful six-cylinder car.

Sturtevant of Boston, USA, market first car with automatic 3-speed transmission.

Engine and gearbox in one unit on French Motobloc and American Stevens-Duryea cars.

Riley of Coventry introduce detachable centre-lock wire wheels.

Introduction of Schrader needle-type tire valve.

1905–1918
The interim years

1905 Moseley of Britain produce detachable wheel rim for easier tire changing.

Renault of France patent a hydraulic shock damper.

Pipe of Belgium make twin high-camshaft engine with inclined overhead valves.

The first Rolls-Royce, the in-line twin-cylinder 10hp, is marketed.

First car by Rover of Coventry has cast aluminum backbone frame embodying engine, clutch housing and gearbox.

Simms-Welbeck car is fitted with pneumatic rubber front bumpers.

1906 Front-wheel brakes fitted experimentally to a Mercedes.

Michelin introduce 'press on' tire gauge.

Rudge-Whitworth market detachable wire wheel.

Electric lighting by accumulator becomes an optional extra.

Porsche joined "Oesterreichische Daimler-Motoren Gesellschaft mbH." in Wiener-Neustadt as chief of engineering and production.

1907 Rolls-Royce adopt one-model policy with 40/50 six-cylinder 'Silver Ghost'.

Chadwick of Pittsburgh, USA, introduce supercharged sporting model.

1908 Ford Model T ('The Universal Car') is introduced (over 15 million built by 1927).

First coil-and-distributor system of ignition introduced by Delco, USA.

First V12 engine by Schebler, USA.

Car heating by exhaust (USA).

Formation of General Motors, USA, the world's first big motor combine.

Sankey of Britain market steel artillery wheel.

1909 Aquila-Italiana introduce aluminum pistons on sporting models.

Isotta-Fraschini standardize front-wheel brakes.

Christie of USA build transverse-engined, front-drive taxi with independent front suspension (the Mini layout).

First dipping device by Bleriot, France, for acetylene lamps.

With the development of light-weight aircraft engines for dirigibles for the Austrian armed forces, Porsche made his first contribution in the field of military technology.

1910 Hydraulic tappets patented by Amédée Bollée Jnr.

Porsche designed the "Big Daimler" (90 hp) and won the "Prince Heinrich Trial" with it.

1911 De Dion V8-engined car marketed.

Delahaye V6-engined car marketed.

1911–1918 Porsche engineered numerous large-scale military projects for the Austrian armed forces. The Austrian emperor awarded him the Officer's Cross with the Bar of Warfare of the Order of Franz-Joseph; the German emperor awarded him the Prussian Order of Merit. The University of Vienna appointed him Dr. Ing. h. c.

1912 Cadillac of USA standardize coil ignition, electric starting and electric lighting.

Hupmobile and Oakland (USA) produce all-steel bodywork.

Triplex introduce splinterproof glass in France.

1913 William Morris (later Lord Nuffield) markets Morris Oxford, using proprietary engine and other major components.

Reo of USA employ centrally-positioned gearchange.

Lagonda of Britain employ unitary construction of chassis and body.

Cable-operated direction indicators introduced in USA.

1914 Loughead of USA (later Lockheed) develop hydraulic braking system.

Adjustable driving seats offered in France and USA.

1915 Cadillac market first American series-production V8-engined car.

Packard of USA market world's first production V12-engined car, the 'Twin-Six'.

Dipping headlights and suction-operated windscreen wipers introduced in USA.

1916 Brake stoplights introduced in USA.

1917 First use of torsion bars in suspension on the Spanish Diaz-y-Grillo car.

1919–1930
The vintage era

1919 Hispano-Suiza of France and Spain pioneer use of servo-assisted 4-wheel brakes. Isotta-Fraschini of Italy market world's first in-line 8-cylinder (straight-8) engined car.

Citroën of France introduce American-type mass production methods to Europe.

Porsche, who had by now been appointed general manager of Austro-Daimler, devoted himself to the construction of a 6-cylinder automobile which, later on, was to become a big export hit. The racing cars completed the same year and fitted with 1.1 liter and 2.0 liter engines scored outstanding successes.

New Bentley 3-litre sports car is announced.

1920 Duesenberg of USA employ hydraulically-operated 4-wheel brakes.

Leyland Motors of Britain announce new 7.2-litre straight-8 luxury model.

1922 Integral chassis/body construction, vertical coil independent front suspension and narrow-angle monobloc V4 engine in new Italian Lancia Lambda car.

British prototype North-Lucas car has all-independent suspension by swinging arms, coil springs and coaxial hydraulic dampers. First British 4-cylinder, 4-seater, 4-wheel braked 'Baby' car, the Austin Seven, is introduced.

Trico of USA produce first electrically-operated screen wipers.

Mercedes of Germany market first European supercharged sports car.

1923 Pratts 'Ethyl' leaded fuel introduced in USA to reduce engine detonation (i. e. 'pinking').

Porsche became chief engineer and a member of the board of directors of Daimler-Benz AG in Stuttgart. His best known creations then were the models "S" and "SS".

1924 Japan takes up motor manufacture with the 10hp aircooled "Lila" light car.

The first MG sports car, based on the Morris Oxford, is marketed in Britain.

Introduction of the low-pressure balloon tire by Goodyear, USA.

'Duco' quick-drying cellulose car finish pioneered by du Pont, USA.

The Technical Academy of Stuttgart awarded Ferdinand Porsche the title of Dr. Ing. h. c.

1925 Electric direction indicators marketed by Bosch of Germany.

General adoption in USA of front and rear bumper bars.

Porsche is dubbed a Knight of the Italian Crown.

1926 Two major German makes, Mercedes and Benz, combine to form Mercedes-Benz. Silentbloc oilless rubber bushes are introduced in USA.

1927 Ford USA replace Model T after 19 years' production with the Model A.

World's largest production road car, the 12.8-litre Bugatti Royale with 14 ft 2 in wheelbase and weight of 2½ tons, is announced.

Epicyclic preselector 'self-change' gearbox developed by Wilson of Great Britain.

Triplex of Great Britain market laminated safety glass.

Tracta of France market 1100cc front-wheel-drive sports car.

1928 Widespread adoption by US manufacturers of chromium plating for bright parts in place of nickel.

Cadillac adopt the synchromesh gearbox. New Morris Minor 'baby' car with overhead camshaft engine is announced in Britain.

The first MG Midget, using the Morris Minor engine, is introduced.

Piloting the Porsche-designed Mercedes SS with super-charger, Rudolf Caracciola won the Grand Prix of Germany at the Nuerburgring.

Foot headlight dipping introduced in USA.

1929 Car radios offered as optional extras in USA.

As a member of the Board of directors, Porsche held the position of technical director of Steyr-Werke AG. His best known designs were the Austria (5.3 liter, 8-cylinder, 100 hp engine) and the XXX (2.1 liter, 6-cylinder engine) models.

1930 Shell-type quickly replaceable 'thin wall' engine bearings developed by Cleveland Graphite, USA.

World's first production V16-engined car by Cadillac, USA.

'Fluid flywheel' hydraulic clutch and epicyclic gearbox adopted by Daimler of Britain.

Wolseley Hornet 'Light 6' using Morris Minor bodywork is announced.

British rear-engined Burney 'Streamline' all-independently sprung car developed by designer of R101 airship.

Britain's first quantity-production £100 car, the Morris Minor, is introduced.

MAJOR LANDMARKS OF PORSCHE HISTORY

1930 Ferdinand established an independent, neutral engineering office in Stuttgart, the Dr. Ing. h. c. F. Porsche GmbH.

1931 The first design by Porsche's own company was a 6-cylinder car for the company of Wanderer, of Zwickau.

1932 Porsche began with the development of a 16-cylinder V-engine which, later on, turned out to be very successful powering Auto-Union's "Silver Arrow" racing cars. Also in that year, he designed the torsion bar suspension conceived for this racing car. For Zuendapp-Werke, he designed the small "Type 12" car with rear-mounted engine. The shape of this car significantly resembled that of the Volkswagen to come.

1934 The Auto-Union racing car became a reality and, right off the bat, won the German Grand Prix.

1935 Following the initiative of the German government, the idea for the construction of a Volkswagen based on Porsche designes took shape. In late 1935, the first VW-prototypes were test driven.

1936 Porsche received an official assigment to plan and carry out the construction of a plant to build the Volkswagen.

1938 On May 26, (Ascension Day) the corner stone was laid for the VW plant near Fallersleben. Porsche continued pushing plans for the construction of the Volkswagen. As a parallel development, a commander car was designed on the basis of the VW concept.

1939 The Volkswagen was exhibited at the Berlin Motor Show.

1940 The Technical Academy of Stuttgart named Porsche a honorary professor.

1940–1945 Porsche designed various military projects, among them the "Leopard", "Tiger" and "Maus" tanks and armored cars.

1945 After the end of World War II, Porsche retired to Zell am See in Austria.

1946–1947 Porsche was arrested by French occupation authorities and detained in various prisons in France.

1948 First Porsche car, Type 356, received official registration permit.

1949 The company of Reutter, Stuttgart, was assigned to build the bodies for Type 356.

1950 Porsche celebrated his 75th birthday anniversary. 298 Porsches were built at Stuttgart-Zuffenhausen.

1951 Professor Ferdinand Porsche died in Stuttgart on January 30. He was laid to rest in Zell am See, Austria.

For the first time Porsche is entrant at Le Mans 24 hours; a 356-aluminum coupé with 1,1-litre-engine is class winner and twentieth overall.

1952 Series production of a so-called "ringsynchromesh-transmission" developed by Porsche begins, to be copied under license by automobile manufacturers all over the world, including Mercedes-Benz in their 300 SLR.

1953 José Herrate's Porsche 550-02 wins the Carrera Panamericana in the 1500 cc class. In the Le Mans 24-hours race, Porsche pilots Richard von Frankenberg and Paul Frère win in the same class in their 550 coupé.

1954 On March 15th, Porsche Nr. 5000 leaves the plant.

1955 This year sees a new high in racing: Richard von Frankenberg is German sports car champion. Together with Helmut Polensky, he wins in the 1500 cc class in the Le Mans 24-hour race.

Porsche has become an institution not only in Europe; it has meanwhile gained a no less extensive and enthusiastic following in the USA. Porsche clubs are being started everywhere; soon, the USA will be one of Porsche's biggest customers.

In the same year, the one millionth "beetle" leaves the Wolfsburg assembly lines.

1956 Porsche Nr. 10,000 is completed at Zuffenhausen.

1957 With Porsche's 1600 speedster (built between September 1955 and August 1958), Richard von Frankenberg, Paul Ernst Straehle and Rolf Goetze quite "privately" set up a series of long-distance records in the 1500–2000 cc class at Monza in March of 1957: in 1000 miles at 186,6 km/h (116,065 mph), 2000 miles 186,1 km/h (115/661 mph), and the 12-hours record with 186,2 km/h (115,720 mph).

1958 It's only ten years since the 356 was introduced, and more than 25,000 sports cars have left the plant at Zuffenhausen.

The 1600 cc coupé is priced at DM 12.700, the convertible at 13.900. The season's dearest model is the Carrera GS convertible at 19.700. At this time, there are 142 Porsche dealers in Germany.

1959 Porsche's annual production amounts to 7.055 cars. German president Theodor Heuss in September confers the Federal Republic of Germany's Distinguished Service Cross, First Class, on Ferry Porsche.

1960 Joakim Bonnier and Hans Herrmann come away from the Targa Florio as overall winners, driving an RS 60. Bonnier also wins the German Prix at the Nürburgring, driving a Formula-2-car.

1961 Porsche has by now gained the upper hand over its competitors at many race tracks. Especially in formula-2-racing, Porsche's cars are always ahead. Joakim Bonnier and Dan Gurney manage to be among the first three no less than fifteen times. And in mountain racing, Sepp Greger in his speedy RSK is the one who usually gets the best results.

1962 Porsche's efforts in Grand Prix racing reach a high with the Formula 1 8-cylinder with which Dan Gurney wins the French Grand Prix at Rouen.

In the same year, however, Porsche retires from costly Formula-1-racing.

1963 When the 911 is presented at the Frankfurt International Motor Show, more than 60,000 of its predecessor, the 356, have been built.

1964 Presentation of the 904 (Carrera GTS), designed by Ferdinand Alexander Porsche. For the first time in the history of Porsche sports cars, the body is made of fibreglass.

1965 This year sees the completion of the last of more than 75,000 Porsche 356's. The 911 has been available for over a year.

Vienna Technical University's honorary doctorship is conferred on Ferry Porsche.

1966 On December 21st, Porsche is able to celebrate a proud anniversary: delivery of Porsche Nr. 100,000, a 912 Targa equipped as a police car.

The 911 S now musters 160 hp.

1967 Swiss Porsche pilots Steinemann, Voegele, Illert, Siffert and Spoerry set up a new world record with a Porsche 911 R. Taking turns driving, they cover a distance of 12,430 miles in 95 hours, 35 minutes and 4,2 seconds, at an average of 130,147 mph—on the Monza track.

1968 Vic Elford and Umberto Maglioli win the Targa Florio in a 907 Porsche. The Sebring 12-hours race is another important 907 victory, Jo Siffert and Hans Herrmann driving; and Vic Elford and David Stone win the Monte Carlo Rally in a 911 T.

1969 For the first time, Porsche wins the International Championship for Makes. And again, the boys from Zuffenhausen win at Monte Carlo, Bjoern Waldegaard and Lars Helmer driving a 911 S. The 911 is now available in three different performance classes: 125-hp 911 T, the 155-hp 911 E and the 180-ph 911 S, all of them based on the 2.2-liter engine.

The 914/4 and 914/6 (mid-engined cars) are presented.

1970 Again, Porsche wins the International Championship for Makes. For the third time running, Porsche wins the Monte Carlo Rally. Again, Bjoern Waldegaard and Lars Helmer are the winners, in a 911 S.

1971 The 911's capacity is increased to 2,341 cc.

1972 The Porsche company becomes a joint-stock company; the Porsche family retires from its active management. The R & D center at Weissach (test track construction had begun as far back as 1961) is ready to take up work.

1973 The beginning of Porsche's pioneering development of racing engines with exhaust-driver-turbochargers. Its apex is the 1100-hp 917/30, the most powerful circuit racing car ever built.

At the International Motor Show, Porsche's "Long Term Car" causes a stir. It's a test vehicle with which Porsche aims to promote development trends suited to modern needs, i. e. with an eye on longer life and greater material economy.

1974 Porsche presents the 911 Turbo, the world's first series car with a turbo charger. It draws 260 hp from a 3-liter capacity.

1975 On January 31st, Austria's Golden Medal of Honor is conferred on Dr. Ferry Porsche in Vienna.

1976 Porsche develops an alternative to its "classic" rear-engine concept, the transaxle concept. It is employed for the first time in the type 924 presented this year.

1977 On June 3rd, Porsche Nr. 250,000 is completed. The type 928, with a V-8 engine, appears in the showrooms. The 930 Turbo, based on the tried and tested 911, draws 300 hp from a 3.3-liter capacity.

1978 The 928 is the first sports car to be voted "automobile of the year."

1979 On September 19th, Baden-Württemberg's prime minister Lothar Spaeth confers the Distinguished Service Cross, First Class with a Star, on Dr. Porsche on the occasion of his seventieth birthday.

1980 In a short time, the 928, presented in 1978, has become the most successful sports car in the upper price bracket. In 1980, the 928 S musters a performance of 300 hp.

1981 As a supplement to its selection of transaxle models, Porsche introduce the type 944. At the International Motor Show, a 911-AWD study is presented in conjunction with the newly developed convertible body.

Peter W. Schutz is installed as chairman of the board of directors of Porsche AG.

1982 The type 956 C is voted "motor sports automobile of the year".

1983 Twenty years after the introduction of the 911, Porsche is still holding on to this successful concept. At the International Motor Show at Frankfurt, the highlight is a study for a Group B competition car. Its high performance is coupled to new AWD technology.

The "latest" 911, the Carrera, now draws 231 hp from its 3.2-liter engine.

1984 The new AWD Porsche 911 Carrera wins the Paris—Dakar Rally. Porsche AG enters the stock exchange at the end of April. On the occasion of his 75th birthday, a professorship is conferred on Dr. Ferry Porsche.

1985 Professor Porsche is made senator for Honour's sake of the Technical University of Stuttgart.

SELECTED BIBLIOGRAPHY

Balestra, N., C. de Agostini, Cisitalia. Milano (Automobilia) 1980

Barker, Ronald, Anthony Harding, Automobile Designers: Great Designers and their work. Cambridge MA (Robert Bentley Inc., David and Charles Ltd.) 1970

Barnes, John W., The Automotive Photography of Peter Coltrin. Scarsdale NY (Jr. Publishing Inc.) 1978

Barth, Jürgen, Porsche Pocket History. Milano (Automobile Publishing) 1982

Batchelor, Dean, Illustrated Porsche Buyers Guide. Osceola, Wisconsin (Motorbooks International) 1982

Beaulieu, Lord Montagu of, Lost causes of Motoring – Europe, Vol. 1. London (Cassel & Co. Ltd.) 1969

Becker, Hans Detlef, Porsche von Fallersleben – Geschichte eines Automobils. Hannover (Sonderdruck »Der Spiegel« Nr. 18–22/1950)

Behr, Lothar, Die Autobosse. München (Verlag Information und Wissen GmbH) 1971

Bellino, Vincent, Porsche Parts Source Directory. Clarkstone GA 1977

Bentley, J. F., Porsche – Ein Traum wird Wirklichkeit. Ein Auto macht Geschichte. Düsseldorf/Wien (Econ Verlag) 1978

–, We at Porsche – The Autobiography of Dr. Ing. h.c. Ferry Porsche. Garden City, N. Y. (Double Day & Co. Ltd.) 1976

Bonatz, P., Leben und Bauen, Stuttgart (Engelhorn-Verlag) 1950

Boschen, Lothar, Das große Buch der Volkswagen-Typen. Stuttgart (Motorbuch Verlag) 1983

Boschen, Lothar, Jürgen Barth, Das große Buch der Porsche-Typen. Stuttgart (Motorbuch Verlag) 1977
English: The Porsche-Book: A Definitive Illustrated History. Cambridge (P. Stephens Ltd.) 1978
French: La Reussite Porsche (Toutes les Porsche). Paris (E.P.A.-Verlag) 1981

–, Das große Buch der Porsche-Sondertypen und -Konstruktionen. Stuttgart (Motorbuch Verlag) 1984

Butz, Evi, Edgar Barth, 30 Jahre Rennen. München (Moderne Verlag) 1966

Campell, Colin, New Directions in Suspension Design. Cambridge MA (Robert Bentley Inc.) 1981

Cancelleri, G., C. de Agostini, M. Schröder, La Legendaire Auto Union. Bologna (Editrice Grafiche Zanini) 1979

Clausager, Anders Ditlev, Porsche: Driving In Its Finest Form. New York (St. Martins Press) 1983

Cohin, Edouard, Paul Couty, Il Historique de la Course Automobile 1894–1965. Clermont-Ferrand 1966

Cosson, L., Ein Auto wird geboren – Porsches Leben. Antwerpen (Edition de Sikke S.A.) 1964

Cotton, Michael, The Porsche 911 and Derivatives: A Collectors Guide, London (Motor Racing Publications, Ltd.) 1980

–, Porsche 911 Turbo. London (Osprey Publishing Ltd.) 1981

–, Porsche. New York (Crescent Books) 1982

Daimler Benz AG, Mercedes-Konstruktionen in fünf Jahrzehnten. Stuttgart 1951

–, Chronik Mercedes Benz – Fahrzeug und Motoren. Stuttgart 1963

Deschenaux, J., Jo Siffert. London (W. Kimber & Co.) 1972

Donohue, Mark, Paul van Valkenburgh, The Unfair Advantage. New York (Dodd, Mead and Co., Inc.) 1975

Editions Briand David, Martini Racing Story. Paris 1983

Edler, Karl-Heinz, Wolfgang Roediger, Die deutschen Rennfahrzeuge. Leipzig 1956

Elfrink, H., Porsche Technical Manual. Los Angeles (Henry Elfrink Automotive) 1965

Frankenberg, Richard von, Porsche macht Renngeschichte. München (Moewig Verlag) 1955

–, Porsche Cars – Porsche Tractors: The success of a Great Man and his Ideas. Mannheim (Book Company for Industry, Commerce and Traffic) 1956

–, Mein geliebter Sport. Stuttgart (Motor-Presse-Verlag) 1957

–, Ferdinand Porsche – Der Weg eines genialen Konstrukteurs. Wien–Zürich–Leipzig (Almathea Verlag) 1957

–, Die ungewöhnliche Geschichte des Hauses Porsche. Stuttgart (Motor-Presse Verlag) 1959

–, Autos. Stuttgart (Steingrüben Verlag) 1962

–, Die ungewöhnliche Geschichte des Hauses Porsche. Stuttgart (Motorbuch Verlag) 1965
English: Porsche, The Man and his Cars. London (Motorraces Book Club, G. T. Foulis & Co. Ltd. 1965

–, Die großen Fahrer unserer Zeit. Stuttgart (Motor Presse Verlag) 1966

Frankenberg, Richard von, Michael Cotton, Porsche: Double World Champions 1900–1977. Somerset (Haynes Publishing Group) 1977

Frère, Paul, Luis Klemantaski, On the starting Grid. London (B. T. Batsford Ltd.) 1957
French: Un des Vingt au Depart. Paris 1956

–, Starting Grid to Chequered Flag. London (B. T. Batsford Ltd.) 1962

–, Das Rennen vor dem Rennen. Stuttgart (Motorbuch Verlag) 1971
English: The Racing Porsches: A Technical Triumph. New York (Arco Publishing Co., Inc.) 1973

–, Cars in Profile No. 5 – The Porsche 917. Windsor, Berkshire (Profile Publications) 1973

–, Die Porsche 911 Story. Stuttgart (Motorbuch Verlag) 1977
English: Porsche 911 Story. New York (Arco Publishing Co. Inc.) 1976 and Cambridge (Patrick Stephens Ltd.) 1980

–, Porsche – Rennwagen der 70er Jahre. Stuttgart (Motorbuch Verlag) 1983
English: Porsche Racing Cars of the 70s. New York (Arco Publishing Co.) 1981

Gregory, Ken, Behind the Scenes of Motor Racing. London 1960

Gretland, P., Historien om Folkvognen. Oslo (Teknologisk For.) 1967

Hack, Gert, Turboautos, Turbomotoren. Stuttgart (Motorbuch Verlag) 1983

Haefli René, Verstummte Motoren. Bern (Edita Lausanne) 1969

Hammer, Henry, Charles Kuell, Kent Schach, Porsche Models International. Miniatur-Auto-Katalog 1978

Harster, Hermann, Das Rennen ist nie zuende. Frankfurt/Main (Verlag Ullstein GmbH) 1969

Harvey, Chris, Great Marques: Porsche. London (Octopus Books, Ltd.) 1980
German: Porsche – Die großen Automobile.

–, The Porsche 911. Oxford (The Oxford Illustrated Press, Ltd.) 1980

–, Porsche – 911 Carrera Superprofile. Sparkford (Haynes Publishing Group) 1982

–, Porsche – The Complete Story. Sparkford (Haynes Publishing Group) 1983

Herrmann, Hans, Helmut Sohre, Ich habe überlebt. Stuttgart 1971

Hill, Graham, Life at the Limit. New York (Coward McCann Inc.) 1970

Hinsdale, Peter, The Fabulous Porsche 917. S. Laguna CA (J. Thompson) 1972

Hirsch, Erich, 25 Jahre – Fahren in der schönsten Form 1949–1974. Stuttgart 1974

–, 100 Jahre Professor Ferdinand Porsche (1875–1975). Stuttgart (Dr. Ing. h. c. F. Porsche AG) 1975

Hopfinger, K. B., Beyond Expectation – The Volkswagen Story. London (G. T. Foulis & Co. Ltd.) 1954

Hornung, Thora, Gerhard Mitter. Stuttgart (Motorbuch Verlag) 1970

Hünninghaus, Kurt, Magier des Automobils. München (Markus-Verlag) 1962

Hütten, Helmut, Schnelle Motoren. Braunschweig-Berlin (C. Schmidt & Co.) 1955

Inouye, Koichi, The Porsche 1978. Neko 1978

–, The Porsche 1979. Neko 1979

–, The Porsche 1980. Neko 1980

–, Porsche IV. Neko 1982

Jenkinson, Dennis, Porsche 356. London (Osprey Publishing Ltd.) 1980

–, Porsche – Past and Present. Sparkford (Haynes Publishing Group) 1982

Jellinek, G., Mercedes, Mein Vater der Herr Mercedes. Wien–Stuttgart–Berlin (Neff Verlag) 1962

Karlmann, J., Porsche, eine namensgeschichtliche Darstellung. Verlag Deutsche Familienchronik 1939

Kirchberg, Peter, Grand-Prix-Report: Auto Union (1934–1939). Stuttgart (Motorbuch Verlag) 1982

Kluke, P., Hitler und das Volkswagen-Projekt. Stuttgart (Deutsche-Verlags-Anstalt) 1960

Knittel, Stefan, Auto-Union Grand Prix Wagen. München (Verlag Schrader und Partner) 1980

Kobayashi, Shotaro, Porsche. Minneapolis MN (International) 1973

Kölling, F., Ein Auto zieht Kreise. Reutlingen (Rardtenschlager) 1962

Koichi, Yazaki, Mareschi, Famous Automobile Museums No. 3: Porsche. Tokyo (Car Styling Publishing) 1980

Langworth, Richard M., Tradition of Greatness. (Publications International Ltd.) 1983

–, Porsche – Die Geschichte einer Denkfabrik. Pfäffikon (Serag AG) 1984

Lapper, Hermann, Porsche KG, Liebe zu Ihm. Stuttgart-Kaltental 1960

Lax, K., Ferdinand Porsche in Gmünd/Kärnten. Kärnten/Klagenfurt (Geschichtsverlag) 1957

Lewandowski, Jürgen, Porsche – Plakate – Posters – Affiches. Konstanz (Verlag Stadler) 1984

Ludvigsen, Karl, Mercedes-Benz Racing Cars. Newport Beach, CA (Bond/Parkhurst Books) 1971

–, Tribute to the Turbo Carrera. Englewood Cliffs NJ, (Porsche-Audi-Division of Volkswagen of America, Inc.) 1976

–, Porsche: Geschichte und Technik der Renn- und Sportwagen. München–Wien–Zürich (BLV Verlag) 1980
English: Porsche: Excellence was Expected. Princeton, NJ (Princeton Publishing Inc.) 1977

Mackerle, Julius, Air-Cooled Automotive Engines. London (M. E. Charles Griffin and Co., Ltd.) 1961/1972

Macksey, Kenneth, John H. Barchelor, Tank, A History of the Armoured Fighting Vehicle. New York. 1972

Matsuda, Yoshiho, Matsuda Collection: Porsche Parade in Japan. Matsuda Collection: Sports and Classic Car Museum. Matsuda Collection: Porsche – Museum of Japan. Tokyo 1981

–, Great Cars of Great Collections. Vol. 3: Porsche 904 GTS. Tokyo Y.M. 1982

Meisl, C., Richard von Frankenberg, Porsche – The Man and His Cars. London (GT. Foulis Ltd.) 1961

Menzel, W., Ferdinand Porsche und die Gebirgstruppe. München (Die Gebirgstruppe) 1960

Merritt, Richard F., Susann C. Miller, Porsche, Broschures and Sales Literature 1948–1965. Scarsdale, NY (John W. Barnes Jr. Publishing, Inc.) 1978

Miller, Susann, Porsche Year 1982. Laurel Hollow, NY (Carrera International, Inc.) 1982

–, Porsche 911/912: A Source Book. Baltimore MD (Bookman Pub.) 1984

–, Porsche Year 1983–84. Laurel Hollow, NY (Carrera International Inc.) 1984

Mönnich, Horst, Die Autostadt. München (W. Andermann Verlag) 1951

Moriarty, Michael G., Porsche, Now and Then. A Portfolio of Frameable Porsche Prints. Waterbury CT (Ambas and Champion) 1976

Müller, Peter, Ferdinand Porsche – Ein Genie unserer Zeit. Graz-Stuttgart (Leopold Stocker Verlag) 1965

Nelson, W. H., Die Volkswagen-Story. Reutlingen (Ensslin & Laibl) München (Piper) 1965

–, Small Wonder. Boston (Little Brown and Co.) 1965

Neubauer, A., Heute lacht man darüber. Luxemburg (Auto Revue) 1951

Niske, Robert, The Amazing Porsche and Volkswagen Story. New York (Comet Press Books) 1956

Oswald, Werner, Kraftfahrzeuge und Panzer der Reichswehr, Wehrmacht und Bundeswehr. Stuttgart (Motorbuch Verlag) 1970

–, Deutsche Autos 1945–1975, Stuttgart (Motorbuch Verlag) 1976

Owen, David, Targa Florio. Somerset (Foulis/Haynes) 1979

Pascal, Dominique, Porsche in Le Mans seit 1951. Paris 1985

Pellow, H., The ABCs and 912s of Porsche Engines. HCP Research, Cupertino CA, Revision 35 1981

–, Secrets of the Inner Circle. HCP Research, Cupertino CA, Version 11 1981

Perini, Giancarlo, Akira Fujimoto, Porsche and Design. Car Styling, Special Edition No. 31½ (Car Styling Publishing Co.) Tokyo 1980

Pietruska, Richard, Perpetuating Porsche Paranoia. Los Angeles (R.P. Design) 1981

Pihera, Larry, The Porsche 917. New York (J. B. Lippincott Co.) 1972

Porsche, Ferdinand, Professor Porsche – 50 Jahre Arbeit. »Automobil Technische Zeitschrift« 1961

Porsche KG, Zehn Jahre Porsche-Wagen (Ferry Porsche 50 Jahre). Stuttgart 1959

Porsche AG, Porsche Ingenieure plaudern aus der Schule. Stuttgart 1981
English: Porsche Engineers Talk Shop

Porsche, Tokyo (Car Graphic Library) 1971

Porsche Sport 1974/75. CBS Publications, Newport Beach, CA 1975

–, Porsche Sport 76/77. Seal Beach, CA (Ruszkiewiecz Publishing) 1977

Porsche Club of America, Up-Fixin der Porsche. Alexandria VA Pubs., Five volumes (1956–1980)

Porsche, Exeter Books of Simon & Schuster Inc. New York 1983

Post, Dan R., Volkswagen, Nine Lives Later. Arcadia CA. (Horizon House) 1966

–, The Racing Sports Cars. London (Vantage Books) 1970

–, Sports Car Championship. New York (W. W. Norton & Co., Inc.) 1972

–, Porsche Owners Companion. Arcadia CA. (Post-Era Books) 1981

Preston, C., The Jokeswagen Book. Canada & New York (Random House) 1966

Pritchard, Anthony, Porsche. London (Pelham Books Ltd.) 1969

Quint, Herbert A., Richard von Frankenberg, Porsche, der Weg eines Zeitalters. Stuttgart (Steingrüben Verlag) 1951

Rasmussen, Henry, European Sports Cars of the Fifties. Arroyo Grande CA (Picturama Pub.) 1978

–, Porsche for the Road. Oscedale WI

(Motorbooks International) 1981

Rathke, K., Wilhelm Maybach, Anbruch eines neuen Zeitalters. Friedrichshafen (Gessler Verlag) 1953

Reutter & Co. GmbH, 1906–1956 Stuttgarter Karosseriewerk Reutter & Co GmbH. Stuttgart 1956

Rich, O. Cee, Porsche: Complete Owners Handbook of Repair and Maintenance. LA & CA (Floyd Clymer Pubs.) 1960

Richter, Craig, How to make an old Porsche Fly. Laguna Beach, CA (Porco) 1983

»Road and Track«, Detroit (Nachdruck). Road and Track on Porsche.
Porsche 1968–1971
Porsche 1972–1975
Porsche 1975–1978
Porsche 1979–1982

Rusz, Joe, Porsche Sport 73. CBS Publications, Newport Beach, CA 1973

–, Porsche Sport 72. Newport Beach, CA (Bond/Parkhurst Publications) 1973

Sasaki, Tatsuro, Porsche: Motor Fan No. 1. Tokyo (San-ei Shobo Publishing Co.) 1979

Scholz, H., Herr seiner Welt – Der Lebensroman Ferdinand Porsches. Augsburg (Adam Kraft Verlag) 1962

–, Ahnenwiege an der Mies – Ferdinand und die Tachauerin. Geislingen (Jahrbuch der Egerländer) 1963

–, Ferdinand Porsche – Ein großes Leben. Bergisch-Gladbach (Bastei/Lübbe Verlag) 1974

Schrader, Halwart, Porsche 356: Auto classic No. 1. Brentford, Middlesex (Albion Scott Ltd.) 1981

Seherr-Thoss, H. C. Graf v., Die Deutsche Automobil-Industrie. Stuttgart 1974

Senger und Etterlin, v., German Tanks of World War 2. New York 1973

Seper, Dr. Hans, 100 Jahre Steyr-Daimler-Puch AG (1864–1964). Wien (Steyr-Daimler-Puch AG) 1964

–, Damals als die Pferde scheuten – die Geschichte der österreichischen Kraftfahrt. Wien (Österr. Wirtschaftsverlag) 1968

Setright, L. J. K., The Grand Prix Car 1954–1966. New York (W.W. Norton & Co. Inc.) 1968

–, The Designers. Chicago (Follett Publishing Co.) 1976

Shoemaker, Howard, Cartoon Book. Stuttgart (Porsche KG) 1964

Siebertz, P., Gottlieb Daimler, ein Revolutionär der Technik. Stuttgart (Reclam Verlag) 1939

Sins, H., Autos, seine Leidenschaft. Vom Klempner-Lehrling zum Auto-Konstrukteur. Düsseldorf (Verlagsanstalt Handwerk) 1968

Sloninger, Jerry, Porsche Guide. New York (Sports Car Press Ltd.) 1958

–, The Porsche Type 356. Leatherhead, Surrey (Profile Publications Ltd.) 1967

–, The New Porsche Guide. New York (Sports Car Press) 1968

–, The Porsche 911 Guide. New York (Sports Car Press) 1976

–, Porsche: The 4-Cylinder Sports and Racing Cars. Reno, NV (Dean Batchelor Publication) 1977

Sloninger, Jerry, Porsche 924/928/944: The New Generation. London (Osprey Publishing Ltd.) 1981

Sloninger, Jerry, Hans-H. v. Fersen, German High Performance Cars 1894–1965. London (B. T. Batsford Ltd.) 1965

Spielberger, Walter J., Porsche, The first Decade 1949–1959. San Francisco (Blutmans) 1960

–, Panzerjäger Tiger (P) Elefant. Leatherhead, Surrey (Profile Publications Ltd.) 1967

–, Elefant and Maus. (& E-100). Windsor 1973

Spielberger, Walter J., Uwe Feist, Panzerkampfwagen 6. Berkeley, CA 1968

Sponsel, Heinz, Porsche – Autos – Weltrekorde. Bleckede/Elbe (O. Meissners Verlag) 1952

Steyr-Daimler-Puch AG, 75 Jahre Steyr-Werke. Oberdonau (Steyr) 1939

Stirling Moss, A Turn at the Wheel. London (W. Kimber & Co. Ltd.) 1961

Strache, Dr. Wolf, Halwart Schrader, (The Sloningers) 100 Jahre Porsche im Spiegel der Zeitgeschichte. Stuttgart (Porsche AG) 1975
English: 100 Years of Porsche Mirrored in Contemporary History.

–, Die Volkswagenstadt Wolfsburg. Stuttgart (Strache-Verlag) 1961

Stuck, Hans, sen., Tagebuch eines Rennfahrers. München (Moderne Verlag) 1967

Tajima, Haru, Racing Porsches: The Matsuda Collection. Tokyo 1984

Tragatsch, Erwin, Das große Rennfahrerbuch. Bern (Hallweg Verlag) 1970

Ulyett, Kenneth, The Porsche and Volkswagen Companion. Burbank, CA (Autobooks) 1962

Volkswagen Werk GmbH, Plaudereien um den KdF-Wagen und das Volkswagenwerk. Berlin-Grunewald 1939

Walton, Jeremy, Racing Mechanic: Ermano Cuoghi Mechanic to a World Champion. London (Osprey Publishings Ltd.) 1981

Weitman, Julius, Wolfgang Graf Berghe v. Trips. Dortmund (Krüger Verlag) 1962

–, Porsche Story. Stuttgart (Motorbuch Verlag) 1968

–, Porsche Story. New York (Arco Publishing Co. Inc.) 1968

Weitmann, Julius, Rico Steinemann, Project 928. Stuttgart (Motorbuch Verlag) 1977

Wyer, John, The Certain Sound, Thirty Years of Motor Racing. Lausanne (Automobile Year/Edita SA) 1981

Zimmermann, P. M., The Used 911 Story. Fox Island, WA (Zimmermann Pubs.) 1981

Zweigardt, Mark, Auto im Zeitblick: Porsche 1949–1958. Köln (Automobilia Shop) 1979

–, Auto im Zeitblick: Porsche 1959–1965. Köln (Automobilia Shop) 1980

Zwickl, Helmut, Weltmeister durch technischen K.O. Stuttgart (Motorbuch Verlag) 1969

Compiled by Lothar Boschen.

ADDRESSES OF IMPORTERS

EUROPE

AUSTRIA
Salzburg (5021)
Porsche Austria Ges. m. b. H. & Co.
Porschehof, Postfach 164
Tel. (06 62) 5 05 81   Telex 06 33 291

BELGIUM
Bruxelles (1050)
Porsche Import
S.A. D'leteren N.V.
50, Rue du Mail
Tel. (02) 5 36 52 54   Telex 24 793

CANARY ISLANDS
Las Palmas
Domingo Alonso, S.A.
C. Diego Vega Sarmiento, 16
Tel. (9 28) 25 20 32
Telex 95 272 dalon

DENMARK
Glostrup (2600)
Skandinavisk Motor Co. A/S
Park Allee 356
Postboks 298
Tel. (02) 63 11 22   Telex 33 651

FINLAND
Hyrylä (04301)
Oy Sport Car Center AB.
Tuusulantie
P.O. Box 25
Tel. (90) 25 55 22   Telex 12 56 45

FRANCE
Saint Ouen l'Aumône (95310)
Sonauto S.A.
1, Av. du Fief
Z.A. des Béthunes
B.P. 479
95005 Cergy Pontoise Cedex
Tel. (3) 0 37 92 62   Telex 69 72 58

GREAT BRITAIN
Porsche Cars Great Britain Ltd.
26–30, Richfield Ave.
Reading RG1 8PH
Berkshire
Tel. (07 34) 59 54 11   Telex 849 180

GREECE
Athens (11526)
Porsche Hellas S.A.
Kifissias Avenue 134
Tel. (01) 6 92 05 11, 6 92 23 57
Telex 215 535

IRELAND
Dublin 12
Motor Distributors Ltd.
Long Mile Road
Tel. (01) 50 33 33   Telex 91 019

ITALY
Verona (37136)
Autogerma S.p.A.
Via Germania 33, C.P. 184
Tel. (0 45) 58 71 11
Telex 480 258

LUXEMBOURG
Luxembourg-Howald (1818)
Autosdiffusion Martin Losch S.a.c.s.
Zone Industrielle
Tel. 49 41 55   Telex 2 760

MALTA
Msida
Continental Cars Ltd.
Testaferrata Street
Tel. 3 68 54, 3 99 60   Telex 232

NETHERLANDS
Amersfoort (3817 CH)
Pon's Automobielhandel B.V.
Arnhemseweg 2–14
Postbus 72
Tel. (0 33) 94 99 11   Telex 79 181

NORWAY
Oslo
Harald A. Møller A/S
Frysjaveien 31
Postboks 3342
Sagene, Oslo 4
Tel. (02) 23 38 85   Telex 7 11 29

PORTUGAL
Lisboa (1200)
Sociedade Comercial Guérin S.A.R.L.
Avenida da Liberdade, 12
P.O. Box 2822
Tel. (01) 36 67 51   Telex 12 307

SPAIN
Porsche España S.A.
Carretera Nacional 2
Madrid – Barcelona Km. 16.400
San Fernando de Henares
Tel. (91) 6 72 56 11, 6 72 56 61
Telex 48 047

SWEDEN
Södertälje (15188)
V.A.G. Sverige AB.
Verkstadsvägen 14
Tel. (07 55) 8 35 00   Telex 10 216

SWITZERLAND
Schinznach-Bad (5116)
AMAG
Automobil- und Motoren AG
Aarauer Str.
Tel. (0 56) 43 91 91   Telex 52 960

ADDRESSES OF IMPORTERS

WORLDWIDE

ARGENTINA
Albert Hermann
Av. del Libertador 1 29 14–22
1640 Martinez
Buenos Aires
Tel. 7 98–57 45 Telex 18 803 saram ar

AUSTRALIA
Norman Hamilton & Co. Pty. Ltd.
576 Princes Highway
P.O. Box 368
Noble Parks 3174, Victoria
Tel. (03) 7 95 70 55 Telex 33 589
Telegramm: porsch aa

BAHRAIN
Performance Cars Bahrain
P.O. Box 26928
Manama
Tel. 72 79 11 Telex 9 735

BRAZIL
Dacon S.A.
Veiculos Nacionais
Avenida Cidade Jardim, 312154
São Paulo
C.E.P. 01454
Tel. (0 11) 2 10 51 05
Telex 01 12384 daco br
Telegramm: Daconveiculos

BRUNEI
Premier Corporation Derhad
Nr. 11–12 Bangunan Menglait Dua
1½ Mile Jalan Gadong
P.O. Box 320
Bandard Seri Begawan
Negara Brunei Darussalam
Tel. 2 17 40, 2 14 31 Telex 2 266 sebati

CANADA
Volkswagen Canada Inc.
1940 Eglinton Avenue, East
Scarborough, Ontario M1L 9Z9
Tel. (4 16) 2 88 30 00 Telex 06-963 588
Telegramm: Volkswagen Toronto

ECUADOR
Tallerer Lothar Ranft Cia. Ltda.
Avenida Los Shyris y
Rio Coca Esquina
Casilla 8388
Quito
Tel. 4 54-2 61 Telex 22 75

GUATEMALA
Auto Marina S.A.
Calzada Raúl Aguilar Batres 34–62
Zona 11
Guatemala C.A.
Tel. (02) 76 29 76, 76 42 26 Telex 5 635

HONGKONG
Jebsen + Co., Ltd.
Scomber Building
No. 1, Yip Fat Street
Wong Chuk Hang
Aberdeen, Hongkong
Te. 5–54 01 11 Telex 73 769

JAMAICA
Sinclair's Garage Ltd.
11, Lower Elletson Rd.
P.O. Box 400
Kingston
Tel. 8 49 11-6, 8 49 18 Telex 2204

JAPAN
Mitsuwa Motors Co. Ltd.
No. 2-16-21, Meguro-Honcho
Meguro-ku
Tokyo
Tel. 03-710-1641 Telex J 24 889
Telegramm: Mitsuwaaut

JORDAN
Motor Trade Company, Ltd.
Station Road
P.O. Box 299
Amman
Tel. 5 13 51, 5 13 38/39 Telex 2 11 68

KUWAIT
Behbehani Motors Company
P.O. Box 4222
Kuwait
Tel. 81 95 74 Telex Kuwait 23 496
Telegramm: Motors Kuwait

MALAYSIA
Forari Corporation Sdn. Bhd.
Suite 3.27, 2nd Floor
Wisma Central, Jalan Ampang
Kuala Lumpur
Tel. 48 10 82, 48 72 57 Telex 3 26 75

MEXICO
Turbo Carrera, S.A.
Apartado Postal 22-217
Calzada Ermita Ixtapalapa 1873
Mexico 14070, D.F.
Tel. 5 94 23 18 Telex 17 72 857

NETHERLANDS ANTILLES
Leo Schnog's Enterprises N.V.
Caracasbaaiweg 83
Willemstad, Curacao
Tel. 5 57 00, 5 57 15 Telex 3 029

NEW CALEDONIA
**Société d'Importation
Automobile »SIA« S.A.**
Marais-des-Joncs, Anse-Vata
B.P. 2245
Nouméa
Tel. 26 12 72 Telex 91 64 81
Telegramm: Sima Nouméa

NEW ZEALAND
European Motor Distr. Ltd.
5 Clemow Drive
P.O. Box 62 026
Auckland 6, Mt. Wellington
Tel. (9) 57 20 19 Telex 21 311 NZ

OMAN
SATA LLC.
P.O. Box 814
Muscat
Sultanate of Oman
Tel. 60 35 44 Telex 51 72

REP. DE PANAMA
Consultenos, S.A.
Via Ricardo J. Alfaro
Apartado 8088
Panama 7, R.P.
Tel. 60 41 11 Telex 2 913

PERU
Dieter Mossier S.A.
Apartado 4976
Lima 18 (Mirafiores)
Tel. 45 09 32, 46 65 72 Telex 21 326

PHILIPPINES
Autohaus Europa
3739 F. Bautista St.
P.O. Box 7322 Airmail Distr. Center
Pasay City, M. M.
Maskati, Metro Manila
Tel. 8 31-39 24 Telex 23 217

PUERTO RICO
Stuttgart Motors Inc.
Avda. Kennedy km 2.2
Puerto Nuevo
San Juan 00920
Tel. (8 09) 7 81 01 92 Telex 32 52 682

QATAR
Gulf Automobiles
& Trading Co.
Salwa Industrial Area
P.O. Box 3899
Doha
Tel. 81 06 55/56/57 Telex: 4 142
Exposition: Saad Road, Doha
Tel. 44 62 70/71/73

REUNION
Bourbon Autmobile S.A.
Route Gymnase
97490 **Ste. Clotilde**
B.P. 699
97474 **Saint Denis**
Tel. 21 09 37
Telegramm: Bonauto

SAUDI-ARABIA
**Consulting and Developing
Engineers Co.**
Dharan Main Road
P.O. Box 266
Al-Khobar, 31952
Tel. 8 64 21 26 Telex 670 037

SINGAPORE
Ngo Hock Auto Spares,
Co., Pte. Ltd.
14 Sungei Kadut Avenue
Singapore 2572
Tel. 3 68 22 23-9 Telex 26 156

SOUTH AFRICA, REPUBLIC OF
LSM Distributors (Pty.) Ltd.
6. Mooi Street South
P.O. Box 261449
Excom 2023
Johannesburg, Transvaal
Tel. (0 11) 29 06 41 Telex 83 958

TAIWAN
Universal Motor Trader Ltd.
349 Tun Hua N. Road
P.O. Box 3051
Taipei
Tel. 7 13 01 73 Telex 11 521

TRINIDAD
Sterling Service (Batoo Bros.) Ltd.
37–41 Charles Street
Port of Spain
Trinidad, W. 1
Tel. 5 11 21-23 Telex 34 26

TRUCIAL STATES
**Orient Automobile
& Trading Co. Pvt. Ltd.**
P.O. Box 10 773
Rashidiya Street
Dubayy
Tel. 25 10 66, 25 10 91
Telex 47 544 Oatco EM

USA
Porsche Cars North America, Inc.
200 South Virginia Street
Reno, Nevada 89501
Tel. (7 02) 7 86 78 51–56

INDEX / PROPER NAMES

CONTRIBUTORS TO THIS BOOK / CREDITS / IMPRINT

CONTRIBUTORS TO THIS BOOK

Juergen Barth
Specialist Supervisor Customer Racing (Porsche AG)

Lothar Boschen
One of the renowned Porsche specialists; has written several books about this topic

Helmuth Bott
Vice President Research and Development (Porsche AG)

Hermann Briem
Former Head of Repair Workshops (Porsche AG)

Gustav Buesing
Freelance motoring writer

Wolfgang Eyb
Chief Engineer Design (Porsche AG)

Peter Falk
Director Racing Development (Porsche AG)

Paul Frère
Former racing driver; has written several Porsche Books; test driver for Second German Television Channel

Paul Hensler
Director Power Train Development (Porsche AG)

Heinz Horrmann
Motoring writer; daily newspaper "Die Welt"

Fritz Huschke v. Hanstein
From 1952–1968 Head of PR- and Racing Department (Porsche AG)

Judith Jackson
English motoring writer; author of the book "Man & the Automobile – A Twentieth-Century Love Affair", London 1977

Henry Keller
Renowned swiss motoring writer

Hans Klauser
General Service Manager Porsche AG (world wide) till retirement. Has been with Porsche for more than 40 years.

Anatole C. Lapine
Director Style-Porsche (Porsche AG)

Hans Mezger
Manager Advanced Engineering (Porsche AG)

Prof. Dr.-Ing. Rudi Noppen
Vice President Production, Quality Control and Supply Economics (Porsche AG)

Bernd Ostmann
Motoring writer; motor magazine "Auto, Motor & Sport"

Prof. Dr.-Ing. h. c. Ferry Porsche
Chairman of the Supervisory Board (Porsche AG)

Peter W. Schutz
President (Porsche AG)

Ingo Seiff
was born in 1928, trained as a businessman in the energy field and then went into the entertainment industry. Since 1970 he has worked as a freelance PR consultant and journalist. Automobile history is one of his specialist subjects, and one on which he has worked extensively both as an author and a photographer. His book on veteran cars has been received with widespread popular and press approval, and his picture archive, comprising over 20,000 photographs of 'old timers' is one of the greatest of its kind in the world.

Reinhard Seiffert
Editor in Chief of "Christophorus," (The Magazine for Porsche Friends)

CREDITS

END PAPERS

The data for the documentation of Porsche sports- and racing cars were kindly made available by Porsche AG.

PHOTOS
(refer to illustration numbers)

Dennis Ashlock 24, 27
Autopresse 75
autozeitung 44
dppi 18, 23, 26, 29, 33
Werner Eisele 6, 17, 19, 30
Gamma 46
Rodolfo Mailander 82
Herbert Novak 38
Porsche-Archiv 41, 49, 50, 51, 57, 68, 69
Press Sport 22, 32
Klaus Reichert 2, 3, 4, 20, 21, 28, 47, 74
Ingo Seiff 1, 5, 7, 8, 9–13, 14, 15, 35, 39, 40, 48, 54, 55, 58, 59, 60, 61, 62, 64, 66, 70, 71, 72, 73
Hans-Peter Seufert cover photo, 31, 42, 43, 45, 52, 56, 76
Haru Tajima 65
Leonard Turner 25, 36, 63, 67
Julius Weitmann 77–81, 83–104
Vandystadt 16, 34, 53
Jürgen Zerha 37

TEXT

The text "From coup to coup" (p. 103–106) by Bernd Ostmann/Hans Mezger is based on the article "Between TAG and Dream. Hans Mezger, the man behind the PORSCHE-TAG-Formula-1-engine", by Bernd Ostmann, published by "Auto, Motor & Sport" 11/1985. By courtesy of that magazine, Hans Mezger has made some additions.

The charts "List of types and quantities" on pages 278–279 were compiled by Lothar Boschen.

The "Major Landmarks of Automobile History" on pages 280–281 were compiled by Cyrus Posthumus, from "Story of veteran and vintage cars". © 1977 by Phoebus Publishing Co., London (a Division of Macdonald & Co. (Publishers) Ltd., London). Ingo Seiff added the Porsche Data from 1875 onwards.

The "Addresses of Importers" on pages 284–285 were excerpted from "Porsche Service", Edition No. 20, 5/1984.

TRANSLATIONS

p. 8 Ferry Porsche relates
From 40 to 1100 hp
p. 33 Peter W. Schutz
"If I were a car, I'd be a Porsche"
p. 89 Lothar Boschen
The Porsche model line from 1945–1985
p. 113 Fritz Huschke v. Hanstein
The Porsche Baron reminisces
p. 160 Peter Falk
33 years of rally successes
p. 174 Henry Keller
Psychograph of the Porsche driver
p. 212 Lothar Boschen
Super-Porsches: From 917 to 962
p. 224 Hans Klauser / Hermann Briem
How it all began

Translated by Patricia Laurel-Baily

p. 40 Helmuth Bott
The rear-engine/rear-drive philosophy
p. 44 Paul Frère
Porsche 911: The living legend
p. 51 Paul Hensler / Wolfgang Eyb
The new Porsches: 924, 928, 944
p. 99 Heinz Horrmann
Into the future with the Porsche 959
p. 107 Reinhard Seiffert
Porsche in Formula 1
p. 153 Gustav Buesing
Porsche and the 24 hours of Le Mans
p. 168 Reinhard Seiffert
The Porsche Mystique
p. 201 Rudi Noppen
First and foremost–Quality
p. 219 Juergen Bath
Customer-Sport Service worldwide

Translated by Stephen Belless

p. 6 Ingo Seiff
"Bella macchina"!
p. 94 Helmuth Bott
Weissach – The Porsche think-tank
p. 103 Bernd Ostmann / Hans Mezger
From coup to coup
p. 207 Ingo Seiff
Porsche styling
p. 273 Ingo Seiff
Afterword

Translated by Oliver Stephan

IMPRINT

Picture editors:
Helmut Mueller, Ingo Seiff

Text editors:
Gerhard Koestner, Ingo Seiff, Norman Zeigler

Cover design: Jan Buchholz and Reni Hinsch
Photo: Hans-Peter Seufert

Graphic design and production:
Helmut Mueller

Original title
DAS GROSSE PORSCHE BUCH
Copyright © 1985 by Hoffmann and Campe Verlag, Hamburg, West Germany
American translation,
Porsche, Portrait of a Legend
Copyright © 1985 by Hoffmann and Campe Verlag, Hamburg, West Germany
Printed and bound in West Germany

Exclusiv distribution rights for the United States of America and Canada
Porsche Cars North America Inc., Reno, Nevada 89501

1953 type 550 Coupé
4 cylinders, 1488 cc, 75 hp, 1212 pounds, 124 mph
1953 Winner, 1500 cc class, Le Mans 24 hours

1954 type 550 Spyder
4 cylinders, 1498 cc, 110 hp, 1212 pounds, 137 mph
1954 Winner, 1500 cc class, Mille Miglia

1956 type 550 A/1500 RS Coupé
4 cylinders, 1498 cc, 135 hp, 1212 pounds, 149 mph
1956 Winner, 1500 cc class, Le Mans 24 hours

1956 type 550 A/1500 RS Spyder
4 cylinders, 1498 cc, 135 hp, 1168 pounds, 149 mph
1956 Winner, 1500 cc class, Nuerburgring 1000 kms

1957/58 type 718/1500 RSK "Sebring Spyder"
4 cylinders, 1498 cc, 142 hp, 1168 pounds, 149 mph
1958 2. place, Targa Florio

1958 type 718 RSK Spyder
4 cylinders, 1498 cc, 142 hp, 1168 pounds, 149 mph
1958 3. place, Le Mans 24 hours

1960 type 718/787 F2
4 cylinders, 1498 cc, 150 hp, 1036 pounds, 155 mph
1960 Winner, Aintree 200 miles

1960 type 718 RS 60 Spyder
4 cylinders, 1587 cc, 160 hp, 1212 pounds, 152 mph
1960 Winner, Sebring 12 hours

1960 type 356 B/1600 GS Carrera GTL Abarth
4 cylinders, 1587 cc, 115 hp, 1720 pounds, ca. 137 mph
1960 Winner, 1600 cc class, Le Mans 24 hours

1962 type 718 W-RS Spyder
8 cylinders, 1981 cc, 210 hp, 1411 pounds, ca. 162 mph
1962 3. place, Nuerburgring 1000 kms

1960–63 type 356 B 2000 GT "Dreikantschaber"
4 cylinders, 1966 cc, 130 hp, 2249 pounds, 143 mph
1963 4. place, Nuerburgring 1000 kms

1962 type 718 GTR Coupé
8 cylinders, 1981 cc, 210 hp, 1477 pounds, 162 mph
1963 3. place, Targa Florio

1962 type 804 F 1
8 cylinders, 1494 cc, 180 hp, 1003 pounds, ca. 168 mph
1962 Winner, French Grand Prix

1964 type 904-Carrera GTS
4 cylinders, 1966 cc, 180 hp, 1433 pounds, 162 mph
1964 Winner, Targa Florio

1966 type 906-Carrera 6
6 cylinders, 1991 cc, 210 hp, 1488 pounds, 165 mph
1966 6. place, Daytona 24 hours

1967 type 910
6 cylinders, 1991 cc, 220 hp, 1323 pounds, 165 mph
1967 Winner, Nuerburgring 1000 kms

1968 type 907 "Langheck"
8 cylinders, 2195 cc, 270 hp, 1323 pounds, 199 mph
1968 Winner, Daytona 24 hours

1968 type 909 "Bergspyder"
8 cylinders, 1981 cc, 272 hp, 948 pounds, 155 mph
1968 2 competitions, no winners

1969 type 908.02 Spyder "Flunder"
8 cylinders, 2997 cc, 350 hp, 1323 pounds, 168 mph
1969 Winner, Nuerburgring 1000 kms

Note for the readers of the English version of this book: The expression "horsepower" is indicated with hp. The hp-va